Fort Riley and its Neighbors

Fort Riley
and its Neighbors

Military Money
and Economic Growth,
1853–1895

By William A. Dobak

University of Oklahoma Press : Norman

This book is published with the generous assistance of Edith Gaylord Harper.

Library of Congress Cataloging-in-Publication Data

Dobak, William A., 1943–
    Fort Riley and its neighbors : Military money and economic growth, 1853–1895 / by William A. Dobak.
    p. cm.
    Includes bibliographical references and index.
    ISBN 0–8061–3071–7 (alk. paper)
    1. Fort Riley (Kan.)—History. I. Title.
UA26.F67D63   1998
355.7'09781'28—DC21   98–13474
                                   CIP

1 2 3 4 5 6 7 8 9 10

For CHERYL COLLINS, JEANNE MITHEN, and the staff of the Riley County Historical Society, who saved the nineteenth-century municipal records of Manhattan, Kansas, from a twentieth-century dumpster.

Contents

Illustrations

Maps

Preface

AN AUTHOR HOPING to drum up customers for yet another book about the United States Army in the nineteenth-century American West had better offer a plausible excuse for the new book's existence and explain what it is, and is not, about. *Fort Riley and Its Neighbors* is not a campaign history or a comprehensive chronicle of a particular fort. It examines, instead, how an agency of the federal government—an army post, a budget-driven bureaucracy—affected the lives of settlers and economic growth in its neighborhood.

More than a generation ago, Nancy O. Lurie predicted that new technologies—photoduplication on film and paper, and the jet airliner—would revolutionize historical scholarship. Limitations on travel and, therefore, access to primary sources have led generations of historians to depend for information on the annual reports of the Secretary of War and the Commissioner of Indian Affairs, which are readily available in the Congressional serial set. Those officials meant the documents to make their agencies look good, or at least busy, when budget time rolled around, and historians have generally adopted the official frame of reference, bestowing the title "the Indian Wars" on the years from 1865 to 1898. A look through the correspondence between any fort and its department headquarters during this period, though, will show that far more letters discussed whether there was enough money left in the current year's budget to shingle the roofs of stables and barracks or to patch a cracked cistern than discussed any Indians, hostile or peaceful. In order to tell a fresh story, therefore, historians should discover what was going on when nothing much seemed to be going on and make it interesting.[1]

Fort Riley differed in important ways from military posts about which historians have already written. Fort Sill and Fort Supply stood in western Indian Territory, where white settlement was forbidden, and did not develop the sort of relations with neighboring civilians that were possible in other territories and states. A recent history of Fort Meade, South Dakota, mentions the nearby town of Sturgis as furnishing recreation for the troops in the nineteenth century. It also notes civilians' successful efforts during the Second World War to turn the buildings of the abandoned post into a Veterans Administration hospital, but it does not develop the economic theme further. Fort Griffin's name appears in the title of a recent work about the settlement of Texas, but the author discounts the army's effect on the local economy.[2]

This book is closer in intent to two other histories: Paul L. Hedren's study of Fort Laramie, Wyoming, during a particularly busy year there; and Frank N. Schubert's analysis of life at Fort Robinson, Nebraska, and the nearby town of Crawford. Hedren's book scrutinizes intensively a fort that stood several days' march from the nearest Indians (on or off a reservation), and through which passed men and supplies headed for the Sioux campaign of 1876. There were no settlements near Fort Laramie in 1876, though, and no railroad came up the North Platte valley until years afterward, so that post lacked the economic elements that figured in Fort Riley's history. Schubert's work is unique in describing settlement by former soldiers and the development of a black community in Crawford. Crawford's growth was stunted, though, when it failed to gain the county seat and a state normal school, and it never developed much beyond being one of John C. Hudson's *Plains Country Towns*—a water tank and a grain elevator—with saloons and brothels thrown in. Fort Riley's neighboring towns, Junction City and Manhattan, were both county seats, and Manhattan was the site of the state agricultural college as well. The combination of settlements, local governments, and railroads gave economic life around Fort Riley a complexity that was lacking in many parts of the West. I have tried to take these factors into account in considering the interplay between national and local interests, and the public and private sectors of the economy.[3]

The same tendencies, of course, exist today. While I was researching and writing my dissertation, there was some alarm in Kansas about the possible closing of Fort Riley, occasioned by reporters' failure, or inability, to distinguish between the alternatives of deactivating the First Infantry Division, moving all or part of it, or closing the fort entirely. I was sitting in the county clerk's office at the Riley County Office Building, going through the minutes of some old commissioners' meetings, and overheard a woman new to Manhattan tell one of the office staff that she and her husband were renting a house until Fort Riley's future was more certain; if the fort closed, they expected residential real-estate values in the adjoining counties to depreciate by 25 or 30 percent. As it turned out, part of the division moved, and Fort Riley's garrison declined from 12,500 to 10,000, although the number of civilian employees stayed constant at about 3,300. Spending on payroll, contracts, and construction, though, dropped from nearly $666 million in 1995 to slightly more than $559 million the following year, a loss of 16 percent. Meanwhile, an organization called the Committee for a Strong Fort Riley lobbies elected officials in Washington, D.C. The general tenor of relations between Fort Riley and its neighbors remains much as it was one hundred years ago.[4]

For help with this book, I am indebted first to the professors at the University of Kansas who read my dissertation: Roy Gridley, David Katzman, Peter Mancall, Rita Napier (who chaired the committee), and Theodore Wilson. Elizabeth Verschelden, a graduate student in the Department of History, kindly took time to read and comment on an early version of the fourth chapter. Since I often sidestepped their suggestions, responsibility for the facts and interpretations offered here is mine alone.

Librarians at the University of Kansas—particularly in Government Documents, Interlibrary Services, and the Kansas Collection—helped immeasurably, as did the staff of the Kansas State Historical Society. Deborah Dandridge, Virgil Dean, and Terry

Harmon deserve special mention. Clerks at the Geary County Office Building, the Junction City municipal office, and the Riley County Office Building let me look at their old city and county records. Cheryl Collins and Jeanne Mithen at the Riley County Historical Society made available Manhattan's early city records, and the staff of the Geary County Historical Society furnished valuable information from their files of newspaper clippings. At the National Archives in Washington, D.C., DeAnne Blanton, William Lind, and Michael Meier were especially helpful.

Paul Dobak, Alaina Drake, and especially John Retherford frequently got me out of tight spots in which my ignorance of computers had lodged me.

Although a dissertation research travel grant from the University of Kansas helped me to get to Washington, D.C., one summer, books that require travel would be impossible to write without the hospitality of friends. Among those who put me up, and put up with me, while I was researching and writing this one were Paul Ceruzzi and Diane Wendt, Timothy and Susan Healy, John Moriarty and Mary White, Edmund O'Reilly, Jeffrey Tarter and Jane Farber, and Daniel and Betty Townsend. Philip and Annelies Dobak opened their home to me for most of one summer and part of another. Mark Moriarty, and Evan Smith and Marlene Mannella, provided welcome resting places on my drives between Kansas and the Atlantic Seaboard.

Lastly, my parents deserve thanks for drawing my attention, at an early age, to the American West.

Fort Riley and Its Neighbors

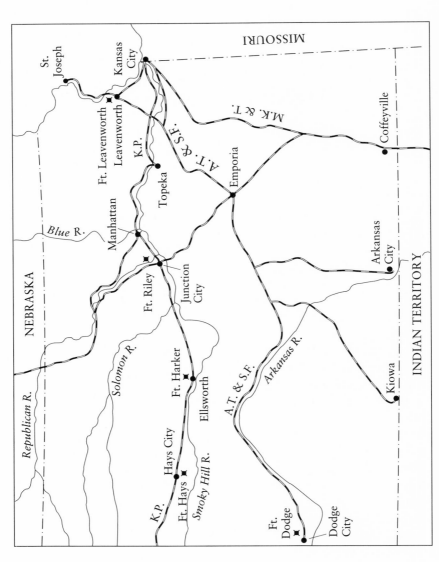

Fort Riley, Junction City, and Manhattan: Their rail connections to cities and military posts in Kansas, late 1870s.

Introduction

Fort Riley and Its Neighbors

ON MARCH 27, 1895, a special train bearing the receivers of the Union Pacific Railroad steamed into Junction City,
Kansas. The receivers—court-appointed officers whose business
was to run the troubled railroad and straighten out its tangled affairs—had come to Junction City to inspect the yards and shops at
the division point there. After lunch in their private dining car, the
train took them to the Fort Riley siding. They met officers of the
garrison at the residence of Colonel Edwin V. Sumner, who commanded the post, and stayed to observe the monthly review of more
than seven hundred cavalry and field artillery troops stationed at
Fort Riley's Mounted Branch School. The receivers "were delighted
with their cordial reception and generous treatment," the Junction
City *Republican*'s correspondent wrote. That afternoon's entertain-
ment seemed an apt acknowledgement of the railroad's part during
the previous thirty years in solving the problem of western distances that had vexed the army and its civilian neighbors and in pre-
serving the existence of Fort Riley itself.[1]

Besides linking the fort to its headquarters, and the neighborhood to the nation, the railroad represented capital. Capitalism
transformed land and life in the American West during the nineteenth century. As the system expanded from its core area in western Europe, it incorporated "new lands" where entrepreneurs found
untapped resources. The western United States was only one such
area. Among the others were adjoining regions of Mexico and
Canada, as well as Argentina, Australia, New Zealand, and South
Africa. The entrepreneurs' usual method of exploiting those lands

was to invest capital from the developed core region and bring resources from the "new lands" to market.

This pattern has been apparent throughout American history, from the time of the earliest settlements on the Atlantic Coast. These seventeenth-century settlements produced staples—timber and tobacco, for instance—for an international economy. Subsistence farming increased during the eighteenth century as the area of settlement outgrew the available means of transporting goods to market. The development of canals, river steamboats, and railroads in the nineteenth century reconnected many farmers to the national and international markets. Town dwellers, who expected immediate commercial benefits, were enthusiastic promoters of railroads. Urban developers—editors, lawyers, merchants—hoped to integrate their towns more thoroughly in the market and make them regional centers of commerce, with the assistance of the government, if possible; without it, if necessary.[2]

As the economy expanded, so did the state. Long before the development of twentieth-century bureaucracy, the law itself fostered the growth of the market. Both the states and the federal government sought to apportion the public lands in order to bring them into production—whether of crops, timber, or minerals—and to develop the means of transporting those products to market. In the West, the federal government was particularly active.

During the second half of the nineteenth century, the federal government confronted the problem of incorporating its newly acquired western territories and bringing them into the national and international economy. National and local interests worked towards these goals, sometimes together and sometimes at cross-purposes. One branch of the federal government in the West, the army, faced daunting transportation costs during this period because of the region's sheer immensity. Both the army and neighboring civilians, therefore, were deeply interested in transportation, particularly the railroad, an innovation that promised to smooth out the seasonal economic fluctuations that resulted from the flow and freezing of rivers.

As the railroads helped to solve the army's supply problems, they also integrated the West into the national and world economies.

Railroads attracted European investors; recruited and imported European settlers who populated the Great Plains states; and exported the raw products of agriculture, logging, and mining, industries that would characterize the economy of the American West throughout the next century. Railroads, as William T. Sherman remarked in 1883, eventually came to be more important than the army in opening the West.[3]

From the outset, though, many westerners grasped the significance of the government's role in economic development. In 1836, when Congress appropriated one-hundred thousand dollars for construction of a military road that would run through Fort Leavenworth, the editor of *The Far West*, a weekly newspaper in Liberty, Missouri, anticipated "increased expenditure among us of the national revenue." Soon after the organization of Kansas Territory in 1854, the *Kansas Weekly Herald* of Leavenworth urged "the fostering aid of our government" for settlers there. Farmers who lived near Fort Riley in 1880 were "much pleased" at the arrival of cavalry companies (the first mounted troops stationed there in four years), because it meant an increased demand for hay and feed grain. When the army decided to build a school for cavalry and horse-drawn artillery at Fort Riley in the late 1880s, a local newspaper exulted, "FORT RILEY BOOMS—The bill appropriating $150,000 passed—the $100,000 contract let will be carried out—Junction City men have a $76,000 slice." Another editor, writing about construction at the fort, headed his piece, "OUR GREAT MILITARY SUBURB." Clearly, neighboring civilians saw a military post as an asset to the local economy.[4]

Fort Riley stands where the Republican and Smoky Hill Rivers flow together to form the Kansas River. The economic effect of the fort on its civilian neighbors varied over the years as the size of the garrison fluctuated according to the army's strategic requirements. By the late 1880s, though, transcontinental railroads and local feeder lines—some of the latter financed partly by county bond issues—had placed Fort Riley centrally in the national rail network. They so reduced transportation costs that Fort Riley became one of the army's largest posts and a linchpin of the local economy. For the next hundred years, the private and public sectors of the economy continued to nourish each other.

Yet while the fort's neighbors welcomed its money, they prided themselves on their independence. Westerners' image of themselves was not one of a people dependent on federal money. The same issue of the *Kansas Weekly Herald* that called for "the fostering aid of our government" boasted that "Squatters have from the earliest settlement of our country, led the van of civilization in its westward course." Missouri's Senator Thomas Hart Benton spoke of "the people going forward without government aid or countenance. . . ." Westerners were already creating their own heroic version of the past, based on true but atypical examples: the rendezvous system of the Rocky Mountain fur trade, rather than the heavily capitalized trading posts along the Missouri River; the overland migration to California and Oregon, places that gripped the popular imagination as Iowa, for instance, did not; and the Santa Fe trade. Missourians were the only residents of a landlocked state to engage in international commerce, with Mexico by way of Santa Fe; St. Louis was the hub of the fur trade; and northwestern Missouri the jumping-off place for California and Oregon. Senator Benton's remarks were true, but only of some of his constituents, some of the time.[5]

Outsiders, particularly army officers, took a different view. "All of the people west of the Missouri river look to the army as their legitimate field of profit," General Sherman complained in 1866, "and the quicker they are undeceived the better for all." Western farmers and merchants competed avidly for government contracts. When contracts were small or nonexistent, local residents used the land and resources—grass, wood, and minerals—of military or Indian reservations as though they were public lands open to settlement. Whether the observer was a westerner or an outsider—a category that included federal officials such as army officers or Indian agents—the connection between the federal presence and economic development was obvious.[6]

The economy worked to integrate westward-moving settlers as soon as they established a foothold in a new region and began to exploit its resources. New means of transportation led to increased traffic and reduced rates during the four decades before the Civil War. Passenger fares declined by more than 60 percent, and freight rates by nearly 65 percent. Steamboats, when and where rivers were navigable, lowered the cost of moving people and goods even more than did the railroads. During these years the army faced the dilemma of policing a vast new territory in which navigable rivers were few. Army officers therefore took a keen interest in the railroads' progress. Throughout the country as a whole, meanwhile, steam power moved an ever-increasing volume of freight and passengers ever more quickly and cheaply.[7]

Army officers had seen the connection between military posts and settlement throughout the nineteenth century. Founded in 1853, the year before Kansas Territory was organized and opened to settlement, Fort Riley attracted artisans, and the 1855 census hints that its proximity to the site of the proposed territorial capital may have drawn a number of lawyers. Tradesmen, laborers, and professionals, as well as nearby farmers, actively sought connections to the national economy from the earliest years of settlement.

Most histories of the army in the American West ignore relations between military posts and the surrounding communities: whether the army and the market it afforded helped to attract settlers; or who got the army's money, how they spent it, and how that affected the community. Those histories do not describe how local civilians competed for contracts and exploited the federal presence, whether cash or land. Nor do they mention the army's detrimental effects: the tracts of nontaxable land sequestered in military reservations, and the wood, hay, and minerals there, private use of which was—in theory—enjoined. That the army's presence affected local residents is clear from a reading of local newspapers and city ordinances. Civilians' reactions reflected the ambivalent attitudes—suspicion and resentment, alloyed with greed—that Americans have always displayed towards their government.

Some historians who write about the federal government seem to imagine it as a unitary, autonomous entity rather than one in which the departments of the executive branch depend on the legislative branch for their annual budgets. Budgets and costs were crucial to the federal government's actual workings in the West, and they explain many of its actions. Congress could easily afford to offer direct aid to railroads in the form of vast grants of unsurveyed land, and the General Land Office, which parceled the land and brought it into the market, was a relatively low-budget operation. The Office of Indian Affairs and the United States Army, on the other hand, had tens of thousands of people to feed, clothe, and house, yet a parsimonious Congress gave those two organizations barely enough to survive, let alone to pursue their goals of "civilizing" the tribes and keeping the peace. Focused more sharply, the image of the federal presence in the West during the nineteenth century should be immediately recognizable to anyone, whether bureaucrat, entrepreneur, or academic historian, who has ever wrestled with a budget.

Local and regional influences on the federal government are worth a closer, longer look than they usually get. Although federal policy, in the shape of land grants, drove the lines of transcontinental railroads through sparsely populated country, local bond issues helped to promote construction of the short lines that filled in the spaces between. At Fort Riley, these short lines helped to perpetuate an immediate federal presence in the neighborhood and, with it, government expenditures. In the nineteenth century, federal policy created opportunities for settlement and the employment of capital. As civilians seized these opportunities, they helped to steer the course of subsequent government action. The interplay of national and local influences shaped federal policy in the West.

To learn how these forces worked on each other, we need to know who received the government's cash or schemed to get its land; see how these people fitted into their communities in terms of wealth and leadership; and, finally, understand now they adapted to external influences imposed by the federal government and the national economy, personified at Fort Riley by the army and the railroads. If the settlers saw federal money almost as a natural resource, they may have been more percipient than they knew, for federal policy could change and affect them as drastically as avulsion could affect the life of a river town.[8]

Some knowledge of the available transportation is necessary in order to understand at least that part of western history which concerns us here: how the American people and their government reacted when they found themselves, after 1848, suddenly faced with *all that space.* Rethinking western history in terms of transportation and its effect on the army's activities yields a different chronology from the usual string of dates, most of which have to do with battles. The army was too small to police the enormous new territory or even to maintain adequate garrisons at its many new posts, Fort Riley among them. Distances posed logistical difficulties. In the central grassland (called "the plains" for convenience, although the distinctive characteristic of the region is its vegetation, not its topography), the seasonal flow of the streams precluded waterborne transportation. The rivers were barely full enough to water draft animals, and as the army moved west, its supply costs increased sharply.

At the same time, acquisition of territory on the Pacific moved the plains from the margin to the center of the country; increased traffic through it; and precipitated hostilities with native peoples whose homeland, up to that point, had lain far beyond the effective range of government power. The advance of railroad lines made possible year-round communications. The buffalo hide trade, which depended on the railroads, nearly exterminated the bison and made plains tribes dependent on government rations. Railroads likewise made possible the rapid concentration of troops, whether to forestall Indian hostilities or to suppress labor disturbances. Such a concentration occurred for the first time in 1885 when an anticipated outbreak at the Cheyenne and Arapaho Agency in Indian Territory brought to southern Kansas more troops than anyone could recall seeing in one place since the Civil War.[9]

Since no shots were fired, 1885 does not figure in the standard military history of the period. Five years later, though, the Sioux Ghost Dance brought another war scare and a similar concentration of troops to Pine Ridge, South Dakota. Because scores of people died, and because it began in the "significant" year of 1890, that incident has received great attention. Often overlooked is the ease with which the army concentrated a large fraction of its strength, a feat that it repeated at Chicago during the Pullman Strike in 1894 and at Tampa when it assembled an invasion force to sail for Cuba in 1898. The success of these troop movements shows that railroads had helped the army to overcome the problems of distance it had faced since the late 1840s. Soldiers from Fort Riley took part in all four operations.

The history of relations between Fort Riley and its civilian neighbors in the nineteenth century falls roughly into three periods. The first was characterized by wagon transportation and ended when the arrival of the Kansas Pacific Railroad in 1866 made possible the removal farther west of Fort Riley's quartermaster depot. During this early period, the fort's presence encouraged settlement and promoted the growth of a class of frontier capitalists to supply the army's wants—food, forage, and firewood—as had happened near Fort Leavenworth a generation earlier. In the late 1870s, during the middle period, the infantry companies that garrisoned Fort Riley required no forage for horses, and as the government's disbursements diminished, local pressure to abandon the post or reduce its reservation grew. The third period followed General Philip H. Sheridan's announcement of a proposed cavalry school in 1884. The school's establishment led to a building boom in the late 1880s that made Fort Riley one of the largest military posts in the United States. The army paid hundreds of thousands of dollars to local contractors, and the fort became the mainstay of the local economy that it has remained ever since.

The arrival of a single railroad in 1866 had signaled the end of the first era of civil-military relations at Fort Riley. An extended national rail network ended the second. General Sherman's annual report of 1882 noted that the growth of railroads had made rapid troop movements possible. This growth also raised the possibility of nationwide railroad strikes more widespread than those of 1877 and suggested the wisdom of concentrating troops in large garrisons at central points where, incidentally, supplies could be furnished cheaply. Sherman's report named posts to be abandoned and those that the army planned to retain permanently. Fort Riley was among the latter. In a later report General Sheridan compared the cost of forts on rail lines with the cost of forts supplied by wagon and called Fort Riley the cheapest post in the country at which to station cavalry and artillery.[10]

Like the corporate decisions of railroads, the army's policy was based on larger considerations than solicitude for local interests. Besides economy, modernization of weapons and tactics concerned the army's commanders during the 1880s. Sheridan had commanded cavalry during the Civil War. General John M. Schofield, who succeeded him as commanding general in 1888, had been an artillery officer before the war. The Mounted Branch School to train cavalry and field artillery was conceived and founded during the years between 1884 and 1895, when these two men commanded the army. The school brought to Fort Riley a far larger garrison than the six companies envisioned in Sherman's report of 1882, and it assured the continuing importance of the fort to the local economy. Between 1887 and 1891, the army spent three-quarters of a million dollars at Fort Riley on construction and other improvements, with more than half the money going to contractors from Geary and Riley Counties.

In regarding federal money as a resource to be exploited, the settlers of Davis and Riley Counties laid themselves open to the same vicissitudes that farmers encounter with the weather; neither federal policy nor the weather can be counted on to respect local convenience, and neither operates in accord with economic reason. To contend successfully with external forces requires a diversified economy, as many towns are discovering again in the post-Cold War era of base closings. The nineteenth-century history of Fort Riley offers an instance of the federal government's relations with local communities at an earlier time, when the West was serving, in Richard White's phrase, as "the kindergarten of the American state."[11]

Prologue

"The Commerce of an Infant State"

THE LOUISIANA PURCHASE added to the United States a vast territory known only in the vaguest way. Traders from St. Louis ascended the Missouri River no farther than the villages of the Arikara and Mandan Indians; rarely did they cross the central grassland to the Spanish settlements on the upper Rio Grande. The United States government at once set about exploring its new lands, appraising the resources and their possible uses. Lewis and Clark went up the Missouri to its headwaters and beyond and reported a country rich in furs. At the same time, Lieutenant Zebulon M. Pike traveled from the Missouri River to New Mexico and described the country between in most unflattering terms, comparing the sandhills along the Arkansas River to "the sandy deserts of Africa." Major Stephen H. Long's report of his explorations in 1820 called the same stretch of country "almost wholly unfit for cultivation, and of course uninhabitable by a people depending upon agriculture for their subsistence."[1]

But the year after Long's expedition, 1821, was the year of Mexico's independence from Spain. This political revolution opened a new market to American manufactures, and traders to Santa Fe began to examine the country along the route more closely. Meanwhile, the United States government continued its efforts to promote commerce and agriculture in the West, fitfully and with varying success. A few years after the trade began, a merchant who had captained one of the Santa Fe caravans reported that "the circulating medium of Missouri now consists principally of Mexican dollars." When Missouri's Senator Thomas Hart Benton orated in later years about "the people going forward without government aid or countenance . . . and compelling the Government to follow . . . ," he was talking about settlers headed for Oregon, but his words applied equally to commercial ventures operating out of his state.[2]

In 1823, when the Arikara Indians attacked William H. Ashley's fur-trading expedition up the Missouri River, Ashley—himself a future Missouri congressman—summoned the U.S. Army to his aid. The Arikara village, which stood where Grand River empties into the Missouri, was a major trading center both for the exchange of buffalo and horticultural products and for guns and horses. The Arikaras were generally antagonistic towards white traders who might undermine their position as middlemen in the trade. The inglorious military campaign that ensued was surely not what Benton meant by "compelling the Government to follow," but Ashley's way of operating—setting out on his own and requesting government assistance when he ran into trouble—has been common in the West ever since.[3]

Far more effective than the Arikara campaign were the less spectacular ways in which the federal and state governments promoted commerce during the nineteenth century. The farthest-reaching of these was the states' prescribing general procedures for incorporation rather than granting charters to individual corporations by act of the legislature. More apparent to the public eye were the river and harbor work of the Corps of Engineers, and state canal projects. Federal surveyors laid out highways, too, whether ostensibly "military roads" or undisguised arteries of commerce. Among the latter ventures was the survey of the Santa Fe Trail in 1825.

Senator Benton had taken an interest in the Santa Fe trade from its inception. William Becknell had gone there with a train of pack mules in 1821; two years later, Missourians carried their goods to Santa Fe in wagons for the first time, and Becknell himself referred to the trail as a "road" in the Franklin *Missouri Intelligencer.* Benton seized on the idea of a road and had printed as a Senate Document the remarks of Augustus Storrs, a merchant who had made the trip as a member of a twenty-three-wagon caravan in 1824. Storrs proclaimed the value of that year's trade as $180,000 "at the lowest estimates"—an amount, Benton told the Senate, "considerable in itself, in the commerce of an infant State" and "an earnest of what might be expected from a regulated and protected trade." Benton proposed, Congress passed, and the outgoing President Monroe signed an act appropriating thirty thousand dollars to survey the road to Mexico and to negotiate with Indian tribes along the way.[4]

Western merchants' eyes were open to various ways of making money, and along with his estimate of the annual worth of the Santa Fe trade, Augustus Storrs offered observations about the country through which the trail passed and its agricultural potential. Between the Missouri and the Arkansas Rivers, the first 250 miles of the route, the soil was "extremely fertile, of a dark color, and loose. The timber is the same as that of Missouri. . . . It grows thickly immediately on the banks of streams, and sometimes extends a short distance up the bottoms." He mentioned again "the richness and looseness of the soil," noting that it contained "very little sand or gravel."[5] This description of the country contrasted sharply with Major Long's of just two years earlier.

In the report of his explorations, Long had stressed the presence of sand and of magnesium salts, "a quality derogatory to the fertility of any soil." He wrote of the Kansas River in particular, "Woodlands are seldom to be met with, except in narrow skirts and small copses along the water courses. Much of the country situated upon its forks is said to be possessed of a good soil, but is rendered uninhabitable for want of timber and water. The bottoms are possessed of a light sandy soil, and the uplands are in many places characterized by aridity and barrenness." Long saw the region only as "a barrier to prevent too great an extension of our population westward."[6] Augustus Storrs, although he was more concerned with his commercial venture to Santa Fe, had an eye towards the country's future as farmland. Their opinions of the land were more cautious than the speculative views of George C. Sibley, who led the government's survey of the road to Santa Fe.

Sibley had first become a federal official in 1805, when he was appointed assistant factor at Bellefontaine, Missouri, a trading post in the U.S. Indian factory system. Three years later, he became chief factor at Fort Osage, on the Missouri River below the mouth of the Kansas. He held that office until 1822, when the government ended its direct participation in the fur trade, largely due to the influence of John Jacob Astor's American Fur Company. As chief factor, Sibley traded goods furnished by the government, at fixed prices, for furs provided by Indians. He dealt routinely with the Kansas and Osages, two of the largest tribes near his post, and in 1811 arranged a peace between them and the Pawnees.

When the federal government abandoned its Indian factory system, Sibley, who by that time had interests in Missouri real estate, obtained a federal license to trade with Indians and went into partnership with two other men, purchasing the government's stock of trade goods at Fort Osage. One of Sibley's partners, Paul Baillio, had been assistant factor at the government trading post on the Marais des Cygnes, or Osage River. By 1825, Baillio had entered the Santa Fe trade and was already in New Mexico when Sibley was appointed one of the commissioners to survey the road to Santa Fe. This shuttling back and forth from government service to private enterprise, as well as the entrepreneurs' various interests in land, furs, and the Santa Fe trade, characterized commerce in the American West throughout the nineteenth century.[7]

What sort of eye did Sibley bring to the Kansas landscape? Although he had never farmed for a living, he grew up in the fall-line town of Fayetteville, North Carolina, between Tidewater and Piedmont, and had lived in Missouri for twenty years. He must have known the current agricultural folklore: a dark, moist soil was more fertile than a light, dry one; hardwoods, and particularly nut-bearing trees like oak and hickory, signaled rich soil. Received wisdom told farmers that the soil of prairies, which lacked trees, was barren, so they settled in the ecotone where grass and woodland met. As early as the 1820s, though, they were beginning to realize that the fertility of prairie soil justified the effort and expense of breaking its sod. Sibley's journals of 1825, when he surveyed the Santa Fe route, and 1827, when he returned to mark it as far west as Council Grove, reflect this growing awareness.[8]

As an Indian trader, moreover, Sibley operated on the frontier between two societies, and he had at least a passing acquaintance with his customers' ways of living on the land. In the spring of 1811 he had made a thousand-mile tour that took him west to the Kansas Indian village near the confluence of the Big Blue and Kansas Rivers, north to the Pawnees on the Loup River, and then south to the Osages. These three tribes lived in earth-lodge villages for most of the year. They grew most of their food in garden plots, which they tended in the creek bottoms nearby. The riverine environment furnished wood and fertile alluvial soil that could be turned with a hoe made from a buffalo's shoulder-blade. Only for a supply of meat did they have to leave their villages, twice a year, to visit the buffalo range in the mixed-grass prairies to the west. They planted their gardens in the spring, hunted in the early summer, returned to their villages for harvest during the buffalo's rutting season, and went on a second hunt late in the fall.[9]

The Kansas' and Osages' location made their trading position different from that of tribes farther up the Missouri, like the Arikaras. Besides growing corn, beans, and squash in their gardens, they could hunt buffalo communally in the grassland during the summer and fall. During the winter they could disperse in small groups to the forest's edge, where firewood was plentiful and where they could hunt deer, bear, and small animals. Moreover, the Lower Missouri and its tributaries—the two largest of which were named for these tribes—put them directly in touch with European traders from St. Louis. The source of horses for the Kansas and Osages was the Plains tribes to their west, as it was for the Arikaras and other tribes farther north, but they obtained firearms and other metalware without the intermediation of tribes to their east. Living in the ecotone and trading directly with whites offered the Kansas and Osages more options than were available to tribes farther up the Missouri.[10]

Sibley arrived at the village of the "Konsees," as he called them, just when they had finished planting their crops and were about to set out on their summer buffalo hunt. "Their little garden patches could be seen in all directions," he wrote, "at convenient distances around the village." En route, he had noted approvingly the presence of nut-bearing hardwoods along the streams and appraised the country as "most excellent land for cultivation; which will at no distant day hold out attractions irresistible to many of our frontier-loving settlers, commonly called *Squatters*." In a few years, as Missouri gained statehood and Sibley's landholdings increased, the opportunity arose to apply his views on proper land use closer to home.[11]

Sibley wrote to Missouri's Senator David Barton in January 1824, describing the part of the state still claimed by the Kansas tribe. He praised "the uncommon excellence of the soil" and went on, "Were this section purchased by [the] Govt. and immediately placed in Market, the rapidity of its settlement and improvements would undoubtedly surpass that of any part of the State or Union. Its rich and exuberant soils would quickly yield a copious overflow of valuable commodities to enrich the State. The water falls which are numerous . . . would soon give life to manufacturing establishments, and our State would be strengthened by the speedy accession of another community of hardy freemen." In June 1825, Sibley helped negotiate a treaty by which the Kansas tribe relinquished its claims to any lands in Missouri and to a vast tract west of the state line in return for an annuity of thirty-five hundred dollars for twenty years and some other considerations. He left immediately afterwards to begin the Santa Fe road survey.[12]

Sibley headed west from Fort Osage at the end of July and reached the Arkansas River three weeks later. Along the way, he noted the quality of the soil, water, and grass and the gradual disappearance of trees. On the day the party struck the Arkansas, about thirty miles downstream from the Great Bend, he wrote, "The soil is apparently fertile and deep, the Herbage tolerably luxuriant; but there is not a single Tree anywhere to be seen on its banks." The commissioners met with the Osages at Council Grove and with the Kansas on the Little Arkansas River. Each tribe granted a right of way through its territory in exchange for "Goods to the value of $300 St. Louis cost," which the commissioners had brought with them, and an order on the nearest licensed trader (Auguste P. Chouteau for the Osages, Cyrus Curtis and Michael Eley for the Kansas) for "Goods such as they may want to the value of Five Hundred Dollars, at fair cash prices." The issuance of licenses to trade with the Indians reflected the federal government's desire to continue to regulate the trade somehow, even after it had ceased to participate directly. The simple words "St. Louis cost" and "cash prices" summarize western economic conditions: high freight charges and precarious credit.[13]

In his 1825 journal, Sibley refrained from predictions about the possibilities of settlement, but when he returned two years later with a party to mark the route with mounds of earth (having in the meantime traveled as far as Santa Fe and spent several months there), he allowed his speculative eye free rein. Standing on a ridge that divided the watersheds of the Kansas River and the Marais des Cygnes, he saw "a Valley of Prairies & forests . . . extremely fertile & beautiful, & I should judge from all that I can See & learn of it that it would afford Room for Several Hund[re]d families of thrifty farmers. . . ." Five days farther west, the expedition reached Hickory Creek, a tributary of the Neosho, and Sibley remarked, "This is a beautiful Cr[eek] & might afford Room for a Number of families near the Road." According to current lore, the stream's nut-bearing hickory trees augured well for the fertility of the soil, and Sibley's mind moved easily from the commercial route of the present to the agricultural possibilities of the future.[14]

So it was that white observers, even before the Indian removal policy of the 1830s, cast an appreciative eye on the prairie. Those eastern tribes from north of the Ohio River who were pressured to move by colluding government agents, missionaries, and traders looked at the unfamiliar land differently. Used to the forests of the Old Northwest, they deplored the dearth of timber and firewood; sugar maples were almost nonexistent. The Indians, of course, were concerned with the land as it lay in their immediate future, not with its possibilities at the indefinite remove of Sibley's conjectural "no distant day."[15]

By the time of Sibley's trips west, wagons had generally supplanted the earlier pack trains in the Santa Fe trade, and the value of the commerce rose steadily during the 1820s. Exact figures do not exist: Augustus Storrs told Senator Benton that $30,000 worth of goods went to Santa Fe in 1824, while Josiah Gregg, writing twenty years later, gave the figure as $35,000. On the other hand, Storrs (a merchant responding to a questionnaire from Benton and eager to promote the trade and possible government assistance for it) estimated the returns of 1824 as $180,000, while Gregg remarked that "average gross returns of the traders has rarely exceeded fifty per cent." Most of the returns took the form of silver and live-stock—asses and mules with a reported average value of $35.[16]

Traders usually sold their wagons in New Mexico and so could not corral the livestock they brought on the return journey. Indians began running off mules as early as 1823; estimates of losses are as uncertain as estimates of the value of goods traded, but surviving records show a loss of about 330 head out of 2,000 (about one-sixth of the total) during the five years from 1823 through 1827. The trade of 1828 was the largest up to that time, with one hundred wag-ons hauling $150,000 worth of merchandise to Santa Fe. In Sep-tember, Comanches and Pawnees attacked different parties of traders on their way back to Missouri, killing four of them and cap-turing 850 horses and mules. Senator Benton proposed a military escort for the 1829 caravan; when Congress adjourned without tak-ing action, Missouri merchants implored the new president, An-drew Jackson, for aid.[17]

The War Department soon issued orders for Captain Bennet Riley and four companies of the Sixth Infantry to take steamboat passage from St. Louis to the recently established Fort Leavenworth and march overland from there, accompanying the Santa Fe caravan as far as the Mexican border, which followed the Arkansas River. The escort was to remain in United States territory and await the return of the traders in the early fall. As it turned out, Indians killed an un-wary merchant who strayed from the caravan a few miles south of the Arkansas, and Riley's troops had to cross the river and escort the wag-ons another two days' march into Mexican territory before returning to their camp. They waited on the north bank of the Arkansas for nearly three months before the merchants appeared, accompanied by a Mexican military escort. By early November, the Missourians were back home and Riley's men were in quarters at Fort Leavenworth.[18]

Commerce on the Santa Fe Trail revived and soon surpassed its previous levels. While 30 wagons had carried $60,000 worth of goods down the trail in 1829, the trade of 1831, borne in 130 wagons, amounted to $250,000. Four soldiers had been killed during the course of the summer, but only one civilian trader. Riley's military escort had accomplished its purpose, and the army's 24 supply wagons were the first on the trail to be drawn by oxen, a practice that the merchants soon adopted. Riley's march to the Arkansas River and back represented the first military intervention on behalf of commerce since Leavenworth's expedition to the Arikara village six years earlier. It was much more successful.[19]

The pattern of federal assistance to commerce, both in the survey of the Santa Fe Trail and in the military escort, is clear. Moreover, Sibley's acquisition of land during his years as Indian factor and survey commissioner, Benton's retainer as counsel for the American Fur Company while he served in the Senate, and Ashley's fur-trading venture between a term as Missouri's lieutenant governor and a term in Congress all illustrate the fluidity with which individuals moved back and forth between government service and private enterprise or sometimes engaged in both at once. During the quarter-century that followed the Louisiana Purchase, American commerce and government took tentative steps into and through the grassland. By 1853, fifty years after the purchase, the extension of United States territory to the Pacific had changed the relative position of the grassland from the country's western margin to its very center; it had given rise to new routes of trade and settlement; and it had severely strained the army's ability to adapt.

Chapter 1

"Steamboat Navigation to Fort Riley
Will Benefit the Settlers"

DURING THE FIRST half of the nineteenth century, the
United States government extended its authority from the Mississippi River to the Pacific Ocean. It acquired valuable mineral lands
that proved their worth immediately and had a tonic effect on the
economy, as well as rich farmlands to be parceled out and the crop
eventually sold in the international grain market. Getting to the
valuable part of the new domain posed a problem, though, for the
way overland led not only through largely unexplored mountains but
across the central grassland of North America, for which the nation
and its citizens had not yet found a use. That one branch of the federal government, the army, played a large part in exploring the region and protecting trade routes is well known. Less often discussed
is the army's role as a conduit for cash, funneling federal money into
the nascent economy of the newly acquired territory. How did the
army arrive in the grassland; what did it hope to accomplish there;
and what were its problems of transportation and supply?

Throughout history, most people of European ancestry have
looked at the North American grassland as a place to traverse on the
way to somewhere more attractive. In the nineteenth century, the
larger eastward-flowing streams usually furnished sufficient water
for travelers and their animals, although the volume was not sufficient to float any but the smallest, lightest boats. Grass afforded
abundant forage. Only after the Civil War did many people seek to
settle permanently in the region. For most of the half-century that
followed the Louisiana Purchase, the grassland was a barrier to
expansion.

Because these lands were marginal (they lay beyond the edge of white settlement, and their agricultural value was unproven), the United States government conceived a plan to remove Indian tribes from the states east of the Mississippi River to the unorganized territory west of Missouri and Arkansas. The army established Fort Gibson at the head of navigation on the Arkansas River in 1824 and Fort Leavenworth on the Missouri in 1827. From these two forts and others like them along a sketchy line from the upper Mississippi River in the north to Red River in the south, the army hoped to monitor and to control, as best it could, relations between the Plains tribes and their new neighbors from the East. The posts' small garrisons of infantry (the army did not raise a mounted regiment until 1832) did not prove very successful.

The acquisition of Oregon in 1846 and of the Mexican Cession two years later made necessary a new scheme of troop deployment. In 1849 the army sent the Regiment of Mounted Riflemen to garrison Fort Kearny, Fort Laramie, and posts farther west along the road to Oregon. In 1850 it established Fort Atkinson on the Arkansas River, and the following year Fort Union in northeastern New Mexico, thus anchoring the middle portion of the road to Santa Fe. The Office of Indian Affairs, transferred from the Department of War to the newly created Department of the Interior, negotiated treaties with the Northern Plains tribes at Fort Laramie in 1851 and with the Southern Plains tribes at Fort Atkinson in 1853. The intention of both treaties was to curtail intertribal fighting and to assure safe passage for travelers on the routes west.

Suddenly, the Plains tribes, who had been living on the farthest margin of United States territory, were right in the middle of it. They were seen as a potential threat by a nation whose view of Indians had been shaped by New England captivity narratives, biographies of Daniel Boone, and fiction like James Fenimore Cooper's account of the fall of Fort William Henry. In fact, Indians killed only about forty white civilians along the Platte River between 1840 and 1860. The army itself, during the first five years after the Mexican War, had only one armed encounter with Indians near Fort Kearny in 1849, another near Fort Atkinson in 1851, and a third near Fort Laramie in 1853. But the expanding military presence in the West meant greater expense, and the army sought a way out.[1]

The army's increasing size was not the primary cause of those higher costs. Its authorized personnel strength grew by less than one-fifth between 1844, the year before the annexation of Texas, and 1849, the year that troops garrisoned new posts in California and Oregon. By another measure, the number of companies had only increased by one-eighth, from 140 to 158 (10 new companies when the Regiment of Mounted Rifles was raised in 1846, and 2 additional companies in each of the artillery regiments the following year). The cause of the army's difficulties becomes clear when the number of companies stationed in the West is compared to the number of western forts. In 1844 sixty-nine companies garrisoned twenty posts, none of them farther west than Forts Gibson and Leavenworth; they averaged 3.45 companies per post. In 1849, with twenty-nine new posts in Texas, New Mexico, California, and Oregon, eighty-six companies were scattered among forty western posts, averaging 2.15 companies to a fort. Territorial expansion meant that the troops were spread thinner; the army's average effective strength had been cut by more than one-third. Distance caused the army's growing costs, and the technology required to overcome distance— the railroad—had not yet penetrated the region.[2]

In 1844 half of the army's western posts had been supplied by steamboat. The others lay an average of 46 miles from a navigable river, five or six days' journey by ox team. The new posts along the routes to Santa Fe and Oregon, though, were supplied by land from Fort Leavenworth: Fort Laramie lay 637 miles to the west; Fort Union, New Mexico, 728 miles; and Santa Fe, headquarters of the Ninth Military Department, 821. In 1845, the army had paid out $130,053.52 for transportation; in 1850–51, transportation cost $2,094,408.51, an increase of 1,500 percent. The cost of forage increased thirteen-fold during the same period, from $99,794.20 to $1,287,327.91, not because of higher prices, the Secretary of War explained, but because the Quartermaster Department, instead of owning 847 draft animals as it had in 1845, had acquired more than 8,000. Between Fort Leavenworth and Santa Fe, though, where a well-developed commerce followed the established trail, civilian contractors hauled the heavier, bulkier supplies, "and this," the Quartermaster General noted, "has been found a far cheaper route than that through Texas."[3]

Military officials searched for ways to cut costs. In 1852 Colonel Thomas T. Fauntleroy of the 1st Dragoons recommended a combined route for the Oregon and Santa Fe Trails, to run along the Kansas River as far west as its confluence with the Republican, where a new military post would be built. He proposed closing Forts Leavenworth, Atkinson, Kearny, and Laramie, as well as Fort Scott, in southeastern Kansas, in order to concentrate ten companies of dragoons and infantry at the new post. From there, troops could patrol the two trails in greater strength than they could from scattered garrisons. "Here are the finest land and the best timber in the western world," Fauntleroy rhapsodized, "capable, the first, of the highest production by cultivation, and the latter affording the most abundant and suitable supply for building materials." Fauntleroy had not looked closely. A post surgeon's report in 1853 listed oak, sycamore, hackberry, and walnut, along with cottonwood, as the predominant species in the river bottoms, but parties of woodcutters with the aid of a steam-driven sawmill soon stripped the neighborhood of usable timber. Cottonwood was known to be poor stuff to build with, yet Fauntleroy ignored the limestone that is still a favorite material for public buildings in the region. Nevertheless, his ill-informed appraisal shows that army officers had an eye towards the future development of the land and its potential market value.[4]

Furthermore, Fauntleroy recommended the colonization of farmers and artisans to serve both the garrison and civilian travelers. He was keenly aware of transportation costs and the higher prices they imposed on the West. "Farmers," he wrote, "can be induced readily to go to this country for the use of the public lands in the vicinity and the promise of St. Louis prices for their products. Mechanics and merchants can also be carried there with the simple hope of selling to, and working for, the emigrants on the several routes which diverge from this point; and thus the government will be enabled at all times, and every season of the year, to have all its work done at prices not to exceed those of old settled neighborhoods in the interior of the States." This colonization proposal echoed an 1848 order from the Secretary of War mandating large military reservations at posts along the road to Oregon. The reservations could be leased to farmers who would supply forage for the mounted troops stationed at the posts. Although the army did not develop a formal colonization scheme—farmers were reluctant to lease part of a military reservation when cheap land was available nearby—a fort did tend to attract farmers and artisans, as well as a small population of discharged soldiers. The fort's expenditures acted as a magnet, without any additional planning or promotion by the federal government. When Fauntleroy concluded that "much expense would be saved to the government . . . , and the efficiency of the troops greatly increased," he touched on matters that were uppermost in the minds of most public officials.[5]

Among those most concerned was Thomas Fitzpatrick, former partner in the Rocky Mountain Fur Company and, in the early 1850s, Indian agent for the tribes on the Upper Arkansas and Platte. Fitzpatrick had expressed his views officially in 1851, when he called Fort Atkinson "a small insignificant military station, beneath the dignity of the United States, and at the mercy and forbearance of the Indians. . . ." Fitzpatrick was a civilian and his comments were published in the reports of the Office of Indian Affairs; his experience in the West dated back to 1823, though, and he was well-acquainted with army officers who served in the central plains. His report said that small posts like Atkinson and Laramie were virtually defenseless. "There is not a single day that passes in which the Indians could not, if disposed to do so, strip and deprive these posts of all their resources, murder the different fatigue parties in detail, and drive off all the horses and stock. . . . What, then, can possibly be the use in keeping up, at such enormous expense, such places? If these men are to be fed and clothed at the expense of the government, would it not be more economical to do it at some other place at a less cost?" Fitzpatrick advocated raising two mounted battalions of about three hundred men each to patrol the Santa Fe and Oregon routes in strength.[6]

In the summer of 1852, while Colonel Fauntleroy was explaining his views to the Quartermaster General, Lieutenant Israel C. Woodruff of the Topographical Engineers was exploring central Kansas and mapping the valley of the Kansas River. Woodruff left Fort Leavenworth during the first week in June and returned about the middle of September. In late October he set out again, this time as part of a board of officers that included Captain Edmund A. Ogden, brevetted major for meritorious conduct in the Mexican War, and Captain Langdon C. Easton, both of the Quartermaster Department, to select a site for a new post in the vicinity Fauntleroy had recommended. The board reported its findings, which the Secretary of War approved in January, and in March 1853 Congress appropriated sixty-five thousand dollars for "barracks and quarters at the Republican Fork of the Kansas River." In May three companies of the Sixth Infantry Regiment arrived at the site, and construction began.[7]

Known at first as Camp Center, from its location near the geographical center of the United States, the new post soon received the name of Fort Riley, after Bennet Riley, who died the month after its founding. During that summer, the garrison averaged 130 enlisted men commanded by five or six officers. Although far fewer than the number of troops recommended by Fauntleroy or Fitzpatrick, they constituted about one-fifth of the troop strength of the Sixth Military Department, which had its headquarters at Jefferson Barracks near St. Louis and included posts in Minnesota as well as those in Kansas and along the Platte. The half-dozen officers present performed a number of functions, taking care of the fort's administrative and logistical business as well as directing the labor of troops in garrison or leading them in the field.

Officers at Fort Riley bore titles and carried out tasks identical to those of officers at other posts throughout the army. The fort's commanding officer, in this instance Captain Charles S. Lovell of the Sixth Infantry, would be the senior officer of one of the line regiments (cavalry, artillery, or infantry) at a post; a second lieutenant of the line would serve as commanding officer, even though a senior officer of one of the staff bureaus, a captain and assistant

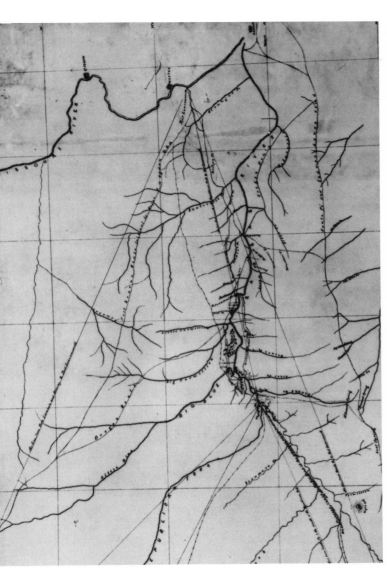

Lieutenant Israel C. Woodruff's map of his 1852 reconnaisance of the Kansas River valley. The road from Independence, Missouri, to Santa Fe runs well south of the river; the road from Fort Leavenworth to Fort Kearny joins the "Oregon Route" between the Big Blue and the Little Blue; and the route from Fort Leavenworth to the confluence of the Republican and the Smoky Hill—the future site of Fort Riley—branches from the Leavenworth-Kearny road. The sparse information in Woodruff's map illustrates the sketchy contemporary knowledge of the central grassland. (Kansas State Historical Society)

quartermaster, say, was present. Captain Ogden, who was an assistant quartermaster, served as post quartermaster at Fort Riley when construction began in the spring of 1853. When he was transferred in June, his duties devolved on Lieutenant Alden Sargent of the Sixth Infantry, whose title became acting assistant quartermaster.

The post quartermaster was responsible for clothing and housing the troops, including construction of buildings, and for transportation, including vehicles, draft animals, and forage. Before and during the Civil War, the post quartermaster advertised army contracts for forage (corn, hay, and oats) and firewood, compared the bids, and awarded the contract. After the war, with the growth of rail transportation, the Chief Quartermaster of the Department of the Missouri handled most bids in Kansas. Fort Riley's post quartermaster reported to this official, whose office was at Fort Leavenworth. The officer whose title was acting commissary of subsistence ("acting" because he was a regimental officer rather than a member of the Subsistence Department, which was headed by the Commissary General) was responsible for the beef contracts and dealt with drovers and local stockgrowers. For the rest of the nineteenth century, these three officers—the commanding officer, the quartermaster, and the commissary—would represent Fort Riley in the army's dealings with its civilian neighbors.[8]

Every military post had an adjutant (administrative officer), a quartermaster, and a commissary of subsistence. Only rarely were the latter two positions filled by officers from the Quartermaster or Subsistence Departments; for the most part, those duties were performed by regimental lieutenants detailed for the purpose. Before Ogden left Fort Riley, Sargent had been serving as post adjutant and ACS in charge of rations. When Sargent assumed the duties of AAQM as well as ACS, Lieutenant Darius D. Clark took over as post adjutant. In addition, each regiment had its own adjutant and a quartermaster, usually the two senior first lieutenants, who also served as the post adjutant and quartermaster wherever regimental headquarters happened to be.

Each post also had a medical officer, referred to as the "post surgeon" whether his actual rank was surgeon (equivalent to a major), assistant surgeon (captain), or acting assistant surgeon (a civilian "contract surgeon," who drew a lieutenant's pay). Fort Riley's post surgeon during the summer of 1853 was Assistant Surgeon Joseph Barnes, who had received his commission in 1840 and had served in that grade ever since. Long service in one grade was the rule. Ogden had been promoted captain in 1838 and was brevetted in 1848.

Ogden set to work with a crew of about forty civilians, mostly masons and carpenters hired in Cincinnati and St. Louis for a wage of two dollars a day and transportation paid. Most of them returned east at the end of their contracts, but a few stayed in the neighborhood, taking up farms nearby, driving teams for civilian freighters, or working at the fort when the quartermaster needed hands. Because Fort Riley was to have been an eight-company post, Ogden had planned on using the labor of two hundred soldiers who would have received a per diem of fifteen cents for extra duty. The three companies actually in garrison could spare only seventy or eighty extra-duty men, though, and construction lagged. Moreover, Ogden was ordered back to Fort Leavenworth in June and could devote only about one-third of his time, much of which was spent in travel, to Fort Riley. By November, only two company barracks and two double sets of officers' quarters (duplexes) were ready for occupancy. Although a small crew of civilians continued to work through the winter, half of the buildings had not even been started when Major Oscar F. Winship visited the post on a tour of inspection the following June. By early autumn of 1854, only two more barracks and another set of officers' quarters had been completed. "The reduced state of the post & the am[oun]t of labor & duty to be performed—absolutely require reinforcements," the commanding officer wrote.[9]

Reinforcements came with a rush in 1855, when the threat of Indian hostilities in the West prompted Congress to authorize two new regiments of cavalry and two of infantry, bringing the number of mounted regiments to five and of infantry to ten. Ogden received orders "to complete as expeditiously as possible, by hired labor, Quarters, barracks, and stables . . . sufficient for Ten companies of Dragoons in addition to the . . . two companies of infantry now constituting the garrison." The additional construction was to be of stone, like the buildings already raised. Wooden buildings, the orders explained, "such . . . as are often appropriate for the frontier, would in a country like that at Fort Riley, where timber is very sparse, involve too much delay for the present emergency, and an expense disproportionate to their value." (Ogden's estimate for 1853 had included fifty thousand feet of rough pine lumber and fifty thousand feet of milled flooring; the freight charge from St. Louis, $1,450, added 50 percent to the cost of the lumber itself.) The work force, hired mostly in Ohio, included one hundred masons and fifty tenders, fifty quarrymen and sixteen stonecutters, besides thirty carpenters and more than one hundred laborers, teamsters, and woodcutters. That they had to travel overland from Fort Leavenworth to Fort Riley, by turns walking and riding in wagons, chagrined Ogden. The Kansas River, he complained to the Quartermaster General, "is lower than ever before known at this season and the Boats attempting its navigation are so unsuitable that I cannot rely upon them for carrying our supplies until some rains visit our arid region and supply the usual depth of water."[10]

One student of the military presence in the antebellum West writes of the army's "initiating" steam navigation on the Kansas River. What actually happened was neither so simple nor so successful as that sounds. Ogden had written to the Quartermaster General in the fall of 1853, "An examination, which was made a year ago, . . . left little doubt of the navigability of . . . the river during the season of high waters. A more careful survey, made a few weeks since . . . , confirms our previous impression, and some enterprizing citizens will, probably, in the ensuing spring, be prepared to take our freight from the mouth of the Kansas to Fort Riley, by Steamers, at rates materially less than the cost of land transportation." Indeed, the *Excel*, partly owned by the civilian contractor Charles A. Perry and loaded with eleven hundred barrels of flour, made the trip from Weston, Missouri, to Fort Riley in two days in April 1854, the first steamer to ascend the river. Another of the *Excel*'s cargoes must have been the seven thousand bushels "of corn, in sacks," that Perry had contracted to ship to Fort Riley "for the sum of $1.15 per bushel, and also such public stores as may be turned over to him at

Fort Leavenworth, for the sum of $1.25 per 100 pounds." The flour and corn were the produce of counties in northwestern Missouri, within the trading area of Fort Leavenworth, where a generation of farmers and brokers had thrived doing business with army quartermasters. Ogden made a round trip on the *Excel* in early June and found the river "so entirely free from obstructions at this season that our pilot though only on his third trip was able to keep the steamer under way by night as well as by day." He went on to remark that "navigation of the Kansas as far as Fort Riley may certainly be regarded as practicable for suitable steamers for at least three months in the year," a statement that the *Messenger* of Independence, Missouri, turned into "at least three-fourths of the year." Steamboats were the essential link to the world downriver and the larger economy.[11]

Although Ogden hedged his statements with qualifiers like "suitable steamers" and "during the season," other forecasters were less restrained. In the fall of 1854, Major Oscar F. Winship, after a tour of inspection in the central plains, reported that "the navigation of the Kansas has opened a way by water for all the supplies that will ever be required at Fort Riley." It was, he wrote, "not only practicable but . . . *un fait accompli*, six successive trips having been made in as many weeks . . . in the months of May and June last, and this steamer was only then withdrawn for want of sufficient business to occupy her for a longer period." A correspondent of the Leavenworth *Kansas Weekly Herald*, writing from the townsite of Pawnee, on the Fort Riley military reservation, declared, "By spring, the whistle of the steamer will be heard at her levee, and then look out, for we are bound to go ahead." The correspondent then soared far beyond reality, declaring the Smoky Hill fork "navigable for steamers over a hundred miles." Navigation was necessary; therefore, the river was navigable.[12]

Thirty-four steamers plied the Kansas River between 1854, the year of the *Excel*'s first trip, and 1866, when construction of railroad bridges put the riverboats out of business. Only three boats made it as far upstream as Fort Riley. This has to do with the nature of rivers in the central plains; rather than carrying snow melt from the mountains, they are conduits for runoff and depend on seasonal precipitation. After the spring floods subside, water levels remain low through the rest of the year. Lieutenant John C. Tidball reported to Ogden from Fort Riley in 1853 on the prospects for navigation: "Throughout the entire course of the stream the evidences were abundant that the water had been from six to eight feet above its level when I descended. . . ." Tidball cautioned, "I have too little experience in matters relating to navigation to form opinions concerning it in which I can rest entire confidence," but still felt "strongly impelled to the belief that there is a period of from two to four months of the year, dating from the first spring rise, during which boats can ascend to this point."[13]

Tidball's belief came from observing the river after a series of wet years. The annual reports of the Commissioner of Indian Affairs contain evaluations of climate, mostly subjective, from agents in the field. In the years following "the unparalleled drought which prevailed in this region during the summer" of 1850, U.S. Indian agents at Council Grove, St. Mary's, and Shawnee Mission had reported "abundant" crops. In August 1853, the month Tidball was descending the Kansas, a missionary to the Ottawas wrote that "their crops have never looked more promising than they now do; they have raised this year much more oats, corn, and potatoes than in any previous year. . . ." The following spring, as the *Excel* was making its trips to Fort Riley, came "almost continuous rains," according to the farmer employed at the Sac and Fox agency. An "extensive and continuous drought" followed, leading to "almost a total failure of crops in the Territory." In spite of the drought (or, rather, because of the spring rains), the missionary at St. Mary's reported that the "Kansas river has proved to be a fine navigable stream in the rainy season, May and June. The facilities of steamboat navigation to Fort Riley," he predicted, "will benefit the settlers in the Kansas valley and adjacent districts."[14]

What the army pioneered in the Kansas River valley in the early 1850s was not so much navigation—which was undertaken by frontier merchants risking their own capital in the form of boats and cargoes, not always in pursuit of a government contract—as the practice, which became a national habit, of observing a sequence of wet years in the grassland and drawing sweeping inferences from it. The reports of Indian agents, agency farmers, and missionaries show that the river's navigability was assessed during wet years and that the *Excel* made its trips to Fort Riley in 1854 during a remarkably rainy spring. To assume that these conditions would prevail consistently showed the same false optimism that was to draw farmers into the plains during the wet 1880s and 1910s, only to be baffled and driven back by the droughts of the following decades. Even observers with several years' experience in the country called the drought of 1850 "unparalleled" and the one that followed four years later "unprecedented." More than "initiating" steam navigation on the Kansas, army officers were helping to initiate a tradition of reckless misinterpretation of rainfall data in the plains.[15]

That army officers chose a site so far west indicated great faith in the navigability of the Kansas River. Fort Riley, at the supposed head of navigation, could serve as an important quartermaster depot. After Woodruff's reconnaissance of 1852, Tidball's descent of the river the following year, and the *Excel*'s deliveries to Fort Riley the spring after that, Major Oscar F. Winship, in a report on military posts in the central plains, expressed the opinion that Fort Riley would eclipse Leavenworth. These hopes were based on the expectation of abundant supplies arriving cheaply by water.

Until the coming of railroads, transportation by water was much faster and cheaper than by land. For instance, Major Winship took three days in June 1854 to travel overland from Fort Leavenworth to Fort Riley, covering about forty miles a day on horseback; the steamer *Excel* made the round trip to Fort Riley from the mouth of the Kansas River and back in that much time. One of the *Excel*'s owners, Charles A. Perry, signed a contract in February 1854 to deliver government freight from Fort Leavenworth to Fort Riley by river for $1.25 per one hundred pounds. The previous summer, when the army had abandoned Fort Atkinson on the Arkansas River, the freighters Russell and Waddell had charged seven dollars per one hundred pounds to move government property to Fort Riley by wagon. Cost differences like these had led to the canal boom of

1825–40 east of the Mississippi, and the 727 steamboats that plied that river and its tributaries by 1855.[16]

Virtually all travel west of Topeka was to be by land, though. Farmers at Indian agencies and army quartermasters at Fort Riley alike complained of drought in the mid-1850s, which meant the river was too low to navigate. In 1853 Major Ogden had estimated the cost of a "military road" from Fort Leavenworth to Fort Riley as $4,525: $675 for soldiers' extra duty per diem of fifteen cents; $3,000 for twenty civilians; and $850 for a "portable sawmill and pile driver." His estimate for a similar road between Fort Riley and the place where the Santa Fe Trail struck the Arkansas River was $7,200. These estimates, like the one for the construction of Fort Riley itself, were "entirely too small," as the Quartermaster General put it while explaining, in his annual report, why another $29,000 was "required to complete the work" on Fort Riley. Army officers who had imagined the benefits of steam navigation confronted reality in the form of steep overland transportation costs.[17]

Ogden continued to insist that Fort Riley was "connected with Fort Leavenworth, by steam navigation, three months in the year," but Lieutenant Edward G. Beckwith, who had traveled the Santa Fe Trail in 1853, wrote that "roads and bridges . . . are of the first importance. . . . I am however, doubtful of the expediency of fixing Fort Riley as the point for their eastern terminus, for it is certain that, if practicable at all for light-draught steamers, *the Kansas River can only be so for a few weeks in each year*, and therefore, upon any unanticipated emergency, supplies can only be received at that terminus by land transportation from the Missouri River." With the initial appropriation of $11,725 nearly exhausted, the Quartermaster General in January 1857 requested another $50,000 to complete bridges and grading. The road, along with others, he wrote, would "afford facilities to emigrants to reach the remote parts of the Territory, by which supplies for the frontier posts will be produced in their vicinity, and the necessity and expense of bringing them from a long distance will be avoided in a few years." Road building, the Quartermaster General reasoned, would pay for itself.[18]

Some "emigrants" were already on hand to help build the route from Fort Leavenworth to Fort Riley, and a few of the earliest contracts between army quartermasters and Kansas residents were for bridges and ferries. The going price for a bridge was sixteen hundred dollars, whether purchased ready made, as when Lewis Vieux sold his bridge over Soldier's Creek in the fall of 1854, or built from scratch, like William F. Dyer's bridge over Grasshopper Creek at Ozawkie, which was to be of "oak timber, 180 feet long, 14 wide, 6 feet above high water mark . . . flooring 2 inches thick, side rails & c." Dyer was president of the Osawkee Association, a town company; William R. Montgomery was the acting assistant quartermaster representing the army; and Dyer's surety was Robert C. Miller, who, like Montgomery, was a member of the Pawnee Association, promoters of a townsite on the military reservation of Fort Riley itself. This was typical of early commercial practices: the names of town promoters appear on contract after contract, either as bidder or surety, in the nascent stage of what Lewis Atherton would call "an inner circle whose own personal interests were so tightly interwoven with those of the community at large that one cannot determine where self-interest ended and public spirit began."[19]

The territory was not so thickly settled in the summer of 1855, though, that Major Ogden could hire local artisans to complete the "Quarters, barracks, and stables" required for mounted troops. As he had during the previous two seasons, he brought in contract workers from Cincinnati and St. Louis. The report of civilian employees at Fort Riley for August 1855 shows 57 quarrymen, 19 stonecutters, 103 masons, and 58 masons' tenders handling the stonework, with 11 limeburners furnishing mortar and 13 brickmakers. There were woodchoppers, sawyers, and carpenters; blacksmiths; painters and plasterers; 45 common laborers; and 105 teamsters. The average monthly payroll in the third quarter of 1855 was $22,506. In the last quarter, as construction slackened and most of the contract men were paid off, it dropped to $13,277. Throughout the summer and fall, under the terms of the contract, one-quarter of their wages had been withheld; when the men left, their money went with them.[20]

The work had gotten off to a slow start that year because the quartermaster at Fort Leavenworth was able to furnish transportation only for the workers and their belongings, and Ogden's construction material and equipment had to be left for another trip. "I take with me of course a much larger quantity of dry pine Lumber than I would do if time permitted the manufacturing and seasoning of enough at Fort Riley," he had written to the Quartermaster General, "but in other respects I have nothing peculiar in my outfit of material except a Pages Double portable Sawmill & patent Shingle Machine driven by a small (20 Horsepower) Steam Engine and Boiler of the Locomotive pattern—which I have deemed necessary in addition to [the] mill now there not only for the more rapid manufacture of Lumber & Shingles—but its utility and economy in ripping, morticing &c and other operations of a similar kind which pertain to carpenter work—The surplus mill which will be on hand at the termination of the work can readily be sold in that new country." When Ogden arrived at Fort Riley on July 18, he found "that notwithstanding the ample time for such preparations not a bushel of Lime was ready or saw log or cord of wood provided." Two weeks later, work was delayed further by an outbreak of cholera that killed Ogden, sixteen other soldiers and military dependents, and an indeterminate number of civilian employees. Nevertheless, by the middle of December the post quartermaster was able to report considerable progress, with three sets of officers' quarters occupied and a fourth near completion, five barracks occupied and a sixth to be finished the next month, and the cavalry stables "all under cover but one." He attached an estimate for labor and materials needed to construct another barracks, a storehouse, a hospital, and a guardhouse in the coming year. The cost of materials was $7,169, of which $2,175, or 30 percent, was "Freight on the above from St. Louis to Fort Riley."[21]

Three of the barracks, each designed to house one company, were "crowded" (the quartermaster's word) with six companies of the Second Dragoons, who had arrived in September. Their horses occupied three of the stables, "whilst the other two which are covered in, are occupied as a Commissary-Store and Forage House; and for sheltering the public mules, there being no Quartermaster's Stables at the post." The average strength of the infantry garrison during

Fort Riley's first two years had been 7 officers and 145 infantrymen. With the introduction of mounted troops, the average strength for the next five years would be 14 officers and 391 enlisted men. The average number of cavalry mounts present when the troops were not in the field was 290. Surviving records of hay contracts at the fort do not show a comparable increase, but the amount of hay provided undoubtedly depended as much on the amount of rainfall as on the needs of the garrison. The purpose of the mounted troops, though, was not to enrich contractors but to overawe the Plains Indians. As it turned out, most of the troops spent the year 1856 trying to keep the peace between pro- and anti-slavery factions in the territory, while others marched to Utah in 1858 to intimidate the Mormons; but their primary concern remained the Plains Indians.[22]

What sort of challenge did the army think the Plains Indians posed? Major Winship's report to the Adjutant General in 1854 contains a revealing anecdote:

> Alluding to [an] attack on the New Mexicans, some one asked a Cheyenne what he thought would be the result, when the news should reach the Government; to which query, he promptly replied 'Our Great Father will send us some more presents. When we want some sugar, and coffee, and blankets, we kill a white man, and straight our Great Father sends us some.' A similar remark was made by an Arapahoe when asked what would be done with the Sioux engaged in the late massacre of Lieut Grattan's party, near Fort Laramie. These tales are doubtless trifling in themselves, and almost always exaggerated, but they are too common and too much in keeping with the general conduct of the Indians to admit of a doubt as to the feeling they indicate toward the whites.

Similarly, some Cheyennes had told John C. Frémont in 1853 that they had stolen five of his expedition's horses and, given a little more time, "they would have stolen a great many more."[23]

Overland travelers to California, Oregon, and Utah totaled more than 125,000 during the emigration seasons from 1852 to 1854. Although the Cheyennes had suffered from white contact along the trails, including a cholera outbreak in 1849 that killed about half of them, they did not have a fight with the army until August 1856, near Fort Kearny, Nebraska. The incident began with a request by some Cheyennes for tobacco. A nervous white man fired a shot and in turn was wounded by a Cheyenne arrow. The fort responded by sending a company of cavalry to attack the Cheyenne camp. Nevertheless, the central plains remained generally peaceful: there was a fight with the Sioux on the North Platte in 1854 and one in 1855; the fight with the Cheyennes in 1856, and another on the Solomon River the following year; and none in 1858. Of these fights, the closest to Fort Riley occurred nearly a week's march west. The reason was simple: Fort Riley lay far to the east of the buffalo range. Buffalo-hunting Plains Indians had no cause to come near the fort.[24]

The quiet ended with the news in 1858 of the discovery of gold in Colorado. Traffic along the Platte route in the seasons of 1859 and 1860 equaled the combined total of the previous four years, and thousands more gold seekers followed the Arkansas River and the even more direct routes up the Smoky Hill and Republican Rivers. The traffic was by no means one-way; disappointed prospectors recrossed the grassland headed east, disturbing the buffalo herds and further annoying the Plains Indians. In 1859, a line of stagecoaches began following a route up the Smoky Hill, Solomon, and Republican Rivers.[25]

While outside pressure increased, changes in Cheyenne society itself made that tribe more likely to respond violently, as more young men began living in villages based on military societies like the Dog Soldiers. The Cheyennes had had a dual, seasonal organization, partly for war, partly for hunting and trade, at least since they moved to the central plains early in the nineteenth century. That tendency now became divisive. By the fall of 1860, "the polarization of the Cheyenne nation between a peace and a war faction was far advanced," and only some of the bands bothered to attend a treaty conference on the Arkansas River.[26]

The crescendo of violence on the Plains continued during the summer of 1864. Colonel John M. Chivington's attack on a village of Cheyennes at Sand Creek that fall "destroyed the last vestige of confidence between red and white man," the U.S. Indian agent at Fort Larned wrote two months after the massacre. It was, by definition, a surprise attack, since the people in the village were peaceably inclined and were on their treaty lands just where their agent had told them to camp.[27]

Sand Creek was exceptional in the history of military campaigning on the plains, though. Any armed encounter between troops and Plains Indians was exceptional. Far more typical was the operation described in the Manhattan *Independent* of August 8, 1864, as a company of Kansas volunteer cavalry returned to Fort Riley from a week-long scout to the southwest: "This expedition has terminated as most people in this vicinity supposed it would, with the exception, that the fruitless chase after escaping savages, was pressed with more vigor and continued longer than any but the commanding officers could imagine the necessity for. The lesson to the red skins would no doubt have been salutary had they waited to receive it: but having left some two weeks before, as most of the rank and file of the pursuing force supposed they would of course do, the lesson was spent on the pursuers, and judging from the humor of the boys on their return it was more impressive than improving." The company's rank and file were local settlers, and expressed their opinions freely to the hometown editor. Plains Indian raiders did not stay around to be caught, nor was the army often able to find and destroy their villages. Rather than far-ranging cavalry, what ended the buffalo-hunting way of life on the plains was the railroad. It enabled the army to maintain supply bases farther west, and within a few years led to the virtual extinction of the buffalo by providing a way to get untanned hides to market.[28]

By facilitating the near-extermination of the buffalo, the railroads opened the grassland to stockgrowers and wheat farmers, who in turn furnished most of the region's rail freight. Railroads expanded and transformed the economy of the American West, integrating it with the national economy by moving goods year-round in all but the most severe weather. Raw material—cattle, grain,

minerals—left the region to be processed elsewhere. Rail transportation made possible industrial mining and increased urbaniza-
tion in the West.

During the five years that followed the Civil War, the nation's
rail mileage increased by half. Most of the additional track was laid
to fill in gaps in the existing network. General Sherman was as
aware of construction connecting Omaha with Chicago and Kansas
City as he was of the two lines heading west towards Denver and the
Great Salt Lake. The road west from Kansas City, at first called the
Union Pacific Eastern Division, and after 1869, the Kansas Pacific,
had strung a telegraph line as far as Lawrence by May 1865 and had
laid track that far by September.[29]

Meanwhile, oxen and mules continued to pull wagons and stagecoaches through the Kansas River valley. In September the Butterfield Overland Despatch began running three stages a week between
Atchison and Denver. Regular communications between the Colorado goldfields and the East had been interrupted by Indian hostilities during the Civil War, but Butterfield's stagecoaches would
run from the late summer of 1865 until the advancing tracks of the
Kansas Pacific gradually superseded them. In November 1865, the
editor of the Junction City *Union* remarked on a seventy-wagon
train headed west "with pine lumber, doors, and window frames and
sash . . . for the construction of military posts . . . on the Smoky Hill
Route." The next month, twenty-five wagons loaded with hay left
Fort Riley to supply cavalry stations farther west. In February 1866
the *Union* noted that an "immense number of trains have gone west
the past week. The roads are now in good order and travel in all directions is brisk." General John Pope at Fort Leavenworth observed
that in spite of "unusually severe weather" everywhere in the West,
"the stream of people crossing the great plains seems to have been
nearly as continuous and as determined as during the summer
months."[30]

Fort Riley and the neighboring town of Junction City were busier
than they ever had been or would be for another twenty years. The
Chief Quartermaster of the Department of the Missouri, believing
that the railroad would reach Fort Riley in the spring of 1866, pre-

dicted that it would be "the great point of departure for [wagon] trains another season. . . ." The *Union's* editor offered to bet "a new hat that nine tenths of the commerce of the plains passes through this place next spring." One reason for the commercial bustle was the fear of Indian hostilities. In February 1866, General Pope ordered that no wagon trains headed for Denver along the Smoky Hill River should venture west of Fort Riley with fewer than twenty wagons and thirty armed men. Fort Riley (or Fort Larned for trains following the Arkansas River) was as far west as travelers could go "without danger." The first locomotive did not steam into Junction City until November 1866, as it turned out, but wagon traffic was heavy all year. Fort Riley's post quartermaster alone employed an average of two hundred teamsters that summer and fall, at a wage of forty-five dollars a month.[31]

As the Kansas Pacific and Union Pacific moved west, the army's freight costs dropped. Even the cost of wagon freight to New Mexico declined 21 percent in two years as the tracks advanced from Fort Riley to Fort Hays and on beyond the Colorado line. In May 1867, the Chief Quartermaster of the Department of the Missouri ordered the depot quartermaster at Fort Riley to transfer his operation to Fort Harker as soon as the railroad reached Ellsworth, three counties and eighty miles west of Junction City. The Junction City *Union* announced the opening of passenger service to Ellsworth and the removal of the quartermaster depot in the same issue. A week later, the editor reflected that "the onward progress of the railroad . . . will render useless to [the] government the keeping up of such a military establishment as Fort Riley. It must before long be abandoned, and the consequence will be that our market will fall to the standard of other towns. . . . The advantages of Fort Riley will soon play out, and the way to secure other and better ones is to encourage liberally the construction of the Union Pacific Railway, Southern Branch [later part of the Missouri, Kansas and Texas]." Diminished government spending caused the editor to look quickly towards Emporia, Indian Territory, and Texas for new fields of action.[32]

While exaggerated predictions of railroad construction and of urban boom and bust proliferated, the commanding officer at Fort

Railroads were the major influence on Fort Riley's history throughout the last third of the nineteenth century. This fanciful, almost woodsy, illustration dates from 1866, the year the tracks of the Union Pacific, Eastern Division (later the Kansas Pacific), reached the fort. (Kansas State Historical Society)

Riley, Major John W. Davidson of the Second Cavalry, took a longer view:

> As a station of troops to protect settlements in [the] event of Indian hostilities Fort Riley has lost its importance, settlements being well in advance of it on both the Smokey Hill and Republican Rivers. But as a Depot for the supply of the posts in our western Territories . . . it is of great importance to the Government. This should be, in my opinion, the Cavalry Depot of the West. The Government owns a large reserve here; the facilities for grazing are unsurpassed in the West. . . . The remount horses of all the cavalry Posts . . . should be kept here. The broken down stock, instead of being condemned or sold at the posts, should be conducted here for recuperation.

A year later, indeed, Fort Riley stabled 146 cavalry horses left behind by deserters from one of the new regiments that had been authorized in 1866, but it would not be considered seriously as a cavalry station again for another eighteen years. Then it would be the large military reservation established in 1855, as well as the fort's rail connections, that attracted General Sheridan's attention. In the years between, the reservation and the railroad would enable Fort Riley to serve as the army's foremost hay farm.[33]

The constant, dynamic change that is inseparable from capitalist development would make Fort Riley a military backwater for nearly two decades. The fort's cash disbursements—the size of its civilian payroll and the quartermaster's contracts—shrank. Local businessmen sought to strengthen their rail links to distant markets and, since the army was not pumping money into the local economy, to open parts of the military reservation to settlement or else to do away with the fort altogether. But the railroads also made possible new uses for Fort Riley—as a hay farm and as a winter dormitory for troops who traveled to their summer campaigns by rail—and the army refused to budge.

Chapter 2

"A Flourishing City May Soon Appear"

THE MOST WIDELY recognized manifestation of the federal government as it helped to shape the economy of the American West was its land policy, which parceled out millions of acres to individual and corporate owners. Less far-reaching in effect, but more immediate, were infusions of government money into local economies. The army, with scores of posts scattered throughout the West, was the chief outlet for federal funds.

Military expenditures took two forms: wages paid to the quartermaster's civilian employees and large disbursements to contractors. Local contracts filled the soldiers' immediate needs—food, forage, and fuel—and varied in size according to the number of troops in garrison, while the army's clothing came from large suppliers in eastern cities. The number of civilian employees at a post, and therefore the amount of wages paid into the local economy, depended on the quartermaster's budget for the department. Often, there was no money to hire civilian artisans, and soldiers who had been driven into the army by unemployment had to ply their civilian trades to make necessary repairs to the fort's buildings. Quartermaster's wages, though they might be one of the few sources of cash in a newly settled region, could vanish overnight at a command from department headquarters. Nevertheless, wage income could be important to a local economy over the years, and particularly at its start.

For the first fifteen years of Fort Riley's history, until the quartermaster depot moved to Ellsworth in 1867, the fort's quartermaster was one of the few sources of wages. In 1855, two years after the fort was founded, nearly one-third of households in the neighbor-hood sent at least one member to work at the fort, augmenting the large crews of artisans and laborers that the army brought from the East. As the population of Davis and Riley Counties increased and the economy grew, Fort Riley employed a smaller percentage of the residents, but they constituted a larger proportion of the fort's skilled workers and laborers. Meanwhile, discharged soldiers began to settle nearby; though few in number, those who remained tended, like other long-term residents, to prosper. Government freighting became big business in the years before the railroad arrived, with major wagon routes running through Manhattan to Denver and Salt Lake City by way of the Platte River, through Junction City to Denver by way of the Smoky Hill, and to New Mexico by way of the Arkansas. Fort Riley served as an engine of economic growth dur-ing the prerailroad era.

The organization of Kansas Territory in 1854 prompted a spate of travel and promotional literature. One such book, simply enti-tled *A Journey Through Kansas*, was published in Cincinnati, where some of the residents were already deeply interested in colonization schemes for the new territory. Its authors praised the tasteful stone buildings at Fort Riley but found the water of the Smoky Hill brack-ish. A little way from the fort, "the evening shadow had begun to soften the outlines of the scene, and a light curling line of smoke, rising from [a] tent, looked the very symbol of quiet and repose. The tent was occupied by some haymakers from the fort, and one of their number . . . informed me that he was so charmed with the spot, that he has selected there his future home." Back at the fort, the authors talked with some officers, who told them that "it is the design of the government, so soon as the settlements in the Kansas valley shall reach upward to the fort, to give up the position, sell out the grounds and buildings, and establish a more western station. Sound policy will doubtless require such a step, and a flourishing city may soon appear at the head of steamboat navigation on the Kansas." Since nearly all of the officers at Fort Riley in 1854 were members of the Pawnee Association, a group of land speculators or-ganized to establish the capital of Kansas Territory within a few miles of the fort, it is hardly surprising that the Cincinnatians' anonymous informants expressed this view.[1]

Lieutenant John Pope, of the army's Corps of Topographical Engineers, succinctly outlined the "well known effect of military posts" on settlement in a report dated 1854, the year after Fort Riley was founded. Forts, Pope wrote, attracted "settlers, who cultivate the country in the vicinity, and who are able in a short time to supply most of the necessities of the garrisons." Settlements eventually outgrew the need for military protection, "and the garrisons can be safely removed farther into the Indian country, to produce in time the same results."[2]

The 1855 census of Kansas Territory, along with the post quartermasters' reports of persons employed and abstracts of bids on contracts, shows what sort of people settled near Fort Riley during its earliest years. Governor Andrew Reeder ordered the census after voter fraud by nonresident Missourians prevailed in the November election of 1854. The Ninth and Tenth Election Districts included Fort Riley and the surrounding country, which had not then been organized as counties. The fort itself lay in the Ninth District. The recorded residents included the quartermaster's clerk, the wagonmaster, the post sutler (licensed civilian trader) and his clerk, and fourteen black residents, three of whom gave their occupation as cook and, along with their families, were listed as free. Phyllis Harris, a minor, was listed as the slave of William A. Hammond, the post surgeon. The census recorded whether residents were native-born or naturalized citizens, their occupations, age (by decades: minor, twenty-one, thirty, forty, and so on), and the place from which they had moved to Kansas. Allowing for the spelling idiosyncrasies of the census-takers and quartermasters, one can get a pretty good idea of how some of the population derived at least part of its income from the Quartermaster Department at Fort Riley.

The quartermaster's monthly Report of Persons and Articles Employed and Hired was a form printed on a folio sheet. It listed persons employed by the month (names, occupations, rate of pay, and dates of employment) and local artisans hired by the job. In later years, items such as telephone service and county clerks' notary fees appeared on the reports, as well as farmers' charges for boarding cavalry horses that gave out on the march while regiments were changing stations. In the 1850s and '60s, ferry rental appeared on the reports. But to say that Fort Riley's quartermasters paid out $46,102.11 in wages during the first two years of the post's existence or that they employed an average of twelve teamsters and thirty-two "mechanics" (all other categories of worker, as listed in the summary in the adjutant's monthly post returns) does not tell much about the post's effect on local civilians. Most of the skilled construction workers at Fort Riley in the summer of 1855 had signed on in Cincinnati or St. Louis for six months' work; one quarter of their pay was withheld until their time was up, after which most of them returned to the East. The territorial census of 1855 is a necessary lens through which to examine Fort Riley's effect on nearby settlement.[3]

The Tenth District, including what would become eastern Riley County, had sixty-eight adult males living in it in February 1855, fifty-six of whom listed their occupation as farmer. The other residents included two lawyers, two physicians, a clergyman, a cooper, a mason, a merchant, a painter, and three men who gave no occupation. During 1853 and 1854, the mason and seven of the farmers had worked at the fort. Thomas Blakely, the mason, had been recruited in St. Louis in the spring of 1853 and continued to work at Fort Riley through the end of the following year. Henry Schepp had signed on as a mason in Cincinnati, worked his six months, and taken up farming. Both he and Blakely worked again as masons in the summer and fall of 1855. Andrew Noll helped drive the mule train between Fort Leavenworth and Fort Riley from May to September of 1853, and Enoch Hinton sawed lumber from February to August of 1854. George DeBotts worked as a teamster from March 1853 to the end of the year and as a sawyer for the last two months of 1854. The Dyers—Abraham, Samuel, and William—cooked or drove teams for a month or two each.

In the Ninth Election District, which included Fort Riley itself and stretched off indefinitely to the limits of white settlement in the west, there were forty-three adult male residents, as well as two minors (a farmer and a teamster). Among the adults were ten farm-

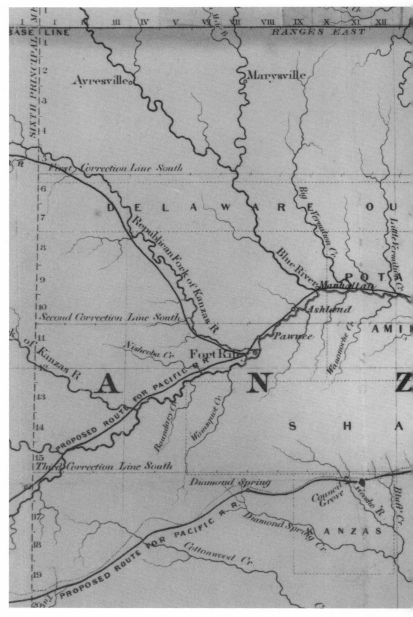

Maps published in 1856 (pages 48–49) and 1857 (pages 50–51), show the rapid advance of white settlers—and speculators—into what had been Indian Territory until 1854. The 1856 map shows "proposed routes" for transcontinental rail lines and the projected town of Pawnee close to Fort

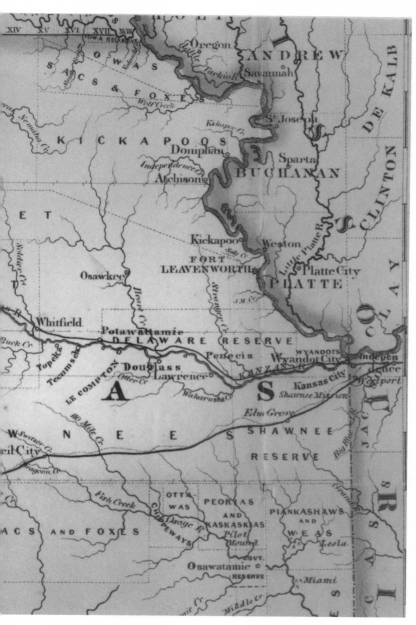

Riley. In the next year's map, the rectilinear survey grid and names of new counties already obscure the still-extant Indian reservations. (Kansas Collection, University of Kansas Libraries)

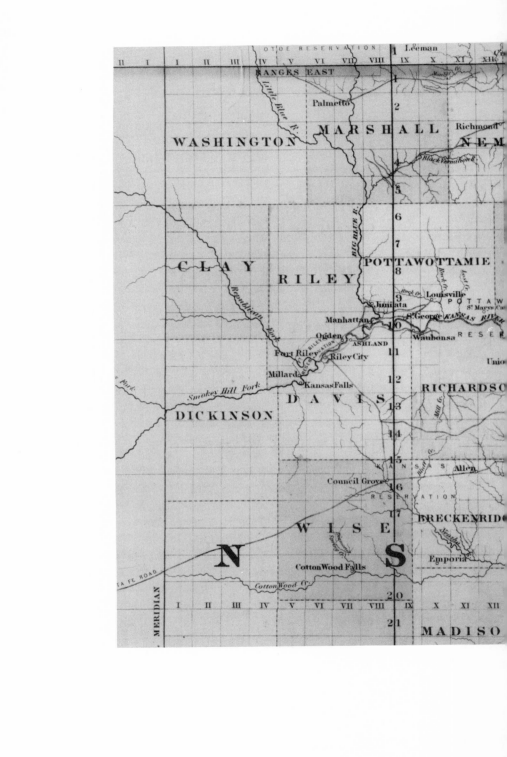

St. Stephens
Rulo
White Cloud
OREGON
Nodaway
ANDREW
SAVANNAH
Rochester
DE K
MAYSV
IOWA TRUST LANDS
Peytonville
Iowa Point
Sabetha
Winona
Hiawatha
Iola
Smithton
Jamestown
MISSOURI RIVER
DONIPHAN
Whitehead
Boyers Setflemer
BROWN
KICKAPOO RESERVATION
TROY
Wathena
ST. JOSEPH
Elwood
Bucklin
Palermo
Petersburg
Stewartville
Powhattan
Geary City
Doniphan
Mission
Whitehead
Helena
SPARTA
BUCHANAN
Rockhouse Prairie
CLIN
Perry
ATCHISON
Leachman
ATCHISON
Platte River
Sumner
Mason
New Market
Holton
Weston
Elm Gro
Kickapoo
Kenda
Jefferson City
Ft. Leavenworth
PLATTE CITY
ALHOUN
Grasshopper Falls
Easton
Summerville
Todds Cr.
Hardville
Leavenworth City
CL
JEFFERSON
Alexandria
Barry
LIBERTY
DELAWARE CITY
Pleasant Hill
Osawkee
Midway
Weimar
Parkville
Liberty Lan
Jacksonville
LEAVENWORTH
Randolph
Wyoming
Quindaro
Indianola
DELAWARE RESERVATION
Wyandott
Kansas City
Topeka
LECOMPTON
Baptist Mis.
Westport
JAC
Friends Mis.
Shawnee Mis.
Washington
Douglas
Benicia
KANSAS RIVER
Big Springs
Dayton
Lawrence
Highland
SHAWNEE
Bloomington
Franklin
Blanton
Midway
Lit. Santa Fe
Brownville
DOUGLAS
Olathe
JOHNSON
Willow Springs
Princeton
Louisiana
Council City
110
Prairie City
Palmyra
Burlingame
Centropolis
St. Barnard
OTTAWAS OF BLANCHARDS FORK
PEORIA & KASKASKIA, PIANKESHAW & WEA TRUST LANDS
SAC & FOX RESERVATION
WELLER
OTTAWAS OF WOLF RAPIDS
Paoli
Morristown
Sac & Fox Agency
Stanton
LYKINS
FRANKLIN
Ossawattamie
A
S
West Point
Oread
Pottawottamie
Shannon
XIV
XV
XVI
XVII
XVIII
XIX
XX
XXI
XXII
XXIII
XXIV
XXV
B
COFFEY
Hyattville
LINN
Burlington
Hamden
ANDERSON
Moneka

ers; four each of carpenters, lawyers, stonecutters, and teamsters; two each of clerks, laborers, and machinists; and a blacksmith, a butcher, a hatter, a mason, a physician, a plasterer, a wheelwright, and the fort's wagon master. The wagon master, H. A. Lowe, was a discharged soldier who had staked a claim near the fort. The mason and three of the stonecutters were squatters whose recent eviction from the military reservation ruled out their employment by the quartermaster, but all of the carpenters and teamsters listed in the census worked at the fort, as did the blacksmith, the plasterer, and the wheelwright.

Opportunities for employment at Fort Riley clearly attracted to the Ninth District a more varied group of workers than the farmers who made up 82 percent of the Tenth District's male population. In December 1856, one of the founders of Manhattan noted in his diary that he had mended his own shoes. "Not a shoemaker this side of Lawrence! With the population, & the time of settlement in this region it seems almost incredible that we have no shoemaker, Harness maker, nor watch repairer. Manhattan has not even a blacksmith!" Because the Ninth District lay west of the Tenth, agricultural settlement may not have caught up with the skilled workers who were drawn to the fort.[4]

Workers at Fort Riley often switched from one job category to another. William Erskine, a free black man, was hired as a carpenter in April 1854 and switched to sawyer in September of that year; George Van Arsdale, who was hired as a carpenter in November 1854, gave his occupation as teamster to the census taker three months later. Judging from quartermasters' reports for the busy years of 1855 and 1865, teamsters and common laborers were mostly interchangeable and equally low-paid, moving back and forth from one trade to the other as the quartermaster's requirements dictated. However crude a worker's skills, he stood a fair chance of earning some wages at an army post.

Workers' pay was slightly higher at Fort Riley in 1854 than it had been the year before. The artisans—carpenters, masons, and plasterers—usually got $2.25 a day instead of the $2.00 they had earned in 1853. Wages rose again in 1855, with brickmakers, carpenters, masons, and stonecutters earning $2.40 a day, and foremen $3.50. Quarrymen and limeburners earned $1.50, and teamsters and laborers one dollar a day. The steam sawmill employed a millwright at $2.50 a day; two steam engineers at $75 a month; a superintendent of the mill whose pay rose from $60 to $65 a month, and later to $3 a day; and sawyers at $2.25 a day.[5]

Pay varied with the quartermaster and according to the employee's abilities and experience. Benjamin C. Card, who clerked for Quartermaster E. A. Ogden in the spring of 1853, earned eighty-five dollars a month. John N. Dyer was hired as a clerk at seventy dollars a month by Lieutenant Alden Sargent in July 1854 and received a raise to one hundred dollars when Captain Thomas L. Brent became quartermaster in November 1855. When one of the seventy-five-dollar-a-month steam engineers left in March 1854, a replacement was hired at sixty dollars. Six months' experience and a change of quartermasters brought him a fifteen-dollar raise.[6] The ability that justified Card's higher salary showed when he obtained a regular army commission in 1861. He received an end-of-the-war brevet of brigadier general for "faithful and meritorious service," and retired in 1889 as Deputy Quartermaster General.

Correspondence from Fort Riley's early years illustrates the precarious nature of civilian employment with the Quartermaster Department. "Should it be intended to continue the building operations at this post," William R. Montgomery, the commanding officer, wrote to the Quartermaster General in Washington on November 10, 1854, "it would conduce to the public interest to retain the present Mechanics, who are anxious to be discharged, and would have left, if not to be continued during the coming winter. They must however soon be discharged unless otherwise ordered. . . . It would be highly desirable to keep the saw-mill running to accumulate Lumber and give it time to season—it is now used green—to the serious detriment of the buildings." Besides the seven workers at the sawmill, four carpenters and a blacksmith, a brickmason, a painter, a plasterer, and a wheelwright stood to lose their jobs.

On December 3, the sawmill shut down, "but the Mechanics remained here till the middle of Dec[embe]r in hopes of a favorable decision from your Dep[artmen]t respecting their continued employment," Montgomery told the Quartermaster General. In orders that took a month to reach Fort Riley from Washington, D.C., the Quartermaster General recommended that Montgomery use his enlisted men to finish the construction. "The working capacity of this command has been taxed to its fullest extent," Montgomery declared. In the summer of 1855, when E. A. Ogden arrived with 373 contract laborers from the East, he found "that notwithstanding the ample time for such preparations not a bushel of Lime was ready nor saw log or cord of wood provided." A few of Montgomery's discharged workers stayed in the neighborhood long enough to be counted in the census. Some worked at Fort Riley again that year, but most of them disappeared from the written record.[7]

Some men found long-term employment at Fort Riley. Thaddeus K. Mills was hired in September 1853 as foreman of carpenters at a wage of three dollars a day. He was one of the few workers Montgomery retained in December 1854, and he stayed on at a monthly salary of eighty-five dollars for more than two years. Wagon masters and quartermaster's clerks also typically held their appointments for years at a time, as did the forage master, whose job was to see that hay was stacked properly when the contractor delivered the fort's annual supply and afterwards to guard against loss by fire or theft. On the other hand, layoffs in skilled and unskilled jobs were common as projects ended or budgets ran out.

During the first two years of Fort Riley's existence, though, more than 30 percent of all adult males in the adjoining census districts worked for the quartermaster at one time or another. The figure climbs to nearly 39 percent if merchants and professional men and the four evicted squatters are excluded from the pool of available workers. Local residents made up only a small fraction of Fort Riley's civilian employees, but the fort provided work for a sizeable proportion of local men.

The beginning of 1860 found civilian employment at Fort Riley at a low ebb. The post quartermaster employed a clerk at sixty dollars a month, and a man who performed the combined duties of wagon and forage master at seventy-five dollars. Both men had been hired in June 1859 and lived at the fort. The clerk owned two thousand five hundred dollars worth of real and personal property, according to the 1860 census. The wagon and forage master, D. W. Scott, listed three thousand dollars worth. A blacksmith, whose home was in neighboring Clay County, was paid forty dollars a month and worked most months, subject to budget constraints. "Has not the blacksmith been ordered to be discharged?" someone jotted in pencil on the quartermaster's report for May 1860. "If not, let the order be given." As it turned out, the blacksmith was not discharged until August and was hired again in January 1861.

With the outbreak of the Civil War, relations between Fort Riley and its civilian neighbors took a new turn. The regular army garrison, reduced to one company of the Second Infantry by May 1861, left that October and was replaced by a succession of companies from Kansas volunteer infantry and cavalry regiments, some of them recruited in Davis and Riley Counties. The volunteers did not keep records as meticulously as the regulars had, but post returns indicate an average troop strength of three or four officers and about one hundred enlisted men from the fall of 1861 through the fall of 1864. Companies from eight different Kansas regiments, as well as a company of Iowa cavalry and an artillery battery from Wisconsin, passed through the fort, the average stay being about four months.

Frequent changes in the garrison made it difficult to prevent deterioration of the buildings at the fort. The volunteers, as one of them recalled soon after the war, were "scattered a company or two in a place, escorting trains, policing the country, hunting bushwhackers, a service more than any other calculated to stimulate individualism among the soldiers and destroy discipline."[8] The inability of small garrisons to detail troops for construction and maintenance labor led to neglect which was exacerbated at Fort Riley by trouble in the quartermaster's department. Exactly what went on is uncertain. There may have been official misconduct or, equally possible, a group of Fort Riley's civilian neighbors may have felt left out when contracts were awarded. In any event, the trouble centered around the new post quartermaster.

When the regular army quartermaster left the post in June 1861,

David W. Scott, the former wagon and forage master newly commissioned in the volunteers, succeeded him. Scott had attended West Point for a year in the late 1830s, held a lieutenant's commission in the regular army during the Mexican War, and afterwards worked at a number of government jobs "measuring roads, erecting buildings, etc.," before getting the wagon and forage master's job at Fort Riley in the spring of 1859. Nearly two years after Scott took over as post quartermaster, the Secretary of War, the Quartermaster General, and the Surgeon General received copies of an anonymous letter signed "many citizens." The letter alleged misconduct by Scott as well as by Fort Riley's commanding officer and the post surgeon.[9]

The surgeon was Frederick Drew, a Junction City physician who had signed a contract as acting assistant surgeon in the summer of 1861 when the regular army surgeon left Fort Riley. Since then, the anonymous letter writers declared, Drew had not "bought *one cents* worth of Medicine for his private practice unless it was something the [Medical] Department didnt issue. . . . Drew is an inveterate drunkard, and it can be proved if necessary that not one single Day passes that he is not more or less under the influence of liquor and *very* often continuously drunk for days. . . . It is no use reporting to the Commanding Officer of the Post, as he and Drew and D W Scott are all in the one clique and between the three, they do as they please and actually act as if they owned the Post and all about and in it." Mention of Drew's failure to buy medical supplies hints that the letter writers were moved by commercial pique. If this were so, it would indicate a local economy sufficiently developed that Junction City merchants could have sold Drew his supplies, had he not been pilfering from the fort's dispensary.[10]

The writers further alleged that Quartermaster Scott was "swindling the Government palpably." In two years, they wrote, he had paid off "a couple of hundred Dollars" in debts, and had recently bought real estate worth three thousand dollars. Moreover, Scott "keeps half a dozen private animals in the QM Stables and feeds them at the expense of the people and along with that he keeps two public mules exclusively for his own private use to haul his buggy. . . .

This Scott has hoodwinked Major Easton [regular army quarter-master] at Fort Leavenworth so much that Easton thinks Scott is a first rate man."[11]

Was Scott dishonest? A look at his wealth as indicated by the censuses of 1860 and 1865 hardly demonstrates the peculation alleged in the letter. In 1860, when he served as wagon and forage master, Scott owned two thousand dollars worth of real estate and one thousand dollars worth of personal property. Five years later, as post quartermaster, he owned real and personal property amounting to three thousand dollars and one thousand two hundred dollars, respectively. The value of Scott's property did not even keep up with the 80 percent inflation of the war years.

The terms of the quartermaster and commissary contracts that Scott signed do not appear unusual either, nor do the names of the contractors. He agreed to pay $.97 a bushel for two thousand bushels of corn in February 1863. The price of corn was $.93 at Fort Scott, in the southeastern corner of the state, where it had jumped from $.55 a bushel since the previous July. It was still $.55 at Fort Leavenworth. Leavenworth was in a more thickly settled region than Fort Riley, though, and had not experienced the dislocations of war as had Fort Scott, which by 1863 had become an important refugee center for former slaves and Unionists from southwestern Missouri and Indian Territory. Quartermaster Scott concurrently held the post of acting commissary of subsistence, and the price of commissary stores varied similarly: in the spring of 1863, flour averaged $4.27 per hundred pounds at Fort Riley, $4.70 at Fort Scott, and $3.14 at Fort Leavenworth; sides of bacon cost $7.47 per hundred pounds at Fort Riley, $7.50 at Fort Scott, and $6.25 at Fort Leavenworth.[12]

The contractors with whom Scott dealt—Thomas Dixon (two thousand bushels of corn), George W. Higinbotham (fifteen thousand pounds of bacon), Edward G. Robinson (two thousand bushels of corn), and Jacob Thierer (one hundred thousand pounds of flour)—were men who continued to have dealings with the army for years after the war and who signed contracts with quartermasters and commissaries whose probity seems not to have been questioned. Of the four, only the names of Higinbotham and Thierer appear in both the 1860 and 1865 censuses: Higinbotham's wealth increased by one-third during the war years, allowing for inflation, and Thierer's by nearly one-quarter. Given the 25 percent increase in population and, consequently, in the size of the market in the two-county area in that time, it does not appear that either man grew outrageously rich by dealing with Captain Scott.

Yet allegations of dishonesty continued. An army inspector's report in the spring of 1865 mentioned that Scott had "been in the employ of the Quartermaster's Department a number of years and should be a better Quartermaster" but noted his "good moral character." A few months later, though, an army inspector reported that Scott "has a farm near the Post, and accusations are made that Government property of all kinds is misapplied, that his clerks discount vouchers at a heavy per centage." The inspector added that although the accusations were "not put in the form of direct charges, whether with foundation or not, an entire change of employes, would, I think, be for the interests of the service."[13]

Another army inspector's report called Captain Scott "slow and inefficient. . . ; so far as I know meant to do right always. Better serve in another state," meaning, perhaps, that Scott had friends in the neighborhood whom he could not refuse favors. The *Smoky Hill and Republican Union* of Junction City had written in 1862, "Captain Scott grants privileges to our citizens consistent with reason and decency," and praised his "accommodating spirit." In November 1865 the Quartermaster General heard "serious charges" against Scott in an oral report from another officer and recommended his removal and discharge. Scott was relieved in January 1866 and mustered out in March. Yet at the same time, other officers testified to his "efficiency and experience" and recommended his transfer to the regular army. Whether Scott was inept or criminal, or tended to make enemies as well as friends and was the victim of small-town gossip, is unclear. What is clear, though, is that neither Scott nor his clerks suffered financially during their time at Fort Riley. Moreover, army expenditures were important enough to the local economy for the anonymous letter writers in Junction City to take a keen interest in the quartermaster's conduct and warn the War Department about it.[14]

The quartermaster's clerks did prosper during and after the war, although no evidence survives to support the anonymous allegations. John T. Price, Scott's $125-a-month chief clerk, was a Mexican War veteran whose employment with the Quartermaster Department began at Fort Union, New Mexico, in 1852. He moved to Kansas when the territory was organized and lived near Fort Riley when the census of 1855 was taken. Price commanded the local militia regiment during the Civil War and signed on as chief clerk in August 1864. According to the 1865 census, he owned two thousand dollars' worth of real estate and nine hundred dollars' worth of personal property. By 1870, after he quit the Quartermaster Department, these holdings had increased to ten thousand dollars and three thousand dollars, and his household employed two female servants and a male farmhand. Price served as Davis County treasurer from 1872 to 1876.[15]

Another of Scott's clerks, William S. Blakely, earned seventy-five dollars a month. The 1860 census showed him as a printer's apprentice who owned no property. After three years of newspaper work in Junction City, Blakely landed the clerk's job at Fort Riley in November 1864. In the following year's census, he claimed to own five hundred dollars' worth of personal property. He was elected to the Kansas senate in November 1865. By 1870 Blakely was a prosperous hardware merchant; the census of that year listed four thousand dollars' worth of real estate and three thousand dollars' worth of personal property in his name. Yet although Price and Blakely did well during and after the war years, official misconduct remains unprovable. Certainly the elective offices they held were not out of the ordinary for "old settlers"—and one of them a close associate of the Junction City *Union*'s editor, to boot.[16]

The census of 1865 showed Davis and Riley Counties with a combined population of 3,002, an increase of 25 percent in five years, and more than twelve times the number of people who had lived there in 1855, when Major Ogden had needed to bring in several hundred contract laborers to build Fort Riley. In 1855 more than one-third of the adult male residents worked at the fort, and the neighborhood could supply only a fraction of the labor required. By 1865 the situation was reversed: a comparison of names on the quartermaster's monthly reports for that year with those on the census rolls shows that only 45 of 389 households (about one-eighth) in the two counties outside the Fort Riley military reservation received wages for work at the fort.

The quartermaster's report for January 1865 shows that of twenty-five clerical, skilled, or supervisory employees, at least eighteen lived in Davis and Riley Counties, and two in neighboring Clay County. Thirteen of thirty-five laborers came from Davis and Riley Counties and one each from Dickinson County to the west and Wabaunsee County to the east. Only one of two wagonmasters and one of thirty-five teamsters at the fort in January 1865 can be identified as a Davis or Riley County resident, but the nature of teamsters' employment made them transient and often subject to transfer from one quartermaster's roster to another's. Fort Riley, from being a major source of wages for the residents of 1855, had declined in importance as the local economy grew. At the same time neighboring civilians, who had furnished only a small part of the fort's work force in 1855, now provided more than 54 percent of all employees and filled 80 percent of the most highly paid jobs. Of these latter, the eight salaried employees earned a total of $680 in January. Artisans earned $3 a day, with the "boss carpenter" and stonemason receiving $3.50.[17]

The level of employment at Fort Riley, as at all military posts, depended on outside factors over which local residents had little or no control. Whether or not the quartermaster had money to employ a clerk or a blacksmith, though, government wagons continued to roll from Fort Leavenworth to Fort Riley and south to Fort Larned, on the Arkansas River, and on to Fort Union, New Mexico. The census takers of 1860 and 1865 listed a total of thirty-eight residents of Davis and Riley Counties as "teamsters" or "freighters" in one year or the other, and the census rolls indicate that business was good during the war years. Seventeen of them appear in both censuses, a persistence rate of nearly 45 percent.

By far the most prosperous of those seventeen teamsters was Calvin M. Dyche, of Ogden, whom the 1860 census showed as a farmer owning no land or personal property. Five years later, Dyche had amassed real estate worth $2,000 and personal property worth $3,000 and employed seven other teamsters who were counted in his household. None of Dyche's employees had appeared in the 1860 census; all were new arrivals. One Riley County resident who switched from driving teams to farming was Henry Brothers, who had owned no property at all in 1860 but by 1865 had $2,000 worth of land and a personal estate valued at $500. Thirteen of the seventeen teamsters seem to have changed occupations during the five-year period, the most notable being a lawyer who had gone into freighting by 1865. Far more usual were changes from teamster to farmer (five) or the reverse (four). Those settlers who survived from 1860, with its devastating drought, to 1865, with its Indian war, were as adaptable as the construction workers in the 1850s who had switched jobs to stay on Fort Riley's payroll.

The remaining settlers had also prospered. In 1860 nine of the seventeen owned no property at all. The two wealthiest each claimed an aggregate worth of just $2,000. By 1865 five of the seventeen had real and personal estates totaling more than $2,000, Calvin Dyche's being the largest. The combined value of their real estate had risen from $6,400 to $9,995, or by slightly more than half; the value of their personal property, from $2,910 to $16,937. (The draft animals that furnished motive power and were the source of their wealth were listed as personal property.) Even allowing for the 80 percent inflation that afflicted the United States during the Civil War, the freight haulers of Davis and Riley Counties were more than half again as rich by 1865 as they had been five years earlier.[18]

The end of hostilities and the mustering out of the armies, North and South, brought boom times to Fort Riley. The number of teamsters employed at the fort averaged 110 a month in the second quarter of 1865, 165 in the third quarter, and 189 in the fourth. Government freighting continued through the following winter. The Junction City *Union* reported in early February that a "large number of government trains have gone west during the past week," and commented a fortnight later, "The number of trains and freighters going west seems not to diminish in the least." Fort Riley's post quartermaster employed a monthly average of 224 teamsters during the first quarter of 1866.[19]

The thousands of veterans who were discharged that summer seem to have been just sufficient to meet the quartermaster's labor demands, for wages remained constant most of the year even though the civilian payroll soared through the first three quarters before dropping slightly in the fourth. Skilled workers like carpenters, painters, saddlers, and tinners earned three dollars a day. Laborers and teamsters earned forty-five dollars a month; they were the lowest paid employees, except for a water boy who earned fifteen dollars a month, and they moved frequently from one job category to the other. The data in Table 1 are compiled from monthly Post Returns (RG 94), filed by the post adjutant, and the Reports of Persons and Articles Employed and Hired (RG 92), filed by the post quartermaster. The two did not always agree exactly. Firing and hiring might occur at any time during the month, and several dozen teamsters might transfer into and out of the fort or from one quartermaster's roster to another's. The table, though, reflects with relative accuracy the number of quartermaster's employees and their earnings during the year.

Wages were often in arrears. The quartermaster's report for July 1865, for instance, shows $17,474.58 earned by workers at Fort Riley that month, and $19,817.33 in "unpaid wages." The paymaster must have visited the fort sometime in August, for that month's figures are $13,507.60 and $6,013.00, respectively. In September, an addition of 311 teamsters brought the balance to $22,967.90 earned and $42,574.48 unpaid. Sporadic paydays were not unusual, for soldiers as well as for civilians. In January 1866 an army inspector noted that companies of the 13th Infantry, which had relieved the volunteers at Fort Riley the previous September, had not been paid in seven months. Infrequent paydays led to practices like the discounting of government vouchers, which Quartermaster Scott's civilian employees had been accused of doing at usurious rates.[20]

Discharged veterans made up a small but significant part of the

Table 1. Quartermaster's Employees and Wages at Fort Riley, 1865

Monthly Averages by Quarter

	Total Worker Force		Laborers		Teamsters		% Unskilled
	Number	Payroll	Number	Payroll	Number	Payroll	
Jan–March	104	$5,594	38	$1,530	38	$1,710	73.1
Apr–June	215	$12,415	29	$1,305	110	$4,935	64.7
July–Sept	276	$17,983	38	$1,655	165	$7,410	73.6
Oct–Dec	301	$16,680	38	$1,743	189	$8,005	75.4

local population and Fort Riley's work force. Since the fort's earliest days, the quartermaster's payroll had drawn some soldiers to linger in the neighborhood after receiving their discharges. As civilians, they helped with construction for wages far higher than a pre-Civil War private's $11 a month. Private John Radley was discharged from the Sixth Infantry on October 17, 1854, and began work that day at the sawmill for $30 a month. He lost that job when the sawmill shut down in December, but he stayed nearby, working for the quartermaster as a woodchopper to fuel the steam-driven sawmill in the summer of 1855 and as a teamster that fall. Both jobs paid $1.25 a day. Sergeant John McHarg worked as a quarryman, providing building stone, for $2 a day in the summer and fall of 1853. Private Patrick Gaffney began clerking in the sutler's store in 1857 when he was discharged from the Second Dragoons. In December 1863 he began earning $100 a month as the quartermaster's foreman, a job that lasted nearly two years. A few other ex-soldiers signed on as teamsters or artisans at Fort Riley. Many more, no doubt, accepted the army's offer of free passage back to the city where they had enlisted.[21]

Some did not return east, though, but remained as civilians, farming or working for wages in Davis and Riley Counties. Former

Quartermaster Sergeant Charles F. Clarke of the First Cavalry ran a ferry across the Republican River after his discharge in April 1860. A year later, he was elected captain of one of the first companies of Civil War volunteers from Davis County. Private Robert Henderson, discharged from the Second Dragoons in March 1857, became another Civil War captain. After the war, he helped to found the Grand Army of the Republic post in Junction City and served at different times as county treasurer and city postmaster.[22]

Three of Henderson's comrades, all discharged in the same month, also settled in the county after serving at Fort Riley for a year and a half. Edmund McFarland headed back to Worcester, Massachusetts, where he and Henderson had enlisted five years earlier, and returned with his older brother a few months later. Although he had acquired a farm worth five thousand dollars by 1870, its value in 1875 was only nineteen hundred dollars—perhaps the effect of the Panic of 1873 followed by the grasshoppers of 1874.[23]

Richard Laurenson's name does not appear in the census of 1860, but he was farming in Davis County by 1865, when the census listed his worth as $580 in real estate and $200 in personal property. He was elected county treasurer that November and reelected two years later. (Henderson followed him in office in 1869.) By 1870 his estate amounted to $10,000 of real and $1,000 of personal property. The hard times of the mid-1870s reduced his holdings to $8,000 and $400, but did not wipe him out. In the 1880s he served two terms as township trustee.[24]

Patrick King shunned public office and stuck to farming. His illiteracy, noted in the censuses of 1865 and 1870, probably kept him out of politics, but by 1870 he owned a farm worth $3,000 and employed three farmhands. By 1875 King's 350 acres had the highest valuation of any of the 207 farms in Jackson Township—$5,000. His maturing offspring enabled him to dispense with hired help.

Former Private William Cosgrove of the First Cavalry stayed poor in worldly goods after his discharge in May 1860, but he became a bartender with a following. When his business changed location, the Junction City *Union* noted the fact. Men like Cosgrove and others—farmers, saloonkeepers, carpenters, a barber, a tailor—

had come to Kansas with the regular army and, once there, decided to stay.[25]

Although hundreds of volunteer troops passed through Fort Riley during the Civil War, most of them belonged to Kansas regiments. When their names appear in postwar censuses of Davis and Riley Counties, it is difficult to say whether they served at the fort and impossible to tell whether a stay there induced them to settle nearby afterwards. Discharged soldiers of the Second Colorado Cavalry, which served at Fort Riley and other Kansas posts from the fall of 1864 through the summer of 1865, were an exception. More than a dozen of them settled near the fort.[26]

Most of the Coloradans who stayed took up farming. In addition to their commercial ventures, three of them entered politics. From November 1865, when John K. Wright was elected probate judge of Davis County, there was hardly a year of the next fifteen when Wright or his fellow veterans Robert O. Rizer and William Lockstone did not hold office as state legislator; county commissioner, treasurer, or probate judge; or mayor of Junction City. Rizer began clerking for Junction City merchants James Streeter and Samuel M. Strickler soon after his discharge. He and Streeter founded a bank in 1867, the year when Rizer first held public office, as city clerk. Rizer served three terms as mayor and two as county treasurer. Lockstone and Wright married sisters, the daughters of Reuben Emick, a former mayor of Junction City, and both spent some time in the hardware business in partnership with their father-in-law. Lockstone's other line of work was as a baker and confectioner, and he sometimes advertised for "two or three hundred pounds of good butter, also one or two hundred dozen eggs, for which he will pay the highest market price in cash." He served two terms as county commissioner and twice ran unsuccessfully for probate judge. Wright took up livestock raising and later became a contractor, grading railroad trackbeds in Kansas, Texas, and Louisiana; he graded many of the roads at Fort Riley during the building boom of the late 1880s. He served three terms as state representative and was one of Rizer's sureties when Rizer was county treasurer in the 1870s.[27]

These men's business ventures prospered more often than not,

John K. Wright came to Fort Riley
as a soldier in the Second Colorado
Cavalry during the Civil War. He
settled in Junction City and became
a railroad construction contractor,
working as far afield as Texas and
Louisiana. In 1888, when Fort
Riley's roads needed grading during
construction of the Mounted
Branch School, Wright got the
contract. (Kansas State Historical
Society)

and they seem to have won at least as many elections as they lost.
Other local businessmen and politicians with no military service
fared as well as Lockstone, Rizer and Wright. As veterans who put
down roots where they were discharged, though, Lockstone, Rizer,
and Wright were an important, if altogether incidental, effect of the
army's presence in the West.

No matter how prominently its discharged soldiers figured in
business and politics, the army's contribution to the local economy,
and to the development of the West in general, lay far more in its
need for freighting—not only in the quartermasters' employment
of teamsters, but in the encouragement of wagon-borne commerce
generally. When Junction City merchants Streeter and Strickler
got a contract in the spring of 1865 for hauling freight from Fort
Riley to posts on the Arkansas River, the *Union* commented, "This
will afford employment to all the teams in this locality. The great
business energy of this firm is adding much to the wealth of our citizens by furnishing remunerative employment to all classes." The
quartermaster's money went to neighboring farmers with oxen or
mules to hire, as well as to wage earners.[28]

The end of the Civil War released thousands of government draft
animals. Daniel A. Butterfield, whose Overland Despatch stage-

coaches offered regular communication between the Colorado goldfields and the Missouri River towns, bought many of the mules. Herds of his animals passed through Junction City during the summer of 1865, headed for stage stations farther west. Those animals that the Quartermaster Department kept went west to haul freight. Civilian contract freighting in the District of the Upper Arkansas, headquartered at Fort Riley, drew to a close by August, but army quartermasters in Kansas continued to employ hundreds of individual teamsters. Quartermaster's jobs would soon disappear, though. The arrival of the railroad and extreme fluctuations in the size of the garrison—effects of either the national economy or War Department policy and far removed from local influences—were responsible.[29]

The number of civilian workers at Fort Riley dropped precipitously in October 1866, the month the Kansas Pacific's tracks reached Junction City. The quartermaster discharged all 393 of his employees. Many of the 250 teamsters no doubt transferred to posts farther west, and local residents returned to their farms. The army's expansion, authorized that July, brought hundreds of recruits to Fort Riley when the Seventh Cavalry organized there in the fall, and these men were able to do many of the jobs that civilians had performed. The post quartermaster hired no more civilians until August 1867, and the number of workers hovered around a couple of dozen for the rest of the year. The number of employees averaged twelve throughout 1868. Establishment of a light artillery school in the spring of 1869 brought the garrison's strength to more than 390 soldiers, enough to furnish clerks and construction details, and the number of civilian employees shrank to two, the wagon and forage master and the quartermaster's chief clerk. Neither of these men was married or owned any property, according to the census of 1870, and neither still lived in Davis County five years later.[30]

From the late 1860s to the early '80s, relations between Fort Riley and its civilian neighbors reached a nadir. The Junction City *Union* occasionally mentioned the military paymaster's arrival and the troops' exuberant misbehavior afterward, but the fort's economic importance had dwindled. The quartermaster depot moved west to Fort Harker, near Ellsworth, in July 1867. "The market afforded . . . through the military demand, has enriched many men in Davis county," the *Union*'s editor wrote a week later. "But the onward progress of the railroad, westward, will render useless to government the keeping up of such a military establishment as Fort Riley. It must before long be abandoned. . . . It behooves farmers, therefore, to look about for another market. The best way to do that will be to build up a large town near their home," and to construct short line railroads north and south, affording access to trunk lines that would offer freight charges competitive with the Kansas Pacific's. "The advantages of Fort Riley will soon play out," the editor concluded, urging his readers "to encourage liberally" a proposed connecting rail line from Junction City to Emporia. "It will now open a new market, as well as make one at home second to none in the state."[31] Local businessmen were alert to the need for connections to the national economy. Steam navigation had failed, but railroads promised a link that would run year-round, barring floods and blizzards, and help to smooth out fluctuations in the yearly business cycle.

Quartermasters' payrolls drew early settlers to the neighborhood of Fort Riley and to other western army posts. Military contracts helped to foster the growth of an agricultural and commercial elite. These business leaders near Fort Riley would turn avidly to railroad promotion in the early 1870s, when the quartermaster's disbursements were no longer pumping cash into the local economy.

Chapter 3

"Uncle Sam Will Soon Make Money More Plenty Here"

MANY WESTERN SETTLERS readily acknowledged the relation of government policy to the economy. A farmer near Fort Riley expressed it clearly after the Panic of 1857. "We hear enough about 'failures' 'broken banks' &c but they do not trouble us much except that they make money scarce," he wrote. "Uncle Sam is buying considerable corn, however, and will soon make money more plenty here." Federal expenditures pumped cash into local economies and fostered the growth of a commercial elite in the neighborhood of military posts. Men who made money supplying the army also took an active part in local government and worked to secure bond issues to help build railroads. Dollars disbursed through army contracts helped to create the class of influential men who directed municipal and county affairs and supported efforts to tie their communities to the national economy.[1]

Newspaper editors wrote of the need for federal funds with a mixture of bravado, envy, and wheedling. The second issue of the Leavenworth, *Kansas Weekly Herald* bore the date September 22, 1854. Page one featured an article titled "Settlements in Kansas." It boasted, "Squatters have from the earliest settlement of our country, led the van of civilization in its westward course" and went on to state that "the Squatters of Kansas . . . are entitled to the fostering aid of our government, and the encouragement and gratitude of the American people." On the second page, the editor noted, "In our immediate vicinity is Fort Leavenworth, from which $600,000 was last year paid out for stock, grain, pay of men, & c., most of which found its way into the pockets of the merchants, farmers and mechanics of Buchanan, Platte, and Jackson counties in Missouri. . . . All this trade has heretofore been enjoyed by the frontier counties above named." Thus from the outset the settlers and their editorial spokesmen voiced their awareness of government's contribution to their developing economy and of the settlers' need for "the fostering aid of our government" while they "led the van of civilization in its westward course." Federal money, though, was dispensed by bureaucrats whose concerns were not local, but national. The flow of money depended on factors over which the settlers had little more control than they had over the weather.

The army was the source of most federal funds that reached the West. Government money bought goods and services contracted for by the Subsistence (rations) and Quartermaster (forage, construction, and transportation) Departments or paid the wages of civilian workers hired by those departments to work at military posts. Payrolls, though, often amounted to relatively small change compared to the sums disbursed for army contracts.

The *Kansas Weekly Herald's* editorialist cited neighboring Fort Leavenworth as an instance. There, a generation before Fort Riley's founding, the business of provisioning military posts and relocated Indian tribes had fostered a group of wealthy farmers and merchants in the nearby counties of northwestern Missouri. Some of these early contractors became prosperous enough, and lived long enough, to supply Fort Riley and other posts farther west. Since contractors required sureties—guarantors of their ability to fulfil the terms of a contract—and the surety, in turn, had to present a certificate that he was "a man of property and . . . able to make good his guaranty," quartermasters' lists of bidders and sureties afford a *Who's Who* of propertied farmers and merchants. Their activities illustrate the growth of the network of frontier capitalists that already existed at the time of Fort Riley's establishment in the 1850s.[2]

Fort Leavenworth, founded in 1827, was the first military post in Kansas. Trade with Mexico via Santa Fe had become important to Missouri's economy during the 1820s, and Missourians soon asked for a mounted military force to patrol the Santa Fe Trail as far as the Arkansas River, which was then the international boundary. Comanche attacks on American traders in 1828 led to more urgent requests, but the expense of mounted troops dissuaded Congress from authorizing the Regiment of Dragoons until 1833. In September 1834 four companies of the regiment arrived at Fort Leavenworth, replacing a garrison of two infantry companies.[3]

The demand for local farm products increased at once. During the three years of 1831–33, the army's orders for corn had averaged just under 1,900 bushels; the average contract amounted to $790. In the five years after the dragoons' arrival, 1834–38, the average order was for 23,400 bushels of corn, for which the army paid $14,000. The price of corn in northwestern Missouri, in other words, increased by nearly 44 percent, from 41.6 cents a bushel to 59.8 cents. With hay and oats contracts besides, the army paid out nearly $19,000 a year to maintain the dragoons' horses alone. Each year, too, Fort Leavenworth's quartermaster bought about $3,500 worth of cordwood for cooking and heating.[4]

The increase in prices does not necessarily mean that the quartermasters at Fort Leavenworth were at the mercy of what one historian has called "price-fixing combinations formed by the few responsible men in small communities who were in a position to bid." Thirteen extant Abstracts of Bids for forage and wood during this period show the names of 132 men, 102 of whom bid on only one contract. Sixteen men bid on two contracts; five bid on three; and so on in diminishing numbers, down to one man, John Boulware, who bid on nine contracts. Boulware was underbid by five and one-half cents a bushel on the corn contract of 1832 but came back the following year with a bid that was two cents lower than his nearest competitor's. It was Boulware's only contract for forage.[5]

The Quartermaster Department's Register of Contracts lists twenty-five contracts for forage and cordwood awarded at Fort Leavenworth in the 1830s. Six men were awarded two contracts each, and thirteen men got only one contract. Boulware managed to get only one contract in nine attempts. James B. Wills, on the other hand, submitted only two bids and got both contracts, underbidding his nearest competitor by fourteen cents a cord on wood in 1835 and four cents a ton on hay the following year. Joseph Todd underbid his nearest competitor by .26 of a cent on the twenty thousand-bushel corn contract of 1835; seven other bids were within five cents of Todd's. The Abstracts of Bids reveal no pattern that suggests price-fixing of the kind alleged elsewhere in the West.

Since army contracts were for thousands of bushels of grain, hundreds of long tons of hay, and hundreds of cords of wood, it should be no surprise that the successful contractors, as well as those whose bids failed, were among the substantial property owners in the neighboring counties. Comparing a list of the men who bid on more than one contract with the 1840 census of Clay and Platte Counties in Missouri, where all the identifiable bidders lived, demonstrates this clearly. The 1840 census form did not have spaces for amounts of real and personal property, but it did list the number of free and slave inhabitants. There were 2,401 households in the two counties, of which 644, or 26.8 percent, listed slave residents. Of the twenty contractors and bidders who can be identified in the 1840 census, seventeen, or 85 percent, held slaves. In other words, more than four-fifths of those interested in government contracts belonged to the slave-holding one-fourth of the white population—clear evidence of their social and economic standing.[6]

These men's backgrounds and the parts they played in their communities show the importance of federal money in promoting settlement and economic growth near army posts. Of thirty-four men who either had wood and forage contracts at Fort Leavenworth between 1832 and 1840 or bid on three or more contracts unsuccessfully during that period, eighteen are mentioned in histories of Clay and Platte Counties. Five were licensed ferry operators. Three ran mills—grist, saw, and textile, powered by water in the early days and later by steam. One owned a tavern on the site of Platte City; another was a grocer in Liberty; a third helped found the town of Weston. Thus, besides farming, which most did more or less, about two-thirds of them had interests in transportation, industry, and commerce.[7]

The eighteen Fort Leavenworth contractors included one state senator, whose service totaled twelve years; three representatives, one of whom also served twelve years; four county judges, two with eleven-year tenures; and three collectors of revenue. Two served in local government as road overseers, one as a city assessor, and another as a township constable. Of thirteen who held office, only four served in more than one capacity. Although they certainly did not by themselves constitute the political elite of the region—none of them served as sheriff, for instance, or held statewide or federal office—they formed a substantial part of it.

While expenditures for forage and cordwood provided annual infusions of money into the local economy during the 1830s, the army awarded other contracts from time to time as improvements at Fort Leavenworth became necessary. The dragoons' horses required a fenced pasture, and John Boulware got the contract, which paid two dollars per hundred fence rails and posts. James B. Wills got a contract "to clear up smoothly, harrow & sew with Timothy seed" part of the military reservation. As ground was broken, plowed and fenced, the Quartermaster Department was able after 1842 to dispense with annual contracts for forage by awarding a three-year lease of "the plantation" to a contractor who then provided corn, hay, and oats grown on the military reservation. The lease obliged the contractor to make good any shortages due to crop failures and freed the government from year-to-year fluctuations in the price of forage.[8]

By far the most ambitious military project of the 1830s, though, was the construction of a "military road" to protect the "permanent Indian frontier" that had been created by the policy of Indian Removal. Members of some two dozen tribal groups, from the Cherokees of Georgia to the Sauks and Foxes of Wisconsin, had been resettled across the Mississippi River, most of them just west of Missouri and Arkansas. During the previous two decades, westward-migrating Indians (for the most part, traditionalists who had left their old lands in the East before they were compelled to) had come into conflict with indigenous tribes like the Osages. In 1836 Secretary of War Lewis Cass announced plans for a road from Fort Snelling, Minnesota, to Fort Towson, on Red River, along which dragoons could patrol the new lands of the resettled Indians. When Congress appropriated one hundred thousand dollars for the work, the editor of the Liberty, Missouri, *Far West* exulted, "This great measure . . . will be received with universal satisfaction. It is just such a measure as we needed, and will give us protection, and also increased expenditure among us of the national revenue." The editor's glee was somewhat premature; not until 1839 were contracts, totaling about twenty-five thousand dollars, awarded to clear, grade, and bridge sections of the road south of Fort Leavenworth, which were among the last to be completed. The War Department was nearly as slow to build the military road as Congress had been to authorize a mounted regiment a few years earlier.[9]

The fostering effect of military money on a local economy, evident at Fort Leavenworth during the 1830s and '40s, became apparent again at Fort Riley a few years later. Transportation costs continually vexed army quartermasters, and since freight moved more cheaply by water than by land, the possibility of steam navigation on the Kansas River influenced the officers who picked the fort's site in 1853. During Fort Riley's early years, contracts for beef, wood, and forage were handled by the post quartermaster rather than by the Chief Quartermaster of the Department of the Missouri at Fort Leavenworth, as they would be when the railroad network grew after the Civil War. Abstracts of bids at Fort Riley show the emergence of prominent farmers and businessmen, several of whom might act as sureties for different bidders on the same contract or enter bids themselves. Many of the Fort Riley bidders had previous experience supplying the garrison at Fort Leavenworth. The first contract at Fort Riley, as it happened, was a small one, but the previous careers of those involved tell a great deal about the kind of men who supported the government's activities in the West during the middle third of the nineteenth century and who were, in turn, nourished by the government.

On August 1, 1853, Charles A. Perry of St. Joseph, Missouri, signed a contract to deliver 250 tons of hay, at seven dollars a ton, to Fort Riley by mid-October. Perry was a thirty-four-year-old native of Maryland who had moved to St. Joseph by 1843. His store there was the first brick building in town. By 1850 he owned property worth $22,425 and ran a ten-wagon supply train from Fort Leavenworth to Fort Atkinson, on the Arkansas River, in partnership with his younger brother Elias and M. L. Young, of Weston, Missouri. The next year, the partners won a two-year contract for all government freighting between the two forts. In 1852 they ran an overland passenger service to California: food and tents provided and fifty pounds of baggage allowed for a fare of $150. That same year, Charles Perry sold forty wagons to a party of Mormons who were at Fort Leavenworth, headed for Utah with machinery to set up a sugar-beet refinery. He seems to have fulfilled the terms of his hay contract in 1853, for the following February he was awarded another "to deliver per steamer at Fort Riley . . . all such public stores as may be turned over to him at Fort Leavenworth." This contract led to his purchase of the steamer *Excel* and its trips up the Kansas River during the wet spring of 1854. Perry's sureties on the 1853 hay contract were his brother Elias and Robert Wilson, the post sutler at Fort Riley.[10]

Wilson, a prominent member of Fort Riley's network of frontier capitalists, had "visited the Mountains" in 1842 and 1843, when he was about twenty years old, and had traded at Council Bluffs before being appointed sutler of the Oregon Battalion, several companies of Missourians who had volunteered for the Mexican War but were sent instead to establish military posts along the Oregon Trail. They established Fort Kearny, Nebraska, in September 1847. Shortly after returning from Fort Kearny in the fall of 1848, Wilson signed a contract to furnish Fort Leavenworth with thirty thousand bushels of corn and five thousand bushels of oats. His sureties on this contract were Hiram Rich, the Fort Leavenworth sutler, and Charles A. Perry, the army contractor from St. Joseph. Wilson's business in 1849 took him as far as Oregon. He returned to Missouri late in the fall. In 1852 and 1853, the year of his appointment as post sutler at Fort Riley, he had annual licenses from the Office of Indian Affairs to trade with the Kickapoo tribe in Kansas. Wilson and Hiram Rich were sureties on the 1854 hay contract at Fort Riley.[11]

Rich had come to northwestern Missouri in 1829 and for years traded with the Indians of the Plains and the Missouri River, sometimes selling provisions to the Office of Indian Affairs for tribes which had been removed to Kansas. He became the post sutler at

Fort Leavenworth in August 1841 and postmaster that October, jobs that he held through Whig, Democratic, and Republican administrations until his death in 1862. During the Mexican War, he had been sutler of General Stephen W. Kearny's Army of the West, making the trip to Santa Fe in 1846 and returning the following year. In 1852, when a "mass meeting of citizens of Nebraska Territory" (an entity that did not yet officially exist) called for the establishment of a territorial government and election of a delegate to Congress, Rich and William F. Dyer were appointed election commissioners for the Fort Leavenworth precinct. After passage of the Kansas-Nebraska Act, Rich became a member of the Leavenworth Association and the Pawnee Association, two speculative town-building ventures in the new territory of Kansas. When Robert Wilson, the post sutler at Fort Riley, got the contract to furnish six hundred tons of hay there in 1857, Rich served as one of his sureties.[12]

Rich's fellow election commissioner of 1852, William F. Dyer, had held licenses from the Office of Indian Affairs to trade with the Delawares, the Kickapoos, or the Potawatomis every year since 1848. In 1854, while licensed to trade with the Kickapoos, he served as president of the Osawkee Association, a town company organized to promote white settlement. At the same time, he contracted with the army to bridge Grasshopper Creek, on the military road between Fort Leavenworth and Fort Riley. His surety on that contract was Robert C. Miller, Indian trader and secretary of the 1852 "mass meeting." It should be clear by now that Perry, Wilson, Rich, Dyer, and men like them were well-acquainted and that they cordially supported each others' endeavors. They would also figure prominently among the organizers and promoters of railroads in Kansas Territory.[13]

These men, like other new arrivals in the West, had an all-consuming interest in transportation. The first government contractors at Fort Leavenworth and Fort Riley lived at a distance because both forts were established in the middle of unceded Indian country. Slow and uncertain means of transportation, though, put the army's contracts in the hands of local residents as soon as white settlers were permitted in the neighborhood: across the river from Fort Leavenworth after the Platte Purchase (the six northwestern counties of Missouri) in 1836, and in Kansas after 1854. During these early years, post quartermasters awarded contracts. Considering that Fort Riley was two days' journey from the Missouri River, whether by stagecoach when all the creeks were low or by steamboat when the river was unusually high, it is easy to see the necessity for local discretion. Distance from larger markets and high transportation costs promoted local enterprise.[14]

Robert Wilson's hay contract of 1857 was the first at Fort Riley to be awarded to a local resident. Only six men entered bids because "the prospect for hay was so slight that very few would venture to bid at all. At present the grass is very poor," the regimental quartermaster of the Second Dragoons commented, "hardly sufficient for grazing purposes, and unless it rains a great deal it will be with great difficulty that the contractor will clear himself." Nevertheless, five local residents and a man from Platte City, Missouri, turned in bids ranging from $11.88 to $20 a ton, and Wilson's bid of $13.40 was accepted. This was nearly twice the amount of Charles Perry's bid four years earlier and shows the importance of rainfall, as the quartermaster had mentioned.[15]

Of the other bidders on the 1857 hay contract, the identities of three remain obscure. Robert Tate, who gave his residence as Fort Riley, does not appear in the census. "Taylor Brothers" of Manhattan probably included Ira Taylor, whose name appears in the censuses of 1857 and 1860. Thomas Dorris lived in Platte City, Missouri. James R. McClure and Philemon Z. Taylor, on the other hand, became long-time residents of Davis County. Both were lawyers and, along with Robert Wilson, were among the original members of the Junction City Town Company. McClure had become acquainted with Governor Reeder and, on his advice, settled with his family close to the projected territorial capital at Pawnee. McClure and Taylor were delegates to the territorial railroad convention in 1860. The census of that year showed both of them among the five richest men in Davis County, each owning ten thousand dollars or more in real estate. Holding a volunteer commission during the

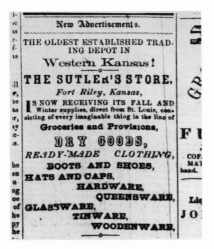

New Advertisements.

THE OLDEST ESTABLISHED TRAD-
ING DEPOT IN

Western Kansas!

THE SUTLER'S STORE,
Fort Riley, Kansas,

IS NOW RECEIVING ITS FALL AND
Winter supplies, direct from St. Louis, con-
sisting of every imaginable thing in the line of

Groceries and Provisions,

DRY GOODS,
READY-MADE CLOTHING,
BOOTS AND SHOES,
HATS AND CAPS,
HARDWARE,
QUEENSWARE,
GLASSWARE,
TINWARE,
WOODENWARE,

Fort Riley's 1867 hay contract went to the post sutler, Robert Wilson, who catered to the needs of civilian settlers and travelers, as well as to those of the fort's garrison. This advertisement for Wilson's wares ran in the Junction City *Smoky Hill and Republican Union* during the fall of 1861. St. Louis, where Wilson got his goods, had not yet been overtaken by Chicago as the commercial metropolis of the central plains. (Kansas State Historical Society)

Civil War, McClure would serve as quartermaster at Fort Riley from August 1863 to October 1864.[16]

The relative anonymity of half the bidders on this hay contract shows the influence of high transportation costs. Hay and wood could be cut on the military reservation with a small crew of local residents. Grain, on the other hand, had to be hauled from a distance and required draft animals and teamsters. Grain contracts therefore attracted wealthier bidders, and although grain dealers might occasionally land contracts for hay or wood, these went for the most part to smaller, local operators.

Businessmen in territorial Kansas were quick to establish the sort of relations that government contractors in Missouri had enjoyed with each other in earlier decades. Taylor's and Wilson's names appear again in the abstract of bids received on the Fort Riley corn contract of 1858, the first surviving list in which the bidders and their sureties are listed. Four of the thirteen bidders on the corn contract—Calvin M. Dyche, George W. Higinbotham, Samuel D. Houston, and Robert Wilson—were sureties for other bidders. Dyche was one of P. Z. Taylor's sureties; Higinbotham and his brother Uriah were two of Houston's sureties, and Houston, in turn, was one of Higinbotham's; and Wilson was a surety for Dyche and P. Z. Taylor. (Wilson and Dyche also served as sureties for five bidders on that year's hay contract, and Dyche bid on that contract himself.) In addition, nonbidders Jesse Ingraham and Andrew J. Mead, both of Manhattan, each guaranteed two bidders from Riley County, Ingraham acting for Higinbotham and Houston, and Mead for Higinbotham and the mercantile firm of John Pipher and Son.[17]

The business elite that coalesced around the new fort was made up of early settlers who wielded political power, too. Samuel D. Houston had squatted in the valley of the Blue River in 1853 and, along with the Piphers and Andrew Mead, had helped found Manhattan in the spring of 1855. Calvin Dyche arrived that fall as a teamster for the freighting firm of Majors and Russell, and the Higinbotham brothers began general merchandising in Manhattan in April 1856. Jesse Ingraham arrived in time to be counted in the census of 1857. During the next ten years, all these men held city, county, or state office for at least one term. Mead was mayor of Manhattan in 1857, while Pipher served as president of the city council and later as county probate judge. Dyche was sheriff of Riley County in 1859; Higinbotham succeeded him. Houston served in the Kansas senate from 1860 to 1862 and was appointed receiver of the U.S. Land Office in Junction City in 1861. Ingraham was a county commissioner in 1859 and went on to serve as coroner of Riley County for the next ten years.[18]

Names from Manhattan and Riley County outnumber those from Junction City and Davis County in the lists of early contractors because Riley was the more populous and wealthier county. It lay to the east of Davis, closer to the river ports along the Missouri. Perhaps more important, the Big Blue River on its eastern edge was part of the busy route to California and Oregon. Riley County, at any rate, had more entrepreneurs ready to execute the bond required of army contractors. The list of bidders on the 1858 hay contract at Fort Riley, for instance, shows twelve from Riley County and three from Davis.[19]

Buying thousands of bushels of corn or hundreds of tons of hay from a single contractor simplified the Quartermaster Departmentc's bookkeeping and, over the years, built up a small group of reliable suppliers, but the practice kept prices artificially high. A few months after the Civil War ended, an army inspector wrote from Fort Riley, "On inquiry of the farmers in the vicinity, I found the price of corn to be seventy five cents per bushel, and if bids for 500 bushels could be received, and contracts let for that amount, all that the country produces could be bought by the Government as far west as Salina, at from seventy five cents to one dollar per bushel." Just five weeks later, Thomas Dixon signed a contract to furnish Fort Riley with ten thousand bushels of corn at $1.19 per bushel. Dixon, along with three of his brothers and two sisters, had arrived as a squatter on the military reservation in 1853 and been evicted; in the ten years since, he had begun a career as one of the army's most consistent suppliers in all of Kansas.[20]

Fort Riley's contracts similarly contradict the allegation of price-fixing. The 1858 hay contract attracted twenty-five bidders, some of them from Council Grove, Topeka, and Wabaunsee County, offering prices that ranged from $5.60 to $12.25 per ton. A Leavenworth man was awarded Fort Riley's corn contract that year, at forty-three cents a bushel, underbidding local competitors G. W. Higinbotham (forty-four cents), P. Z. Taylor (forty-eight cents), S. D. Houston (fifty cents), C. M. Dyche (fifty-four cents), and Robert Wilson (sixty-three cents). Although many of the same names appear in the Register of Contracts from year to year and even from decade to decade, the size of the market the army provided in Kansas—as many as nine forts for a few years in the early 1870s—and the rudimentary means of communication at the bidders' disposal ruled out sustained, systematic collusion on any wide scale. Kansas contractors were too mobile and venturesome to be characterized as a "few responsible men in small communities," but they were not Goulds or Rockefellers, either.[21]

Besides the contracts, records of which have survived, some of the army's suppliers seem to have operated under less formal arrangements. In November 1855 two men named Neally and Whiteside— neither of whose names appears in the census of that year or in the Register of Contracts—took eighty-three bushels of Isaac Goodnow's corn to Fort Riley and gave Goodnow $1.25 a bushel after selling it there. No corn contract at Fort Riley was recorded in 1855, but Charles A. Perry's price the year before, for seven thousand bushels of corn in sacks, delivered by riverboat, was $1.65 a bushel. There is no record of what Neally and Whiteside charged the army, but Goodnow did not seem satisfied with his share. "Must be some mistake," he wrote in his diary.[22]

There are gaps in the records from Fort Riley's early years of the sort one might expect to result from fires, mice, and misfiling, and any reader of the adjutant's monthly post returns from the Civil War years will see at once that the volunteers did not keep as meticulous, or even legible, records as did the regulars. The post quartermaster's advertisements for contract bids survive in the old files of local newspapers, but the official record becomes much sparser. After the war, as the Kansas Pacific laid track west, the Chief Quartermaster of the Department of the Missouri at Fort Leavenworth reviewed bids and awarded contracts. The railroad encouraged this sort of centralization, a development that characterized all of American society in the final third of the nineteenth century.

During the post–Civil War era, contractors' prices declined gradually, not only because of the prevailing deflationary trend and an influx of farmers who produced more grain, but because the expanding network of railroads brought down transportation costs as well. For example, in 1864, the price of corn was $2.14 a bushel at Fort Leavenworth but $4.74 at Fort Zarah on the Arkansas River near present-day Great Bend, a difference of 120 percent. Four years later, with the Kansas Pacific running trains nearly to the Colorado line, corn was 88 cents a bushel at Fort Leavenworth and $1.47 at Fort Hays, a difference of slightly more than 67 percent. Between the two points, corn cost 97.6 cents a bushel at Fort Riley and $1.27 at Fort Harker, near Ellsworth. In the 1870s, after the Santa Fe reached Dodge City, Junction City contractor Thomas Dixon could supply Fort Dodge with corn at 61 cents a bushel; his price at Fort Leavenworth was just over 48 cents. The cost at the western post was only 27 percent greater than in the more densely settled country on the Missouri River. Clearly, the ease with which the railroad moved supplies in bulk had become a more important factor in provisioning military posts and reducing costs than the presence of farmers nearby.[23]

Table 2 shows the declining price of corn at Fort Riley as railroad expansion drove down transportation costs. Garrison strength is from monthly post returns for January, April, July, and October of each year, except for 1866. That fall, the Seventh Cavalry was being organized at Fort Riley, and the figures show the regiment was short of horses. In the spring of 1868 the Tenth Cavalry had just completed its organization and left for Fort Hays. In 1870 the garrison consisted of four batteries of light artillery and their horses, and in 1872, of several Sixth Cavalry companies. From April 1873 to November 1880 the garrison consisted almost entirely of infantry. After that, the post served as a base for cavalry companies who traveled by rail to field service in Colorado and the Indian Territory.

As noticeable as the just over 63 percent decline in price between 1866–70 and 1888–90 is the decline in the number of contractors needed to scrape together enough grain to meet the fort's requirements. In 1866, a very busy year on the plains, civilian and military wagon trains, as well as the track-grading crews of the Kansas Pacific, competed for forage. Fort Riley required seven men, who signed ten contracts between March and July of that year, to furnish the corn, in quantities ranging from 500 to 53,100 bushels. In 1890 one man, whose office was in Leavenworth, could supply the amount needed.[24]

The career of Thomas Dixon affords some idea of how a contractor operated over the years. Dixon was one of a family of stone-cutters who squatted on the Fort Riley military reservation in 1854. They were evicted the following year, and their names do not appear in the 1860 censuses of Riley or Davis Counties. Dixon was back by February 1863, when he signed a contract to furnish two thousand bushels of "corn in ear" at Fort Riley, just over 28 percent of the fort's requirement that year. In July he contracted to provide Fort Larned with eight hundred tons of prairie hay, at $13.94 a ton. The price of prairie hay at Fort Riley that year was $4.87, a difference explained by more abundant grass and less likelihood of the

Table 2. Corn Contracts at Fort Riley, 1866–1890

	Cost/bushel (in cents)	Bushels (1n 100s)	Garrison Strength		No. Contractors
			Men	Horses	
1866	91.10	811	547	264	7
1868	80.00	35	205	(?)	1
1870	86.25	4,088	322	305	2
1872	63.73	2,488	246	325	2
1874	74.00	1,848	74	32	1
1876	42.50	1,320	77	33	1
1878	[illegible]		137	5	—
1880	42.50	1,960	78	2	1
1882	43.00	5,600	208	169	1
1884	[volume lost]		238	207	—
1886	44.00	4,480	305	262	1
1888	32.50	5,600	383	319	1
1890	30.80	7,280	670	497	1

crew's being interrupted by Indian raiders. In 1865 the Riley County census listed Dixon's occupation as farmer, with real estate worth six thousand dollars and personal property worth four thousand dollars. That year, he furnished all ten thousand bushels of Fort Riley's corn.[25]

For the next few years, Dixon supplied a few thousand bushels of corn a year to Fort Riley; the fort's firewood in 1867 (1,600 cords at eight dollars each); and several hundred tons of hay to Fort Harker and to army camps guarding the construction of the Kansas Pacific. In 1869 General John M. Schofield, commander of the Department of the Missouri and a former artillery officer, decided to establish an artillery school with four batteries and about 300 horses at Fort Riley. Dixon's business boomed. The previous year, the fort's quartermaster had bought 3,500 bushels of corn; in 1869, he ordered nearly 10,000. Five contractors were needed to provide that amount. In 1868 the hay contract had called for 170 tons; in 1869, 900. The artillery horses needed 357,000 pounds of oats, and Dixon supplied 165,000 of them, at $1.67 per hundred pounds. He also delivered 4,000 bushels of corn and more than 20,000 bushels of oats to Fort Hays. In 1870, he furnished Fort Riley with 250,000 pounds of corn and 180,000 pounds of oats, and he shipped 1,500,000 pounds of corn and 160,000 pounds of oats to Fort Hays. Dixon's gross of $21,405 made him the third-largest contractor supplying military posts along the line of the Kansas Pacific. That year, the census listed him as a "grain dealer" worth $15,000 in real and $3,000 in personal property.[26]

The 80 percent increase in Dixon's wealth during the five-year period does not imply uninterrupted success. The grain business involved risks as great as the potential profits. Dixon's business records have not survived, but there is an account of one of his reversals. Mattie M. Coons, the daughter of an early settler who had farmed in Riley County during the 1860s, recalled, "One year there was a particularly good corn crop." The army's corn contract that year went to Dixon. "The morning after the news was received," Manhattan merchants George W. and William P. Higinbotham "started out a lot of men on horseback to buy up all the corn in the country at one dollar a bushel. Such prices had never been thought of and all the farmers sold to the limit. In a few days, Dixon started his men out to buy corn to fill his contract and there was none to be had. As the contract had to be filled he was compelled to come down [from Junction City to Manhattan] and buy Higinbotham's corn at two dollars per bushel. And many of the farmers who had sold too much were compelled to buy back before spring at double the price." Coons remembered the Higinbotham brothers starting out "about 1857" as "two peddlers with packs on their backs." By 1859 they had opened a dry goods store, and they later engaged in freighting, army contracting, and railroad promotion. In 1867 they supplied 3,500 bushels of corn to Fort Riley, the same amount Thomas Dixon furnished that year. The Quartermaster Department's Register of Contracts does not show any hiatus in Dixon's business activities that would be attributable to a ruinous reversal, so it is impossible to substantiate Coons's anecdote.[27]

Thomas Dixon seems to have stuck to farming and grain dealing for most of his life; the only public office he ever held was as treasurer of Ogden Township in Riley County. A businessman who operated in a wider sphere was Nathaniel A. Adams, of Manhattan. Adams and his wife moved to Riley County in the spring of 1859. The next year's census showed them aged twenty-four and twenty-one, with one thousand five hundred dollars' worth of real estate and four hundred dollars' worth of personal property. In the summer of 1862, when the Eleventh Kansas regiment was raised, Adams' neighbors elected him captain of their company. He commanded Fort Riley for seven months while the company was stationed there. In 1864 he was promoted to major, the rank he held when the Eleventh Kansas was mustered out in June 1865. That year's census listed his estate as three thousand dollars worth of real and five hundred dollars worth of personal property. He gave his occupation as farmer, as he had five years earlier.[28]

Adams had increased the range of his acquaintances while he was in the army. In 1869 the three former majors of the Eleventh Kansas—Adams, Martin Anderson, and Edmund G. Ross—found themselves in Manhattan at the same time. Ross was Adams's guest during his stay. "Maj. Ross has served three years in the U. S. Senate," the Manhattan *Standard* noted, "Maj. Anderson two years as State Treasurer, while Maj. Adams has been actively engaged in business pursuits." By August 1866, as the Kansas Pacific tracks drew near Manhattan, Adams had built a warehouse, and when the trains began running he was ready for business as a commission agent, ordering

Manhattan businessman Nathaniel Adams, former major of the Eleventh Kansas Cavalry and, by 1868, "the heaviest grain dealer in the state." Judging from his appearance, the photogaph seems to date from the period of Adams' early ventures in army contracting and railroad promotion. (Kansas State Historical Society)

goods at wholesale prices for local customers. "For the low commission of 5 per cent he will procure from Leavenworth or Lawrence, lumber and all kinds of building materials, also the heavy articles of provisions such as flour, salt, sugar &c. and he keeps good apples constantly on hand." A year after the railroad arrived, Adams, with hardware merchant Henry Booth and three other businessmen, incorporated the Manhattan Flour and Meal Manufacturing Company.[29]

Grain dealing and army contracts made up a large part of Adams's business. In 1867 he had begun with three contracts at Fort Harker, near Ellsworth, and two at Fort Riley, where he delivered nine thousand bushels of corn and one thousand five hundred of oats. The following year he expanded the scope of his operations considerably, with contracts at Forts Leavenworth, Riley, Harker, Hays, and Wallace—all the posts along the line of the Kansas Pacific. The *Standard* described him as "the heaviest grain dealer in the state. We mention this to show that Manhattan has live business men," the editor continued. "And this is only a specimen of what is going on." Indeed, the next month Adams and the *Standard*'s editor, L. R. Elliott, opened a real-estate partnership.[30]

The Quartermaster Department's Register of Contracts (Table 3) shows that Elliott's description of Adams as "the heaviest grain

Table 3. Contractors Furnishing Corn and Oats, 1868

	No. Bushels	Posts
Oats		
N. A. Adams	11,900	Harker, Hays, Riley
S. E. Hoffman	24,000	Hays
P. G. Lowe	20,000	Hays, Leavenworth
H. R. Hammond	10,000	Leavenworth
A. H. Whitcomb	10,000	Harker, Hays
Five others (total)	12,500	
Corn		
N. A. Adams	34,000	Hays, Leavenworth, Wallace
L. F. Bartels	24,500	Harker, Wallace
Thomas Dixon	14,000	Hays
Owen Duffy	14,000	Harker, Hays
A. S. Van Meter	10,000	Hays
Five others (total)	22,500	

dealer in the state" was more than a local editor's hyperbole and probably close to the truth. Adams handled more than 13 percent of the oats and more than 28 percent of the corn that reached military posts in northern Kansas that year. He was the only contractor who supplied all five posts and the only one whose name appears on both lists.[31]

Of the ten contractors who can be identified in the censuses of

1865 and 1870, Adams and Dixon lived farthest west, in Manhattan and Ogden. Seven of the others lived in Leavenworth County, which is not surprising. Leavenworth was the largest city in the state, and Fort Leavenworth was the headquarters of the Department of the Missouri, where the Chief Quartermaster accepted bids for contracts at posts throughout Colorado, Kansas, New Mexico, and Indian Territory. What Leavenworth and Riley Counties had in common was the railroad.[32]

The railroad and the telegraph line that ran along the right of way enabled contractors to live at a distance from the places they supplied. Many of them found it advantageous to live close to the central authority, the Chief Quartermaster of the department at Fort Leavenworth. Recipients of the government's "fostering aid" took an intense interest in the transportation and communication revolutions of the post–Civil War era. Merchants of Davis and Riley Counties tried to connect themselves to the national economy, first by a wagon road between the Missouri River and the Colorado goldfields, and eventually by promoting short-line railroads to connect with the transcontinental lines to their north and south.

Chapter 4

"The Aid of Cities and Counties . . .
Will Build It"

SETTLERS IN THE West sought connection to markets. No matter the degree of self-sufficiency to which they might aspire or how they loathed the high rates a monopolistic railroad charged on freight, settlers wanted manufactured goods. To that end, county governments surveyed roads to carry farmers' produce to mill or to town, while merchants constructed informal alliances and chartered corporations, first to promote the construction of wagon roads and later of railroads. Railroad schemes often provoked opposition among farmers in the townships, but when a proposal for a bond issue could get on a county-wide ballot, voters in the county seat outnumbered those in the rural precincts and could decide the question in favor of the town's interests. Cash-poor farmers, on the other hand, felt threatened by burdensome taxes. They saw nothing wrong, though, with county roads that led to gristmills and grain elevators, and every county commission spent a good part of its time granting farmers' petitions for new road surveys.[1]

To a degree, of course, all people and governments in the West were cash poor. Capital resided in the East, and for the most part money from outside the West built the transportation routes through it. Governments provided much of this money, particularly in the early years, as when the army established Fort Riley at the supposed head of steam navigation on the Kansas River. One of Manhattan's early promoters, himself a resident of Ohio, urged the Secretary of War to improve the military road connecting Fort Riley and Fort Leavenworth. That, incidentally, would have linked Manhattan to the Missouri River and the markets of the East. Such

Freight costs and shortage of specie vexed western businessmen throughout the nineteenth century. As late as 1880, Manhattan businessman Edward Purcell—DEALER IN EVERYTHING—would paint "CASH HOUSE" on the side of his building to advertise the advantages of cash transactions over barter or long-term credit. (Kansas State Historical Society)

extensive projects were the federal government's to undertake. County governments played the least expensive part, declaring roads and licensing ferries.

By the 1850s railroads offered a new solution to the problem of distance. The nation's rail mileage increased by 245 percent, from 8,879 in 1850 to 30,636 ten years later.[2] The federal government, and the cost-conscious army in particular, saw advantages to be gained from the expanding rail network. Merchants and farmers and the local governments that they constituted saw opportunities for closer integration into the national economy.

Railroads would not only link the frontier to the East: they would span the continent. The transcontinental line, a Junction City editor exulted in 1862, would "connect the *Leavenworth Fort Riley and Western Railroad of Kansas* with the Central Pacific Railroad of California."[3] Imagining the Pacific Railroad as a feeder line for the Leavenworth, Pawnee & Western (as the name appeared in the corporation's charter) reflected more than the editor's local chauvinism. Behind it lay a geographical determinism of almost mystical character that had already affected public discourse. "God has marked out by topography the lines of commerce," the editor of the *Western Journal of Commerce* had informed Kansas Citians in 1858. Those who studied "these great tracings of the Almighty's finger" could clearly see the confluence "of the Missouri and Kansas as the last great seat of wealth, trade and population in the westward march of commerce. . . . If men will only study topography," the editor concluded, "the problem is solved." Bishop Berkeley had given Americans a faith to live by.[4]

To set out on the course of empire, a town required young and nimble entrepreneurs. Entrenched capital was slow to respond to the opportunities railroads offered. During the 1850s, merchants in Keokuk and Galena, on the Mississippi River, were deeply committed to river transportation and saw their commerce fall behind that of Davenport, Dubuque, and other towns which were better able to accommodate the railroads. Farther west, many members of St. Joseph's economic elite owed their fortunes to the existing system of overland freighting. Similarly, Independence was home to several manufacturers of freight wagons. Entrepreneurs in the new towns of Kansas Territory were ready to entertain a variety of possibilities. Since railroads required an unprecedented amount of organization and capital, the easiest avenue of commerce open to Kansans was a wagon road from the Missouri River to the Colorado goldfields.[5]

A wagon road—little more than a long-distance county road, in effect—was attractive because so many difficulties had impeded construction of railroads. Settlers in Kansas had been projecting railroads since the territory was opened to settlement in 1854, but political questions—popular sovereignty and extinguishing the title of immigrant tribes in the eastern part of the territory—occupied public energies for the first few years. After 1857 a nationwide depression made raising capital still more difficult.

Even in the most favorable times, railroads required extraordinary financial backing. Operators of stagecoaches and canal boats did not own the roads and canals they used. Navigation of rivers and lakes was free to the owners of steam and sailing vessels, and the federal government helped with channel dredging and harbor maintenance. Railroads, on the other hand, had to own land (on which they paid taxes), lay track and acquire rolling stock, and keep the track and rolling stock in running order. It is no wonder that when the gold rush to Cherry Creek began in 1859 only one rail line west of the Mississippi River, the Hannibal & St. Joseph, was nearing completion.[6]

Businessmen interested in outfitting gold seekers and in supplying the new settlements in Colorado (then still the westernmost county of Kansas Territory) needed to locate and publicize a central route to the diggings. Issues of the Manhattan *Express* from the early autumn of 1859 contain a call for a citizens' meeting "to see what can be done for a road from Manhattan to Denver City" and a record of the proceedings. "This is a road which we absolutely need," the editor urged, "if we are not disposed to be left behind in the general strife of securing a portion of the travel to the gold mines next Spring." The sense of the meeting was in favor of a route "from Leavenworth . . . , by way of Manhattan and Ft. Riley, thence up the Solomon Fork." One advantage of this route was that the stretch from Leavenworth to Fort Riley had been marked, and the streams bridged, by the army. The meeting appointed a committee "to confer with the citizens of . . . places along the said route." Because the committee was not an organ of city or county government, and because of frequent gaps in the file of the *Express*, no record of its work survives.[7]

The next stage in the development of a wagon road west of Fort Riley began in late March 1860, when Green Russell, one of the discoverers of gold near Pike's Peak, showed up in Leavenworth and offered to explore a central route. According to the Leavenworth *Times*, the city council eagerly agreed to his $3,500 fee; on that same day alone, an express from Denver, following the Platte River road, had brought in gold dust amounting to $1,446.63. Russell and his party passed through Manhattan a week later. He reported in the *Times* that he had "traveled the well known road from Leavenworth City via Manhattan and Fort Riley to Junction City"—the military road—and then headed up the Smoky Hill. By May 5 he was in Denver. "There is plenty of wood and water on this road," he wrote. "We found good grass all the way through." Reaction was immediate. The issue of the *Times* that printed Russell's report announced a meeting at City Hall that night to plan further steps. "Not only is the Smoky Hill the best and shortest route," the editor averred, "but the energy of Leavenworth, with the aid of cities and counties along the line, will build it." The promoters said nothing about the army, which had already improved the first hundred miles of the route, from Fort Leavenworth to Fort Riley.[8]

The city of Leavenworth sent emissaries to Lawrence, Topeka, Manhattan, and Junction City. In Manhattan they addressed a mass meeting. One of Leavenworth's representatives predicted that "if we all done our duty," by early September "there would be a daily mail and a tri-weekly express from here to Colorado City." The editor of the Manhattan *Express* took the floor. "Would we stand back," he asked, "while Junction City had done so nobly?" Junction City, he said, had pledged $500 in municipal bonds and offered to double the amount "if necessary." Robert Wilson, the sutler at Fort Riley, offered $150 worth of supplies to the surveyors who would mark the route that summer, and he announced that he would double his contribution if Junction City increased its subscription to $1,000. Individual residents there reportedly pledged more than $600. "I have no money," the Manhattan editor went on, "but I have City property; a number of lots, and I am willing to give any of them for this glorious enterprise." In the end, Manhattan decided to buy seven yoke of oxen for the surveying expedition, levying a special tax for the purpose. The details were still being debated at a city council meeting a month later, when the surveyors "were daily expected."[9]

Yet amid reports of bustle and energy was a querulous editorial note. When the editor of the Leavenworth *Times* wrote, "Nor can government be idle or negligent," he clearly meant the federal government, for he went on at once to point out the military advantages of the Smoky Hill route. "When rightly asked, then, for action which . . . will save it money," the government "cannot refuse. . . . Government owes the West something. It ignores it often, but it cannot ignore it when *all* the interests of the land demand this action." He called for a federally sponsored survey of the route. Once the road was open, the editor of the *Express* pointed out, the "property of our City, towns and farms would very materially advance in value, thus offering a just reward to those who have been living here for years, struggling against thousands of obstacles, submitting ourselves to all manner of privations and sacrifices in order to settle the country and thus prepare homes for hundreds of others."[10]

This indignant, injured, self-righteous tone is very different from that of the Leavenworth *Herald* five years earlier, during the first months of Kansas settlement. Then the *Herald*'s editor trumpeted, "Squatters have from the earliest settlement of our country, led the van of civilization in the westward course. They have hewed away the forests and carried tilth and beauty and abundance everywhere." Even then, though, the editor hinted that virtue was not to be the squatter's only reward. "If such be the mission of the Squatters of Kansas (and judging of the present by the past, we have a right to think it no less), they are entitled to the fostering aid of our government, and the encouragement and gratitude of the American people." By 1860, the editor of the Manhattan *Express* wrote, the debt had come due. The settlers of Kansas had a definite idea of their place in the scheme of national development and did not wait for the passing of a generation, or even of a decade, to assert it.[11]

As westerners often did when the federal government proved slow or ineffective, promoters of the wagon road went ahead with their plans anyway. In early June Leavenworth's "Executive Committee on the Smoky Hill Route" announced that the city council would issue $3,000 worth of municipal bonds and that money, goods, and oxen worth $2,165 more had been pledged in other towns. By the third week in June an expedition of thirty-seven men, with six wagons drawn by fourteen yoke of oxen, was headed west. Under the direction of the Leavenworth County surveyor, who had been sent along, they marked the road with mounds of earth, just as George Sibley's party had marked the Santa Fe Trail in 1827. By mid-August they had arrived in Colorado City.[12]

Local preparations for the road went forward, although the presidential election of 1860 and the subsequent secession crisis all but crowded transportation news out of the columns of Kansas newspapers. In April 1861 the Manhattan *Express* noted that a bridge over the Blue River was "progressing rapidly towards completion. In a few more weeks" it would be ready "to accommodate the Pike's Peak travel." The following year, the *Smoky Hill and Republican Union* of Junction City mentioned twelve wagon trains loaded with provisions, headed for Colorado. How many followed the Smoky Hill route, though, is open to question. Towns on the Missouri River boasted of the volume of their commerce but did not specify whether the traffic was headed for New Mexico, Colorado, or Utah, or by what route. In March 1865, for instance, the Atchison *Freedom's Champion* claimed that the tonnage of goods shipped from there in 1864 had been three times that of 1863 and the trade of 1865 was "opening up lively, and the shipments promise to far exceed those of any previous years." With the Civil War drawing to a close, businessmen could turn their attention once more to developing the West's resources. Throughout the postwar decades, railroads furnished the motive power of capitalist expansion.[13]

While promoters before the Civil War planned and surveyed wagon roads and oxen hauled thousands of tons of freight each year, railroad development in Kansas had been awaiting an infusion of eastern capital. Kansas products were lacking, too, to furnish freight for eastbound trains. Unlike Santa Fe merchants, who could sell their wagons and draft animals at the end of the trail, a railroad could not dispose of its rolling stock at its western terminus and therefore faced higher fixed costs than any other mode of transportation. Railroads needed freight to help pay the cost of the return trip from the West. Soon after the Civil War, cattle shipments from Abilene began to furnish the needed carloads on the Kansas Pacific, but during the pre-war period, New Mexican wool did not offer sufficient inducement to lay track through an unsettled country. Gold in the Rocky Mountains and a growing population of farmers between the river and the mountains provided the impetus.[14]

The territorial legislature of Kansas chartered at least fifty railroads between 1855 and 1861. Nearly all of them were speculative ventures; their organizers hoped merely to sell some stock and then, as the president of the Kansas Central wrote, "get some good and reliable company to take the road and build it." The acts incorporating railroads in Kansas usually specified a one-hundred-foot right of way and authorized the issuance of stock in amounts that ranged from one to five million dollars. After a certain percentage of stock had been sold (in 1857 the legislature began to include the words "actually paid," reflecting the promoters' difficulty in collecting money from subscribers), the company could elect a board of directors and open the company's books for the sale of stock to the public. The investment required for a railroad was far greater than for a steamboat company; the Kansas River Navigation Company was authorized to issue only $350,000 worth of stock.[15]

The legislature chartered five railroads during its first session. Names of territorial officials were prominent in the lists of organizers, which were published as part of the corporate charters. Chief Justice Samuel D. Lecompte's name appeared in three of them, while those of Associate Justice Rush Elmore, U.S. attorney Andrew J. Isaacs, and territorial secretary Daniel Woodson each appeared once. At least two of the organizers had practical railroad experience: John Duff of the Kansas Central and Charles Passmore of the South Kansas both had construction contracts with the Hannibal & St. Joseph. But experienced railroaders were few; far more common were the usual sort of western entrepreneurs.[16]

The organizers of the Leavenworth, Pawnee & Western, chartered to run from Leavenworth to the western edge of Kansas by way of Fort Riley, typified frontier capitalism. Best-known among them were Judge Lecompte; the Missouri freighter William H. Russell; Amos Rees, a member of the Leavenworth Association; Robert Wilson, the Fort Riley sutler; and William F. Dyer, town promoter and army contractor. Charles H. Grover, a Leavenworth attorney, was also associated with the Leavenworth & Lecompton line. As important as any of them, though, were James Findlay and M. Pierce Rively. Findlay had attended the "mass meetings of citizens of Nebraska Territory" in 1852 and 1853. Rively's trading post near Fort Leavenworth (formerly owned by Robert Wilson) was where a squatters' association had formed in June 1854, preliminary to the Leavenworth Association's drawing up its articles of agreement. Findlay had been a trader with the Ottawa tribe, licensed by the Office of Indian Affairs, since 1838. Rively had clerked for Robert Wilson when Wilson held a license to trade with the Kickapoos in 1852 and 1853.[17]

Indian traders were important to early Kansas railroads because land cession treaties had yet to be negotiated with the immigrant tribes in the eastern part of the territory. All five of the company charters of 1855 name at least one trader with years of experience and influence among the people whose land the railroads wanted. Senior among the traders was Cyprian Chouteau of the Kansas Valley Railroad. Chouteau, a member of the St. Louis fur-trading family, had been operating near the mouth of the Kansas River since 1825. That same year Albert G. Boone of the Leavenworth & Lecompton had gone to the mountains to trap beaver, but he had returned and begun trading with the Sauks and Foxes by 1838. Thomas N. Stinson, also of the Leavenworth & Lecompton, had begun as a blacksmith at the Potawatomi agency in 1843, obtained a trading license in 1849, and married a woman of Chippewa and Shawnee ancestry the following year. With these agents already among the tribes, the railroads were well prepared for land-treaty negotiations.[18]

Traders were not the only potentially influential men whose names appear in the company charters. The Reverend Thomas Johnson, who had founded the Methodist Shawnee Mission in 1830, was among the organizers of the Leavenworth & Lecompton. Johnston Lykins of the Kansas Valley line had been a Baptist medical missionary since 1831. The railroads had influential representatives among the tribes, and their selection indicates the same attention and care that a successful town company required in its membership. Capital proved hard to attract, though, for the political turmoil of 1856 discouraged investment. As the violence subsided, the Panic of 1857 gripped the national economy, and Kansas remained without a railroad.[19]

Although no track had yet been laid west of the Missouri, residents of Kansas were well aware of the railroads' presence east of the river. Beginning in the summer of 1859, the Manhattan *Express* carried an advertisement for the Hannibal & St. Joseph Railroad each week; that October, one appeared for the Chicago, Burlington & Quincy. The following March, they were joined by one for the Michigan Central. Their advertisements occupied an entire column in each week's edition. The advertisements disappeared in 1861 when service on the Hannibal & St. Joseph was interrupted at the beginning of the Civil War. At the same time, political and military developments crowded economic news and promotional pieces out of newspapers' editorial space.

As the war ended, railroads readied themselves for a push across the plains. The Union Pacific's first locomotive arrived at Omaha in July 1865, by riverboat because the nearest railroad to the east stopped at Des Moines, 160 miles away. In Kansas, the tracks of the Kansas Pacific reached Lawrence that September and Junction City in October 1866. Although the gap east of Omaha was not closed until February 1867, the Union Pacific tracks had by then reached the forks of the Platte River at North Platte, Nebraska, more than 300 miles to the west.[20]

Always troubled by transportation costs, army officers were fully aware of the importance of railroads. Colonel Joseph A. Potter, quartermaster at Fort Leavenworth, predicted in September 1865 that "the great point of departure for [wagon] trains another season will be Fort Riley, or that vicinity." Completion of the Kansas Pacific that far would make it "much cheaper for the department to pay transportation direct to Fort Riley, and send across from that point to Kearney," on the Platte River and the Union Pacific, than to dispatch government wagon trains from Leavenworth. Also at Fort Leavenworth, commanding the Department of the Missouri, was John Pope, who in 1854 had reported from Texas on "the well-

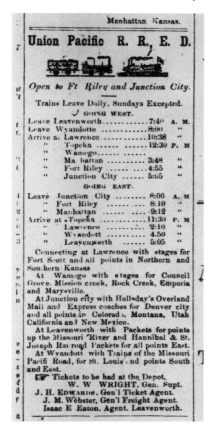

Manhattan Kansas.

Union Pacific R. R. E. D.

Open to Ft Riley and Junction City.

Trains Leave Daily, Sundays Excepted.

GOING WEST.

Leave Leavenworth	7:40	A. M.
Leave Wyandotte	8:00	"
Arrive at Lawrence	10:38	"
" Topeka	12:30	P. M
" Wamego		
" Manhattan	3:48	"
" Fort Riley	4:55	"
" Junction City	5:05	"

GOING EAST.

Leave Junction City	8:00	A. M
" Fort Riley	8:10	"
" Manhattan	9:12	"
Arrive at Topeka	11:30	P. M
" Lawrence	2:10	"
" Wyandott	4.50	"
" Leavenworth	5:05	"

Connecting at Lawrence with stages for Fort Scott and all points in Northern and Southern Kansas

At Wamego with stages for Council Grove. Mission creek, Rock Creek, Emporia and Marysville.

At Junction city with Holladay's Overland Mail and Express coaches for Denver city and all points in Colorado, Montana, Utah California and New Mexico.

At Leavenworth with Packets for points up the Missouri River and Hannibal & St. Joseph Rail road Packets for all points East.

At Wyandott with Trains of the Missouri Pacific Road, for St. Louis and points South and East.

☞ Tickets to be had at the Depot,
W. W WRIGHT, Gen. Supt.
J. H. EDWARDS, Gen'l Ticket Agent.
J. M. Webster, Gen'l Freight Agent.
Isaac E Eaton. Agent. Leavenworth.

The tracks of the Union Pacific, Eastern Division (later the Kansas Pacific) reached Fort Riley and the neighboring towns in the fall of 1866. This timetable ran in the Manhattan *Independent* late that year. (Kansas State Historical Society)

known effect" of military posts on settlement. He now believed that "with every foot gained by [railroads] in their progress westward, a large public expenditure is lopped off. The speedy and complete solution of our Indian difficulties lies largely in the completion of these roads, and . . . the end of Indian hostilities will do away at once with the necessity of troops, and the enormous expense of maintaining them in such remote regions."[21]

Western civilians, as well as army officers, paid close attention to freight costs. Although a jubilant reception always greeted the first locomotive to arrive in town, residents along the line of the Kansas

Pacific soon came to realize that the sole carrier of freight could set whatever rates it chose. Local businessmen and editors were alive to the advantages of competition, between the rival commercial centers of Chicago and St. Louis as well as between railroads. As the Kansas Pacific laid track westward and the Fort Riley quartermaster depot prepared to shift to Fort Harker, near Ellsworth, in the summer of 1867, the Junction City *Union* asked, "Without a second line of road, is there a market at present which can be reached with profit by Davis county farmers, should Fort Riley be taken from them?" In 1869 the *Union*'s editor was still fuming. "It is impossible that so large a population, and interests of such magnitude, should for any length of time submit to such exactions as are imposed upon the district of country now tributary to the Kansas Pacific Railway." During the late 1860s Kansas entrepreneurs began to incorporate railroads that would connect with existing lines at Omaha, St. Joseph, and Kansas City and lead to the larger markets of Chicago, St. Louis, and even Galveston and New Orleans. To do this, they sought capital from the East and bond issues from local governments.[22]

The activities of railroad promoters in Junction City and Manhattan are important because they helped to build the short lines that connected Fort Riley to the Missouri, Kansas & Texas (Katy) and Atchison, Topeka & Santa Fe lines at Emporia and to the Union Pacific at Kearney, Nebraska. These connections put Fort Riley in the middle of the country's rail network just as decisively as national expansion to the Rio Grande and the Pacific during the 1840s had put the Great Plains in the center of the United States. Low freight costs eventually made Fort Riley the cheapest post in the country to supply and led to the Mounted Branch School's establishment there, which extended the fort's economic importance for decades into the twentieth century. This was not at all what local railroad promoters had planned on, for many of them had favored reducing the size of the military reservation and opening the land to settlement. Their immediate interest, though, was in access to competing railroads and a variety of markets.

Municipal efforts to attract railroads usually took the form of outright land grants. In November 1865, months before the tracks of the Kansas Pacific neared Manhattan, the city offered the use of its riverfront Battery Park, "or twenty acres of Central Park to be used for Depot Buildings, Machine Shops, or any other purpose whatsoever," as well as rights of way. Two years later, the city council considered damming the Kansas River in order to offer the Kansas Pacific free water power and forty acres of land, "provided they will locate the machine shops of their railroad at this point." A division point and its machine shops meant a payroll. Junction City was a division point from 1866 to 1870, when the census showed the Kansas Pacific as Davis County's second largest employer. The railroad employed 199 men, while Fort Riley's garrison numbered 413, of whom 305 were privates, whose base pay was only thirteen dollars a month. Clearly, the railroad was an employer to be courted.[23]

County governments, on the other hand, usually offered railroads a bond issue to help finance construction. Although the constitution of Kansas prohibited state assistance for internal improvements, it contained no similar restriction on local governments. By 1870 Kansas counties, cities, and townships had issued railroad bonds amounting to $1,189,000. During the next two years, they issued $1,880,000 more. Davis County's aid to railroads worked out to eighteen dollars for every man, woman, and child; Riley County's per capita indebtedness was thirty-seven dollars. How did this difference come about? Bond issues required elections, and the differing views of expansive town dwellers, who stood to benefit directly from railroad jobs as well as lower freight costs, and cautious rural voters stand out clearly. Junction City's municipal records go back only to 1871, but a look at railroad agitation in Manhattan, and its organizers, shows how these bond issues got on the ballot and how they passed.[24]

Preeminent among Manhattan's railroad promoters was Nathaniel A. Adams, the army contractor and grain dealer. His business activities gave him a keen appreciation of the advantages to be gained from competitive freight rates. In December 1868, Adams and six other men—his old army comrade, State Treasurer Martin Anderson, among them—incorporated the Manhattan and Chicago Railway Company.[25]

The objective of the Manhattan & Chicago was more modest than its name implied. Plans were to lay track between Manhattan and Elwood, a town in Doniphan County just across the Missouri River from St. Joseph, there to connect with the Hannibal & St. Joseph and, at the other end of that line, with the Chicago, Burlington & Quincy. Five months after the company's incorporation, the Riley County Board of Commissioners received a petition with 230 signatures requesting a special election for a one hundred thousand dollar bond issue to aid the Manhattan & Chicago. At the same meeting, though, opponents presented two remonstrances signed by 396 residents, and "after a lengthy discussion and arguments on both sides," the commissioners decided against an election. L. R. Elliott, editor of the *Standard* and Nathaniel Adams's real-estate partner, expressed "much regret that they did not let the people have a chance to vote on the proposition." The people of neighboring Pottawatomie County, through which the tracks would run, did get a chance to vote on a bond issue but rejected it, effectively killing the Manhattan & Chicago.[26]

During the weeks before the election, partisans on both sides wrote long letters to the Manhattan *Standard* and the *Pottawatomie Gazette*, published in Louisville, in which their remarks expressed not only the arguments but also the tone that characterized debates over railroad bond issues. The rhetoric reflected the speculative fervor of town-dwelling merchants on one side and the wariness of farmers on the other. With less than a month to go before the election, Elliott's *Standard* printed a letter from a writer who identified himself only as "one of the largest taxpayers" in Pottawatomie County. "Tax Payer" argued that competing railroads—one leading to St. Joseph and Chicago, the other to Kansas City and St. Louis—would be forced to lower their rates. Then, after a statistical demonstration that increased property valuation would lead to lower mill levies, he launched into his peroration. "I presume there may be a few of the old fogy style of men who do not care to see the country filled up with men who are always building school houses, churches, mills, manufactories, bridges and good roads, and developing the country generally, making money themselves, and assisting others to make money. I hope all the live men of the county will be at the polls on election day and have their neighbors there, and give such an overwhelming vote for the bonds that our fogy friends will travel farther westward in search of a people who do not believe in improvements." The *Standard*'s printing a letter about an election in another county was in accordance with a resolution passed at a meeting of the prorailroad bond forces of Riley County. In it they pledged "to second the efforts of the people of [Pottawatomie County] in securing the vote of bonds." Nathaniel Adams had been the principal speaker at that meeting; Elliott, the *Standard*'s editor, had served as secretary; Henry Booth had helped draft the resolution. These influential men realized that the issuance of railroad bonds was a question that transcended county boundaries and would affect the entire region.[27]

Meanwhile, Adams had written to the *Pottawatomie Gazette*, urging passage of the bond issue. His letter excited the wrath of Durant V. Sprague, a young farmer. "The Chicago and Manhattan Railroad Company is either very poor or wants the Bonds for speculation," Sprague wrote. "If we have a surplus of cash we had better use it to shield the people from the rascality of some of the corporations that now hold sway in Kansas, than in establishing others." Adams response the following week presented the usual argument about increased property values and lower mill levies and challenged Sprague, "If the men composing the Company are humbugs and not to be trusted, show them up individually—give facts, figures and particulars." "We have less than one thousand voters in this county," Sprague replied. "Upon the handful of poor men, just starting in property and desiring to secure homes for large families, they propose to throw a burden of $150,000. . . . I believe you asked for figures; there they are." Farmers' fear of debt could defeat a bond issue unless voters in the county seat outnumbered those in the townships.[28]

To secure a bond issue, then, it was necessary to select a group of incorporators that would appeal to a broad constituency. The three

Riley County incorporators of the Manhattan & Chicago were not the right men to get the bond issue on a county-wide ballot. Adams himself was well enough connected but, like the other two, lived in Manhattan. One of the others, D. E. Ballard, had only arrived in July 1867, and his job as U.S. revenue assessor may not have made him many friends. Six months after his arrival, he had raided and temporarily closed the brewery at Ogden. The third of the organizers from Manhattan, Edwin C. Manning, had founded and edited the *Kansas Radical,* one of two newspapers that had existed in Manhattan because the question of saloon licenses had split the local Republican Party. Although the *Radical* and its prohibitionist rival, the *Independent,* had been bought and combined in Elliott's *Standard* in the summer of 1868, Manning and the *Radical* had antagonized some of Manhattan's wealthiest and most powerful people. By 1869 he was secretary of the Kansas Senate and, if physically present in Manhattan at all, did not figure prominently in the railroad meeting or the newspaper controversy. When a bond issue was next at stake, Adams would have more numerous and more effective associates.[29]

Proponents of railroad bond issues had to take into account local interests (retail sales, or real estate values, for instance) as well as national (both the corporate, in the form of the Kansas Pacific railroad, and the federal government's) in conducting their businesses. As a commission agent, Adams imported finished goods by rail; as an army contractor, he shipped grain to military posts along the Kansas Pacific. His livelihood depended on the railroad, and the defeat of the Manhattan & Chicago bonds did not deter him from undertaking further projects. A month after the voters of Pottawatomie County decided against the bond issue, Adams and at least ten other delegates from Riley County attended a railroad meeting at Clay Center that launched the Manhattan and Republican Valley Railroad. This road was to run from the Kansas Pacific at Manhattan, northwest through Clay, Cloud, and Republic Counties, connecting with the line of the Union Pacific along the Platte River in Nebraska. Representative Sidney Clarke introduced a bill in Congress to provide a federal land grant. The bill did not pass,

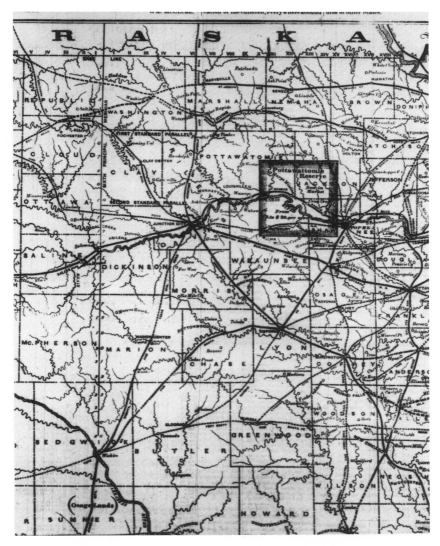

True to the nineteenth-century newspaper's role as civic booster, the Junction City *Weekly Union* of March 11, 1871, printed a map that showed its town as a rail hub, and—equally important, and equally characteristic of newspaper boosterism—neighboring Manhattan with no short line connections at all. Besides the Kansas Pacific, existing or projected lines connect Junction City with Clay Center to the northwest (and, beyond it, Kearney, Nebraska, and the Union Pacific's main line), as well as to Emporia and Wichita, on the Santa Fe, and several towns along the line of the Missouri, Kansas & Texas. (Kansas State Historical Society). Solid lines indicate completed track; dotted lines, track yet to be laid.

but the next year Adams and four of the other Riley County delegates to the Clay Center convention joined with other Manhattan residents to incorporate the Manhattan & Nebraska and the Manhattan & Southern. In June 1871 several of these men incorporated the Manhattan & Northwestern Railroad and went to work to secure a county bond issue to support it.[30]

A look at their backgrounds shows why the organizers of the Manhattan & Northwestern were much better able to do the job than those who had organized the Manhattan & Chicago (Table 4). Adams, Gove, Griffin, and George Higinbotham were old settlers, having come to Kansas in time to be counted in the census of 1860, and Green had arrived by 1865. Adams, Gove, Higinbotham, and Purcell were among the town's wealthiest residents; all four had held elective office. Adams, as mayor, had headed the proliquor license ticket in 1869, while Purcell had sat as an antilicense councilman. Higinbotham had run on both tickets from time to time. Nehemiah Green, former governor and Methodist minister, was also an official of the state Temperance Society. After 1870, when Albert Griffin bought the *Standard* from Elliott and renamed it the *Nationalist*, Elliott devoted himself to his real-estate business and a monthly promotional sheet, the *Kansas Homestead*. Adams, Griffin, and Higinbotham were members of the Masonic Lodge. Horatio Barner, the most recent arrival, was the law partner of R. B. Spilman, who was then serving as mayor and had twice been elected county attorney. Together, the eight men were admirably placed to secure public backing for their enterprise.[31]

Success depended on circulating their views widely. Griffin spoke with the editorial voice of the *Nationalist*. Apart from well-publicized civic meetings, what other means the organizers of the Manhattan & Northwestern used to influence the voters must remain conjectural. Perhaps they followed an editor's advice to Kansas City merchants years earlier. "Make it a *business rule* to never let a farmer go out of your store until you have said more or less to him about Railroads. By constantly keeping up this rule, you soon have all our farmers in the habit of thinking about our Railroads, and then, and not till then will they see their worth and help us to

Table 4. Founders of the Manhattan & Northwestern—Manhattan Residents

	Clay Center	Man & Neb	Man & South
Nathaniel A. Adams 34 Railroad agent Major, 11th Kansas $44,000/11,000 Township trustee, 1866 Mayor, 1869	X	X	X
George W. Higinbotham 41 Merchant Sheriff, 1860 $40,000/35,000 Mayor, 1866	X	X*	X
Edward B. Purcell 33 Merchant Councilman, 1869 $35,000/50,000	X	X	X
Moses J. Gove 55 Stock dealer Mayor, 1863, 1864 $24,500/7000	X		X
Horatio G. Barner 49 Lawyer $———/556	X		X*
L. Richard Elliott 34 Editor *Standard*, 1868–70 $4561/3800 *Kansas Homestead*, 1870-		X	X*
Nehemiah Green 32 Minister Lieutenant Governor $7000/3000 and Governor, 1867–69		X*	X*
Albert Griffin 36 Farmer Editor *Nationalist*, 1870- $3000/1240			

* = held office in company
X = present at the Clay Center convention, or organizer of the Manhattan & Nebraska and Manhattan & Southern Railroads
Occupations and values of real and personal estates as given in 1870 Census.

The Manhattan real-estate and insurance office of L. Richard Elliott, Nathaniel Adam's partner in railroad promotion. Elliott himself stands second from left. A hitching rail runs between the up-
rights that support the signs "LAND OFFICE" and "RAILROAD
AGENT." (Kansas State Historical Society)

build them."[32] It would take more than talk, though, to overcome
the caution of Riley County's rural voters.

A farmer on Wildcat Creek who opposed the earlier bond issue
had raised the chief objection. "This road is of no value to any one
out[side] of Manhattan city, and but few in the city." Albert Griffin,
in the *Nationalist*, denied the imputation of narrow, selfish interests.
"We do not propose that Manhattan shall array itself against the
County," he wrote. "Let it be understood that hereafter the interests of the city and County *as a whole* are to be considered and cared
for, not those of individuals. . . ." Despite his expressed solicitude,
Griffin's next step was to attack two of the county commissioners by
name, something the editors of the *Independent* and the *Radical* had
avoided even during elections that hinged on the emotionally
charged issue of liquor licenses. Petitioners for the railroad bonds
had asked for an election "at the earliest practicable·day," and the

commissioners had put the issue on the November ballot, four months in the future. Having attacked the commissioners, who lived in the rural townships and did not respond promptly to the desires of Manhattan, Griffin tried to rally the voters of Riley County by raising the bogey of interference from Junction City. "The truth is," he wrote on the eve of the election, "that [Junction City's] business men know full well that if the bonds are voted the roads will be built, and that a great deal of trade that they now get . . . will thereafter go to Ogden and Manhattan. . . . They want to make Riley County tributary to Junction—which they cannot do if these bonds are issued."[33]

The bond issue passed, 949 to 425, but despite Griffin's attempts to unify the county, it was Manhattan's vote, 517 to 12, that carried the election. In the precincts outside Manhattan and Ogden, the vote was against the bonds, 382 to 308. The farmers' suspicions were correct. Two years after the election, in 1873, the mill levy to pay the 7 percent interest on the Manhattan & Northwestern bonds had risen to equal the levy for general revenue, and represented 37.5 percent of the total county assessment, aside from school taxes. Repayment of its bonded indebtedness would trouble the Riley County Commission for years to come.[34]

By 1874, though, crews were laying track towards the Union Pacific at Kearney, Nebraska, and Fort Riley's civilian neighbors already had a connection to the Santa Fe and the Katy at Emporia. These feeder lines would center Fort Riley geographically and in the minds of military planners. They would affect the army's use of the fort, the fort's future existence, and therefore its effect on the local economy, well into the next century.

Town dwellers, as well as army officers, had a vital interest in railroads. Railroads—two or more in competition—meant survival and prosperity for towns and could pull the residents together, as Manhattan's lopsided vote in the 1871 county bond election showed. Even men on opposite sides of a heated question like prohibition could join forces to promote a railroad. In fact, such broad-based support was necessary if the road were to amount to more than an entry in the Register of Corporate Charters. Outside the city limits

This lone water tank stood where the tracks of the Junction City &
Fort Kearney met those of the Kansas Pacific. Twin spouts enabled
the tank to water locomotives on either line. At its other end, the
Junction City & Fort Kearney connected with the main line of the
Union Pacific at Kearney, Nebraska. By the 1880s, the network of
short lines had made Fort Riley the cheapest post in the country to
supply. (Kansas State Historical Society)

townships that would not be directly served by the railroad recorded
similarly lopsided majorities against bond issues. The hopes of rural
voters were not easily inflated. Nevertheless, if a bond issue could get
on the ballot, the favorable majority in the county seat would assure
success. The only problem remaining was to find "some good and
reliable company" to "take the road and build it."

Railroads created a bond between local and national interests.
They promoted commerce and military efficiency at the same time,
and while the army used the railroads, the railroads changed the
army. "For a hundred years we have been sweeping across the continent," General William T. Sherman wrote in 1882. "Now we are
across, and have railroads everywhere." The following year, in his
last annual report before retirement, Sherman concluded, "I now
regard the Indians as substantially eliminated from the problem of

the Army," and credited the rail network as an even more important cause of that development than the advance of white settlement or the activities of the army itself. Yet the railroads, Sherman went on, "constantly call for the protection of the military" (it was only six years since the nationwide strikes of 1877), and the army needed to reorder its entire scheme of garrisons and depots, concentrating large bodies of troops where they could be moved rapidly and supplied cheaply. Lieutenant General Philip H. Sheridan, headquartered in Chicago, described his own command, the Military Division of the Missouri. "The extension of railroads in all directions over the vast region between the Missouri River and the Rocky Mountains now affords an opportunity for concentration, . . . and economical results are anticipated." As always, the general had his eye on transportation costs.[35]

Fort Riley stood in the middle of Sheridan's division on the Kansas Pacific between Denver and Kansas City, with branch lines running northwest to the Union Pacific in Nebraska and southeast to the main lines of the Katy and the Santa Fe. Local civilians, hoping to secure the advantages of competitive freight rates and connections to wider markets, had put their county governments heavily in debt to build some of the branch lines. These railroads made Fort Riley a convenient base for supplies and field operations and led the generals to reevaluate the fort's place in their strategic plans.

Chapter 5

"Where They Can Be Housed and Supplied at the Least Expense"

"THE INTERESTS OF the country are so intimately connected with the success of the Railway Company, that any measure promoting the interests of one, almost necessarily advances the interests of the other," an army inspector wrote in January 1866, the winter before the Kansas Pacific reached Fort Riley. During the decades that followed, the army found itself faced with changing responsibilities. As railroads helped to bring new lands and their resources into the market, less and less did troops patrol open country to protect isolated homesteaders from Indian attack, as they had in the valleys of the Republican and Solomon Rivers in the 1860s. More often, the army had to prevent incursions on Indian lands by rapacious land-boomers and miners. Moreover, railroads carried the mail, which gave a pretext for federal intervention when labor disputes threatened to interrupt delivery. At the same time that they presented the army with new duties, the railroads suggested a new scheme of troop deployment and offered a new means of supplying military posts.[1]

Fort Riley's importance—indeed, its existence—depended on its location. Army officers had chosen the site because they entertained hopes, soon disappointed, of supplying it cheaply by riverboat. After the Civil War, the extension of railroads west of the Missouri River provided another cheap means of moving supplies to the post. During the twenty years that followed the war, the advancing network of rails afforded new uses to which the army might put Fort Riley and its twenty-thousand-acre military reservation. The Kansas Pacific, the first railroad to reach the fort, turned it into a backwater. Later rail connections put Fort Riley at the center of a transportation network that assured not only its survival but its selection as the site of one of the army's largest garrisons.

Transportation routes influenced the size and shape of the army's administrative regions as well. Departmental boundaries within the Military Division of the Missouri—the central third of the country—make little sense at first glance. The Department of the Platte, for instance, included Illinois, Iowa, Nebraska, Wyoming, and Utah. The Department of the Missouri included Missouri, Kansas, Colorado, and New Mexico. The shape of the departments makes sense only when the lines of major transportation routes are drawn on the map. The Department of the Platte covered the line of the Union Pacific Railroad, which connected with the Central Pacific in Utah. To the south, the Department of the Missouri included the Kansas Pacific, between Kansas City and Denver, as well as the Atchison, Topeka & Santa Fe. These railroads followed older wagon routes and took advantage of the same easy grades and available water. Steam locomotives, like the draft animals of wagon trains, needed water. The importance of cheap supplies and the routes by which those supplies moved explains the military map of the West.[2]

As soon as railroads became available, the army began using them to move troops. A company of infantry on its way to Fort Harker, near Ellsworth, was detained at Fort Riley for nine days in June 1867, "trains on R.R. westward having been suspended on acct. of high floods." There were many posts, of course, that railroads did not reach until years later. In October 1876 a battery of artillery took nine days to march 159 miles from Fort Sill to Caddo, Indian Territory. At Caddo the troops took the cars of the Missouri, Kansas & Texas, and they arrived at Fort Riley thirty-six hours later. The next month, Fort Riley's garrison was reinforced by a company of infantry that had made the trip from Fort D. A. Russell at Cheyenne, Wyoming, in about thirty hours. Long-distance movement of troops by rail became commonplace.[3]

Cavalry, though, continued to march cross-country when the move was not urgent. Companies of the Sixth Cavalry stationed at

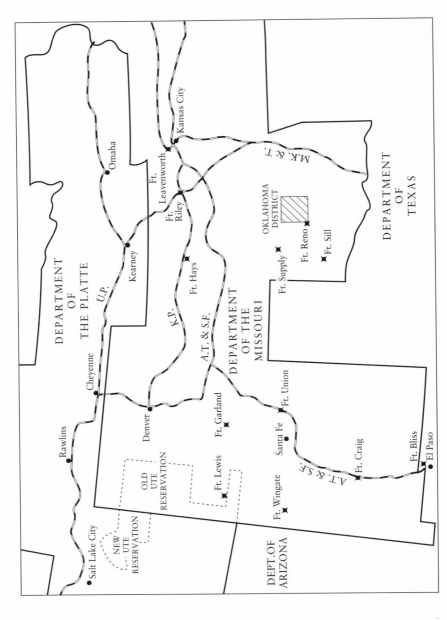

The Department of the Missouri in the 1880s: Where Fort Riley's soldiers campaigned and where the Quartermaster Department shipped the fort's hay.

Fort Riley during the early 1870s spent the summers tenting near Fort Hays, 150 miles to the west. The march took seven days, but by the time they reached their destination, men and horses were ready for field service.[4]

The summer camps at Fort Hays in the early 1870s were not mere exercises. When the Cheyennes and Arapahos signed the Treaty of Medicine Lodge in October 1867, they had "reserve[d] the right to hunt on any lands south of the Arkansas as long as the buffalo may range thereon in such numbers as to justify the chase." The next spring, the Sioux reserved the right to hunt buffalo on the Republican River in an identically worded clause of the treaty they signed at Fort Laramie. The Medicine Lodge and Fort Laramie treaties thus assured the whites of a central region free of Indians, through which railroads could pass to California, Colorado, and New Mexico. Within a few years, these railroads would abet the commercial slaughter of the buffalo and obviate the hunting rights guaranteed in the treaties.[5]

Meanwhile, though, protection of the transportation corridor became the responsibility of Brigadier General John Pope, commanding the Department of the Missouri. Pope deplored the retention of off-reservation hunting rights; encounters between Indian hunting parties and white settlers, he wrote, were sure to end badly. But the railroad offered a solution to the problem of policing the plains; Pope declared that it "furnishes cheap and rapid communication and puts most of the posts within easy reach of supplies. . . . Summer camps of cavalry or infantry sent out in the early spring to important points from some large central posts accomplish all the objects to be expected from small posts kept up all the year at the same points . . . much more completely and at vastly less cost." So troops from Fort Riley took to the plains each summer, and Indians continued to hunt while the buffalo lasted. Most livestock thefts, the troops discovered, were the work of white rustlers.[6]

The railroad's greatest importance, though, lay not in the movement of troops but of supplies. If all else failed, soldiers could march to their destination; supplies could not. Railroads moved more goods more quickly and cheaply than wagons could, and brought lower freight rates generally. With no railroad west of Lawrence, Kansas, freight charges were high in 1865. Quartermaster General Montgomery C. Meigs listed the transportation costs per hundred pounds of "corn, hay, clothing, subsistence, lumber, or any other necessary" from the Missouri River at Fort Leavenworth to Fort Riley at $2.46; to Fort Union, New Mexico, $14.35; to Fort Kearny, Nebraska, $6.44; to Fort Laramie, Wyoming, $14.10 and to Denver $15.43. The rate averaged about $2.50 per hundred pounds per hundred miles. As the Kansas Pacific laid track westward, the rates charged by wagon freighters plummeted. Army freight contracts allowed for a seasonal variation of as much as 65 percent (low from April to October, when the grass was good; higher from November through March). The yearly average rate, though, dropped by one-third in four years, from $1.81 per hundred pounds per hundred miles in 1867–68 to $1.18 in 1870–71. In 1872 General Pope reported that the Atchison, Topeka & Santa Fe was running trains as far as Fort Dodge, "which enables us to dispense with a large part of the wagon transportation, which has hitherto been a heavy expense in this department."[7]

By moving supplies cheaply and in large quantities, the railroads allowed troops to travel farther and stay in the field longer. In October 1868 the Kansas Pacific Railroad made possible the establishment of an army post far to the south, in a corner of Indian Territory where none had existed. The new post was called Camp Supply, and its purpose was to support a late-autumn punitive expedition of a kind never before attempted on the plains. Sheridan wanted to move troops against Indians whom he suspected of harboring raiders while cold weather immobilized them in their villages. This operation required an enormous store of rations, ordnance, and quartermaster's supplies. For years afterward, the number of civilians employed by the Quartermaster Department at posts in Kansas rose and fell in response to the needs of Camp Supply, first at Fort Hays, on the Kansas Pacific, and then at Fort Dodge after the Santa Fe reached there in 1872.[8]

The civilian payrolls at Fort Hays and Fort Dodge illustrate nicely the effect of railroads on military posts. The Kansas Pacific

Table 5. Sheridan's Winter Campaign and the Fort Hays Payroll

	Employees	Teamsters	Payroll
October 1868	430	222	$11,838
November	470	220	19,784
December	446	234	23,132
January 1869	241	115	10,095
February	244	114	10,132

reached Fort Hays in October 1867. From February to July 1868, the Fort Hays quartermaster employed an average of 29 civilians, from half to two-thirds of them carpenters and plasterers, earning an average total of $1,711 a month. In September as Sheridan began to prepare his winter campaign, the payroll rose to 149 employees, including 84 teamsters, earning $4,840. As Camp Supply was established and the troops took the field, Fort Hays boomed (Table 5). As 1869 wore on, activity became more regular, with the number of employees averaging 140, 105 of them teamsters, and a monthly payroll of about $5,060.[9]

In September 1872 the tracks of the Atchison, Topeka & Santa Fe reached Fort Dodge, bringing a rail line eighty miles closer to Camp Supply. During most of 1872 the Fort Dodge quartermaster had employed only a clerk, a blacksmith, and a saddler, with combined monthly earnings of about $270. With the railroad came the boom. The quartermaster's payroll peaked from January to April 1873 (Table 6). During the remainder of that year it settled at about forty-six employees, twenty-six of them teamsters, earning about $2,170 a month.

The railroad's arrival at Fort Dodge had diminished the importance of Fort Hays. In the summer of 1872 the quartermaster there had employed an average of 72 men, 38 of them teamsters, with a payroll of about $2,760. After wagon freighting was transferred to Fort Dodge, the number of quartermaster's employees shrank to 25,

Table 6. The Santa Fe Railroad and the Fort Dodge Payroll

	Employees	Teamsters	Payroll
October 1872	22	6	$1,246
November	55	22	[illegible]
December	45	27	2,080
January 1873	72	51	3,112
February	71	51	2,405
March	69	51	2,562
April	70	51	2,968

with average monthly earnings of $1,120. In March and April 1873 no teamsters at all worked at Fort Hays. That May, when five cavalry companies from Fort Riley arrived for a summer camp, the quartermaster hired twenty teamsters, and the Fort Hays payroll hovered around $1,420 through September.[10]

The establishment of military posts farther west made the future of Fort Riley uncertain. In 1866 and 1867, anticipating Indian hostilities, the Department of the Missouri named Fort Larned the assembly-point for wagon trains headed for New Mexico; Fort Harker, on the Smoky Hill, for those going to Colorado; and Fort Riley, for trains headed up the Republican River. No trains were to go west of those posts with fewer than twenty wagons and thirty armed men. Fort Riley was already home to the principal quartermaster depot between Fort Leavenworth and Fort Union, New Mexico. It employed an average of 166 teamsters and wagon masters in the months following the Confederate surrender and twice that many during the peak freighting months of 1866. On a tour of inspection, Sherman remarked that "the country out as far as Fort Riley is as much a settled country as Illinois and Missouri." He added, "There is no necessity for troops east of Fort Riley."[11]

As the Kansas Pacific pushed beyond Fort Riley, the army decided to move its quartermaster depot to Fort Harker on the Smoky Hill, five or six days farther west by ox team but only about five hours by rail. Fort Harker and the nearby town of Ellsworth lay about eighty-five miles west of Fort Riley and Junction City, at the place where the shortest good wagon road ran between the Smoky Hill and the Arkansas Rivers. Bulk goods would be far cheaper if moved by rail to a depot at Fort Harker. That was the logical place from which to supply military posts on the Santa Fe Trail, which followed the Arkansas.[12]

Local opinion was pessimistic about Fort Riley's future as an army post. The Junction City *Union* observed that "the onward progress of the railroad . . . will render useless to government the keeping up of such a military establishment as Fort Riley. It must before long be abandoned." The army, though, was already casting about for uses to which they could put the fort's twenty thousand acres. Brigadier General Rufus Ingalls, who had been Chief Quartermaster of the Army of the Potomac, had written in July 1866 to Quartermaster General Meigs, "The Reservation is an immense one, but I saw no cultivation of any consequence upon it. Corn, wheat, potatoes and grasses would grow luxuriantly there if cultivated. I do not pretend, however, that farming by the government is an economy to the service." Meigs queried Sherman, who was then commanding the Military Division of the Missouri, about leasing the reservation to farmers, suggesting that "the sure market and high prices of the frontier should . . . be sufficient inducement." Sherman, occupied at that moment with military operations from Kansas to Montana, commented, "Our men seem to be too busy to garden," before passing the letter on to his Chief Quartermaster, Langdon C. Easton.[13]

Easton was one of the three officers who had chosen the site of Fort Riley fourteen years earlier, and he saw a different future for the fort. He thought that the idea of leasing the reservation to civilians was a poor one, unlikely to succeed. Most settlers, he wrote, would prefer to invest their labor and money in a claim under the Homestead Act, on equally attractive land nearby but outside the limits of

"Fort Riley . . . must soon be abandoned, and the consequences will be that our market will fall," the editor of the Junction City *Weekly Union* wrote in 1867. Twelve years later the fort was still open, but this photograph of North Washington Street suggests the tiny garrison's diminished economic effect on Junction City throughout most of the 1870s. (Kansas State Historical Society)

the military reservation. Moreover, Easton thought that Fort Riley would still prove useful to the army. "The object in having the very large reserves referred to by the Quartermaster General, is to secure timber, and grass for hay and for grazing, both of which are very scarce at the most of our western posts." It would be years, though, before the railroads' extension westward enabled the army to ship Fort Riley's hay to posts in New Mexico and Wyoming.[14]

During the years before the army found a new use for Fort Riley, the size of its garrison swelled and shrank spasmodically. Beginning in the fall of 1866, while two new cavalry regiments were organizing, the average troop strength was well over five hundred. The departure of the Tenth Cavalry in 1868 left the fort with a garrison of two infantry companies, and finally of one, with an average strength of seventy-five officers and men. Then, in March 1869, Ulysses S. Grant resigned from the army to become president, causing a string of promotions and reassignments and bringing a new commanding general, John M. Schofield, to the Department of the Missouri.[15]

Schofield planned to use the mobility that the railroad afforded to gather batteries of field artillery at Fort Riley and train them there. He was an 1853 graduate of West Point who had served eight years as a lieutenant in the artillery before the Civil War brought him quick promotion. Schofield attained the regular army rank of brigadier general in November 1864 and was serving as Andrew Johnson's Secretary of War in 1869, when Grant's resignation and the promotions of Sherman and Sheridan opened a major general's position. Schofield remained in Kansas only a year before moving on to San Francisco to command the Military Division of the Pacific, but during that year he attempted to use Fort Riley and its enormous reservation as a school of instruction for light artillery.[16]

Schofield's concern for tactical training reflects a professionalism that is seldom recognized by historians and popular writers who characterize this period as "the Indian Wars" and lavish attention on the cavalry. The post-Civil War army included five regiments of artillery, each made up of twelve companies. According to the reorganization of 1866, ten companies in each regiment were assigned to harbor fortifications from Maine to Florida and along the Gulf and Pacific coasts. The other two companies (referred to as "batteries" just as cavalry companies were called "troops") were mounted and served as field artillery, often stationed near large cities where they might be useful in riot control. Schofield was convinced that the light batteries of the regular army needed to train together and that Fort Riley, with its stone barracks and stables and its spacious reservation, provided a suitable place. In July 1869 four batteries of field artillery arrived at Fort Riley. One came from New Orleans; another from the Presidio of San Francisco, by way of the Central and Union Pacific Railroads, whose lines had joined in Utah only two months earlier.[17]

Despite Schofield's professionalism and his keen eye for the potential uses of railroads, the first artillery school at Fort Riley was a failure. Training was compromised from the start by the army's need for troops in the field during the summer after Sheridan's winter campaign. Soon after arriving at Fort Riley, two hundred of the artillerymen were issued carbines and cavalry saddles and sent off to patrol the Republican and Solomon Rivers. The garrison dwindled to less than half its normal strength during the summer of 1869 and again in 1870.[18]

A more serious detriment to training, because it persisted year-round, was the army's practice of detailing enlisted men to nonmilitary duties keeping up the fort's buildings and grounds and doing other manual labor and clerical work. Each battery provided the post hospital with at least one man as a cook or an orderly; the post bakery took another man; at least one other cared for the company garden (required as a source of fresh vegetables) in season; and noncommissioned officers were needed to serve as post sergeant major, commissary sergeant, stable sergeant, and provost corporal. Most voracious was the Quartermaster Department, which gobbled up enlisted men experienced in the building trades, blacksmithing, leatherwork, and most of all, teamsters and common laborers. The surviving bimonthly muster rolls show that an average of 17.5 percent of the available men (those not in the hospital or the guardhouse or absent from the post) were occupied with these chores.[19]

This policy of "frittering away the men" gave rise to repeated complaints to Department of the Missouri headquarters at Fort Leavenworth and to the Adjutant General in Washington, D.C. The commanding officer wrote that one battery, "after supplying its quota of extra duty men, has about one man to six horses present at Stable call. Our instruction therefore necessarily consists more in teaming, carpentry, masonry &c. than the use of arms. . . . Under the circumstances, I do not know that the state of affairs can be avoided." Matters were exacerbated by a reduction in the number of civilian employees from twenty-six to three just as the batteries were arriving at Fort Riley. This false economy, initiated by Langdon C. Easton himself, as Chief Quartermaster of the Department of the Missouri, effectively stymied instruction during the two years of the batteries' stay at the fort. Although troops supplied cheap labor for the army throughout the post–Civil War years, a training program was impossible to conduct under those circumstances. When Schofield left the Department of the Missouri, John Pope returned as commanding general. Pope disbanded the school, and Fort Riley reverted to a small garrison, usually of infantry. Schofield's first attempt to found a school had failed, but his second try would succeed fifteen years later. By that time, additional railroads had made Fort Riley's location even more attractive. More important, the railroads had forced new responsibilities on the army and had brought new opportunities as well.[20]

One wholly unforeseen circumstance in which railroads played a part was the trade in raw buffalo hides, which in a few years destroyed the Plains Indians' chief source of food, clothing, and shelter. About 1870, a new tanning technique made possible the use of buffalo hides for shoe leather and industrial drive belts. The new railroads on the plains were the only profitable means of shipping high-bulk, low-value freight like hides. Hays, on the Kansas Pacific, became a major shipping point as commercial hide hunters slaughtered the herds in western Kansas. In 1872, when the Santa Fe reached Dodge City, the hunters extended their operations south of the Arkansas River and into the Texas panhandle. By the late 1870s the buffalo had been virtually exterminated in the southern plains. Their disappearance nullified those treaty provisions that allowed Plains Indians to leave their reservations to hunt. For the army in Kansas and Indian Territory, this meant that instead of camping out in the summer to keep an eye on Indian hunters, the troops might be called on at any time of year to prevent white encroachment on Indian lands.[21]

By the end of the 1870s, new railroad lines were able to carry troops from Fort Riley to several campaigns in such overwhelming force that no armed conflict occurred. These operations are not much written about, nor does the army appear frequently in tribal histories of the early reservation period unless a fort was adjacent to the agency, like Fort Sill on the Comanche and Kiowa reservation or Fort Reno on the Cheyenne and Arapaho. Yet these demonstrations of federal authority took much of the army's time and manpower and incurred extra expense, to the consternation of administrators. Operations in which troops from Fort Riley participated were more typical of the army's activities during the last two decades of the century than were the more violent incidents that have usually received historians' attention.[22]

Just south of Kansas lay Indian Territory, the home of five tribes that had been removed there from the Southeast before the Civil War. Most of these people had sided with the Confederacy during the war, and the tribes signed a series of punitive treaties in 1866, forfeiting about one-third of their lands. Some of the ceded area was assigned to the Arapahos, Cheyennes, Comanches, and Kiowas as reservations, and some to tribes who were moving south from Kansas, where their old, prewar reservations were being opened to white settlement. In the middle of Indian Territory lay the Oklahoma district, nearly two million acres that had not been assigned to any tribe. As settlement in Kansas approached the ninety-eighth meridian (approximately the twenty-inch rainfall line) and the extermination of the buffalo confined the Plains tribes to their reservations, railroad promoters, land speculators, and farmers turned towards Oklahoma.[23]

The Boomers (named for the land boom they hoped to create) argued that in not assigning the Oklahoma district to any tribe, Congress had implicitly added it to the part of the public domain that was open to settlement. Secretary of the Interior Carl Schurz expressed a different view in a letter to the secretary of war. Schurz requested the army's help to forestall the Boomers' colonization scheme and, if necessary, to arrest their leaders. Not only had Congress failed to authorize settlement in Oklahoma at any time since the treaties of 1866, Schurz pointed out, but recent legislation had explicitly placed the district and the rest of Indian Territory within the jurisdiction of the federal court at Fort Smith, Arkansas. Schurz asked that troops be sent to Coffeyville, Wichita, and Arkansas City, Kansas, three towns where the Boomers were assembling.[24]

The request brought troops by rail and steamboat from as far away as Michigan. Fort Riley's contribution was a company of infantry sent to Wichita and a ten-man detachment sent to Coffeyville. The residents there took much the same view of their military visitors as did other civilians throughout the West. When a company of cavalry from Camp Supply reinforced the Fort Riley contingent, the Coffeyville Journal's editor remarked, "our farmers now have a purchaser for their corn." The following week, he noted the arrival of a quartermaster from department headquarters "to settle accounts of the troops stationed here." The editor's preoccupation with the army's money seemed to bear out the observation of a U.S. Indian agent the year before that white settlers would annoy the Indians until military protection became necessary. "It is preferable to be at war than to be without money."[25]

No war ensued in Indian Territory, though. The only penalty for trespassing on Indian lands, according to federal statute, was a fine for the second offense. Since the Boomers who were convicted owned no property and could not pay a fine, they were repeatedly released and invariably prepared another invasion of the territory. Officials of the Office of Indian Affairs and the War Department urged imprisonment as punishment for trespassing, and bills providing stiffer penalties were introduced in session after session of Congress, but none passed. Finally, the death of David L. Payne in 1884 deprived the Boomer movement of its guiding spirit, and the question of the Oklahoma district merged with the larger issue of the allotment of Indian lands in severalty and the opening of reservations throughout the plains, which led in 1887 to the General Allotment Act.[26]

During these years, companies from Fort Riley camped for months at a time along the southern boundary of Kansas. When Colonel Edward Hatch and three companies of the Ninth Cavalry arrived by rail during the winter of 1885, the Arkansas City *Republican* exulted; "This is another luscious plum for Arkansas City. Poor old Caldwell. This will be a bitter pill for her to swallow. The *Journal* has boasted that that city was the headquarters for the soldiers while Arkansas City was for the boomers. We are headquarters for both now. Gen. Hatch pronounced this city the natural gateway to Oklahoma and accordingly moved the troops here. . . . They will be stationed here for quite a while, and as the companies will draw their pay here lots of shining shekels will find their way into the coffers of our merchants." The troops had moved through town and bivouacked in Indian Territory before an army paymaster arrived and, according to the *Republican*, "drew some $17,000 out of the bank here and departed to pay the boys in blue for their services." As the troops moved beyond the reach of Arkansas City's merchants, they disappeared from the pages of the *Republican*.[27]

The economic motive for cordiality was transparent. The town of Kiowa, just north of the state line and about eighty miles south-west of Wichita, was host to seven companies of cavalry and in-fantry in the summer of 1885 because of a threatened outbreak at the Cheyenne and Arapaho agency. A month after the troops ar-rived, the Kiowa *Herald* dismissed the rumors of trouble that had brought the troops but discouraged immigration. "The Indian busi-ness is scarcely spoken of any more. The scare, as we predicted from the beginning, was without foundation." Nevertheless, the paper welcomed the army quartermaster who "spent several days in Kiowa last week, looking up the grounds on which to build a government supply depot at this point." According to the Herald, the soldiers "[thought] it probable that a permanent post [would] be established near here." The season ended, though, with a disappointed snarl. "The battalion of infantry that has been encamped on Mule Creek for several weeks, left yesterday for Fort Riley, where they will go into winter quarters. Fort Riley is situated in the center of the state in one of the most populous counties in Kansas. And there can be no earthly use to keep a large command stationed there. If the troops are needed at any place at all, it is on the border and it is a short sighted policy that will concentrate troops at a place like Fort Riley, and leave the border unprotected, even though there is no danger apprehended." The *Herald's* editor ignored completely the doctrine of stationing troops cheaply at central points, which Sher-man, Sheridan, and others had been propounding for years in their annual reports. At Kiowa, as elsewhere throughout the West, the in-terests of local merchants ran a poor second to those of the federal government.[28]

The railroads, moreover, enabled troops from Fort Riley to man-ifest the federal presence in neighboring states, hundreds of miles distant, both to help quell civil unrest and to avert possible Indian hostilities. Since before the Civil War, army officers had complained of tiny garrisons and the inability to concentrate a large body of troops to meet an emergency. The railroads solved that problem. Two companies of the Sixteenth Infantry from Fort Riley were able to travel by rail to St. Louis and spend a couple of weeks there dur-ing the railroad strike of 1877. A few years after that, deployment of the fort's garrison to Colorado became almost commonplace. When the Sixteenth Infantry moved to Texas in the late autumn of 1880, four companies of the Fourth Cavalry arrived from the Ute reservation in Colorado and stayed until the following spring. "The agricultural community are much pleased, and speak as if they feel indebted to General Pope, for sending a cavalry command to occupy the post," a correspondent wrote to the *Army and Navy Journal,* "as it gives them quite a market for their surplus produce." After spending the winter in good horse country, most of the Fourth Cavalry returned to western Colorado, leaving a detachment of one officer and two dozen men to mind the fort for the next six months.[29]

The Fourth Cavalry's sojourn was part of a years-long effort to move the Ute tribe off its mineral-rich lands in the western third of the new state of Colorado to a much smaller reservation in Utah Territory. With rail transportation available, considerably less serious alarms could evoke responses that would not have been possible ten, or even five, years earlier. When Navajo herdsman were reported to be grazing sheep off their reservation during the winter and spring of 1883, two Ninth Cavalry companies went by rail from Fort Riley to Fort Lewis, in southwestern Colorado. The Navajos were a large tribe, numbering perhaps sixteen thousand, with an estimated eight hundred thousand sheep. Patrols of the Ninth Cavalry "saw no Indians with herds" off the reservation, though, and "found no trouble." The troops returned to Fort Riley in the fall.[30]

Yet for all the ease with which troops could be shunted back and forth by rail, more important for Fort Riley's future was its twenty-thousand-acre reservation. The army turned it into an immense hay farm, and rail transportation made possible the shipment of hay to posts as far away as Fort Wingate, New Mexico, in Navajo country. An entire cavalry regiment was always stationed in New Mexico, and the Quartermaster Department there employed hundreds of draft animals. In the spring of 1879 the tracks of the Atchison, Topeka & Santa Fe reached Fort Union, the quartermaster depot of the District of New Mexico. Fort Riley's hay harvest, which far exceeded local requirements, and several railroads by which to ship the hay made it unique among army posts and assured its survival in the face of local efforts from 1871 on to reduce the acreage of its military reservation and open the land to settlement. Records of Fort Riley's hay shipments before 1880 have not survived, but those from later years give some idea of the quantities and destinations, and the difficulties that the quartermasters faced in providing forage for posts throughout the Department of the Missouri. A quartermaster's duties at any post were onerous, and required "patience, . . . energy, . . . courtesy [and] imperturbability," but Fort Riley's quartermaster needed the abilities of a railroad manager, as well.[31]

The first recorded hay shipments from Fort Riley were in January 1880. They went to Fort Garland in southern Colorado to supply the Fourth Cavalry troops that would garrison Fort Riley the following winter. Six companies of the Fourth Cavalry had recently arrived at Fort Garland from Texas, en route to the Ute reservation after fighting broke out there in October 1879. The Fort Riley quartermaster shipped more than three hundred tons of hay—about forty carloads—to Fort Garland in January and more in early April. Winter weather held the Fourth Cavalry at Fort Garland until May 1880, when they moved north into a country "barren and bleak, and with no grass or timber suitable to build a post or to furnish forage of any kind for the animals." After a summer in the mountains, the cavalry was "drawn in to posts along the railroads, where they can be housed and supplied at the least expense," with four of the companies finally spending the winter at Fort Riley.[32]

Although the Ute Reservation was in Colorado, which lay within the Department of the Missouri, its mountainous terrain dictated that supplies for the army camp on White River, in the northern part of the reservation, be shipped by rail to Rawlins, Wyoming, in the Department of the Platte, and from there overland by wagon to the camp. During the last five months of 1880, the Fort Riley quartermaster sent at least nineteen carloads of hay—about 160 tons—to Rawlins. On November 17 he reported 80 tons of hay already baled at Fort Riley, 576 tons more on hand that could be baled, and 672 tons not yet delivered on that year's contract. Fort Riley itself would require 750 tons to feed 360 horses and 164 mules through June 1881. Should he, the quartermaster asked, "continue baling for

The soldier's uniforms show that Fort Riley continued to be a center of military hay shipments well into the twentieth century. (Kansas State Historical Society)

the present?" The Chief Quartermaster's answer must have been affirmative, for two-thirds of the hay destined for White River was shipped to Rawlins in the month of December.[33]

Drought often diminished the hay crop in the District of New Mexico, and in the late winter of 1884 Fort Riley's quartermaster dispatched nineteen tons of hay to Fort Wingate in the northwestern part of the territory. Seven tons went to Fort Craig, south of Socorro on the Rio Grande, to augment ten tons that had been sent the previous October. In 1880 Fort Riley furnished hay to detachments of troops watching the Boomers at Baxter Springs and Coffeyville, and in 1885 to Colonel Hatch's troops at Arkansas City and Caldwell. The cost of shipping baled hay from Kansas was sometimes lower than the bids offered by local contractors in Colorado, Indian Territory, and New Mexico.[34]

Shipments could be impeded by a lack of railroad cars. "Hay will go forward as soon as cars can be had," Fort Riley's quartermaster wrote when shipments to Rawlins stopped suddenly in December 1880. Baling the hay could present difficulties, too. In July 1880 the quartermaster intimated that a new hay press would enable his crew to bale eight tons a day, but two months later he acknowledged that the old press was "ready for use with very little repair." The following January he could find "no baling wire in Junction City or vicinity and [it] cannot be ordered and obtained in less than 10 days." When a replacement for the old hay press finally arrived in June 1881, he informed department headquarters, "wire received with baling machine cannot be used unless man is hired to cut, straighten & prepare it, as it is in coils." He asked whether "proper baling wire" would be sent or he should buy it locally. Using the latest technology meant that military operations might depend on privately owned rolling stock over which the quartermaster had no control, or else on his authority to purchase the right kind of wire or to hire a civilian to fix the defective wire. Nevertheless, the increased overall efficiency that the railroad afforded outweighed minor inconveniences.[35]

In October 1883, on the eve of his retirement, William T. Sherman reflected on the changes that had occurred during his nearly fifteen years as Commanding General. "I now regard the Indians as substantially eliminated from the problem of the Army," he wrote in his annual report to the Secretary of War.

> There may be spasmodic and temporary alarms, but such Indian wars as have hitherto disturbed the public peace and tranquility are not probable. The Army has been a large factor in producing this result, but it is not the only one. Immigration and the occupation by industrious farmers and miners of lands vacated by the aborigines have been largely instrumental to that end, but the *railroad* which used to follow in the rear now goes forward in the picket-line in the great battle of civilization with barbarism, and has become the greater cause. . . . I therefore renew the recommendation of last year, as contained in my letter to you of October 16, 1882, that the strategic points therein named shall be adequately enlarged, with permanent barracks, so as to accommodate suitable garrisons, and that all minor places be abandoned by the military. This will in the end result in economy as well as efficiency.

In his earlier letter to the secretary, Sherman had sketched the future military needs of the country, listing harbor defenses and inland posts that "should be held permanently," with buildings "of brick or stone of the most permanent character, meant to last forever." Fort Riley's name appeared on the list alphabetically between Omaha and San Antonio, two rail centers. Chicago, Cincinnati, St. Louis, and Kansas City all had military garrisons close by. Troops from Fort Riley had gone to St. Louis during the nationwide labor troubles of 1877 and would go to Chicago during the Pullman Strike in 1894. Railroads—both their use and their protection— had come to be of prime importance to the army. As the railroads brought new responsibilities they presented new advantages in moving supplies and troops, advantages which would guarantee Fort Riley's survival into the next century.[36]

Chapter 6

"To Appropriate Everything Within Their Grasp"

FOR THIRTY YEARS the army hung on to Fort Riley, housing large garrisons and small in the barracks and stables and, as rail transportation became available, using the twenty thousand-acre reservation to grow hay for shipment to posts farther west. From the outset, civilian neighbors saw the fort as a potential source of income, whether from government expenditures or, in the years of small garrisons and small budgets, from the land of the military reservation itself. At one time or another, local residents sought to rearrange the boundary of the reservation in the interest of a town-promotion scheme; to cut off a portion of the reservation in order to benefit a private company; and finally, to reduce the reservation's acreage drastically and open most of the land to settlement. All of these enterprises were aimed at bringing into the market land and resources that the federal government had set aside for the army's use. Depending on the garrison's size and the amount of the quartermaster's disbursements, civilian entrepreneurs could easily view the government's acreage as a brake on economic development.

The first attempt to diminish the reservation failed in 1854, the year after the fort's establishment, but another, more surreptitious, maneuver successfully detached nearly four thousand acres soon after the Civil War. After the quartermaster depot, with its large civilian payroll, moved to Fort Harker in 1867, rumors of Fort Riley's closing circulated continually. By the early 1880s, though, the fort's enormous reservation and its central position in the nation's railroad network ensured its retention as a permanent post. With many local residents benefiting from the fort's presence—the horses of a large mounted garrison consumed grain grown by neighboring farmers, and local builders got construction contracts—efforts to close Fort Riley or to reduce its reservation ceased. The first twenty years of the fort's history, though, saw a couple of bold grabs, and even after the establishment of the Mounted Branch School in the late 1880s, civilians continued to help themselves to the reservation's abundant wood, hay, and sand. The behavior of Fort Riley's civilian neighbors clearly evinced the acquisitive instinct that has always characterized westerners. As the lawyer Joseph G. Baldwin wrote in 1853, the year Fort Riley was founded, the frontier was a place where "avarice and hope joined partnership."[1]

The earliest attempt to acquire part of Fort Riley's reservation failed partly because of the haphazard combination of army officers, territorial officials, and private citizens involved. It was a scheme to redraw the reservation boundary and provide a site close to the fort for the projected town of Pawnee, which members of the town company (including the territorial governor) hoped would become the capital of Kansas. As casually as the Pawnee Association was thrown together, it might have succeeded, had it not been for national politics: the pro- and antislavery struggle for domination of Kansas Territory, and bureaucratic feuding between Secretary of War Jefferson Davis and Commissioner of Indian Affairs George W. Manypenny. Evidence is inconclusive, but the pro-slavery Davis may have used his office to destroy the Pawnee Association out of spite towards two of its members: the antislavery territorial governor, Andrew H. Reeder, and Fort Riley's commanding officer, William R. Montgomery. Whatever Davis's motives (and the story of the Pawnee Association is replete with personal animosities, great and small), the incident illustrates the national influence on local economic development.

As squatters entered any new territory, army posts offered attractive sites for settlement. During the 1850s Fort Leavenworth was the largest post in Kansas, a river port on the opposite bank from Platte County, Missouri. In 1854 Missourians staked out a town on land that may have been part of the Fort Leavenworth military reservation or may have belonged to the Delaware Indians. In neither case was it open to settlement. The Missourians' impunity emboldened six settlers near Fort Riley to ask its commanding officer, William R. Montgomery, to exclude a similar townsite from its military reservation, the limits of which had not yet been surveyed.[2]

Montgomery had arrived at Fort Riley in the middle of May with orders to survey and mark "a tract of land . . . sufficient . . . to afford all the advantages of timber, fuel, hay and other requisites." Accordingly, he declared a 180-square-mile reservation, 10 miles from north to south and 18 from east to west, in order to exclude settlers while he assessed the grass, wood, and mineral resources. The tract was "much more extensive than absolutely necessary," Montgomery later explained, "with a view to keeping liquor venders at a proper distance, though sadly failed of that object." In 1848 the Secretary of War had suggested 100-square-mile reservations (64,000 acres) for new posts along the Oregon Trail. Shortly after Jefferson Davis became Secretary of War, he suggested 25,000 acres for new posts in California and New Mexico. Fort Riley's reservation, 115,200 acres, would clearly have to be reduced.[3]

Given the size of the military reservation at Fort Riley and the Leavenworth Association's success in staking out its town that summer, it was not surprising that six "Citizens of Kansas T[erritor]y" should have requested that a half-section of land (320 acres) fronting on the river "be thrown off the said reserve for the purpose of locating a town site. . . . [T]he wants of the country," they declared, "demand some eligible point on a navigable stream as a shipping and receiving point." Montgomery agreed fully "as to the propriety and necessity for such a Mart to supply the present and prospective commercial wants of the citizen community now locating in this vicinity" and promised them a site on the Kansas River. A week after receiving Montgomery's letter, a group of civilians and army officers formed the Pawnee Association to plat and promote a town of that name.[4]

Montgomery accepted election as president of the association, and before the year was out he had an interest in several tracts of land adjoining the original 320-acre townsite. By late November the association's membership had swollen to include five newly arrived civilian officials of the territorial government, as well as three army officers at Fort Leavenworth (among them Major Edmund A. Ogden, in charge of Fort Riley's construction) and the Chief Quartermaster of the Department of the West in St. Louis. Federal officials, civil and military, were as alert as other westerners for opportunities, and few worried about what a later age would call conflict of interest. So matters stood on December 25, when Montgomery ordered Captain Nathaniel Lyon, commander of one of the infantry companies at Fort Riley and a member of the Pawnee Association, to survey the limits of a diminished reserve.[5]

Trouble awaited the association, though. Lyon, a prickly character with a sadistic temperament, was at odds with Montgomery because of the severe punishments Lyon inflicted on his men, as well as the marriage of an enlisted man in Lyon's company. Permission for the marriage was Lyon's prerogative as the soldier's company commander, but Montgomery forbade the union because the prospective bride was the servant of another officer, who had brought her from the East and stood to lose not only her services but the cost of her transportation besides. Nevertheless, the marriage took place and Montgomery, the post commander, put Lyon in arrest. Lyon swore vengeance.[6]

The instrument of his revenge would be a family of squatters named Dixon—four brothers, two of them married—who appeared on the military reservation the first week in November 1854. They settled on a site that H. A. Lowe, a civilian employee at Fort Riley, had preempted as soon as the limits of the military reservation were declared. The Dixons paid Lowe $225 for his interest in the site. They possessed some capital, part of which, witnesses at Montgomery's court martial later agreed, was in the form of whiskey that they sold to the soldiers at the fort. When Governor Andrew H. Reeder paid his first visit to Fort Riley in November and inspected Pawnee's townsite, he remarked to Montgomery that a clan of Irish whiskey sellers squatting just outside its limits would blight the town's prospects.

Montgomery set about removing the Dixons. Accusing them of

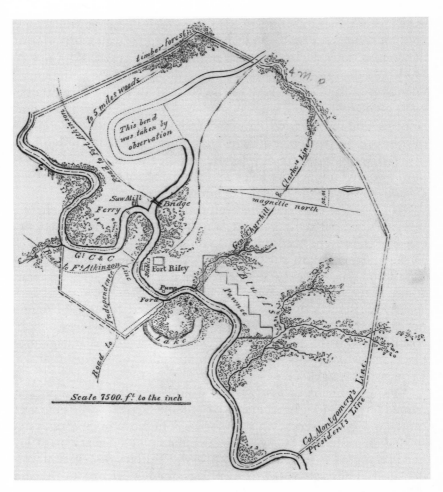

This map, based on a preliminary survey in 1854, shows Fort Riley's military reservation and the proposed townsite of Pawnee on the left bank of the Kansas River a short distance below the fort. Pawnee was a speculative venture by army officers and civilians at Fort Riley; the project's collapse ended the regular army career of the fort's commanding officer. (Kansas State Historical Society)

"depredating upon public timber" on the military reservation, he twice sent troops—commanded by officers who, like almost all the others at the fort, were members of the Pawnee Association—to destroy the Dixons' dwellings. Although Lyon commanded one of the parties, he preferred charges against Montgomery for official misconduct. After the Dixons' improvements had been razed a second time, Thomas Dixon filed a deposition in the district court of Platte County, Missouri. Its "serious accusations of official misconduct" led to the appointment of a board of officers to investigate the military reservation at Fort Riley and with it the affairs of the Pawnee Association.

Members of the board took testimony in May 1855 and rode over the reservation to assess its resources. The board found no impropriety in Montgomery's reducing the reservation by nearly four-fifths but questioned his wisdom in setting aside so close to the post a townsite over which he would have no jurisdiction and on which whiskey sellers already were squatting. While the board was writing its report, Montgomery and Lyon received orders to move with their companies to another station, leaving only two military members of the Pawnee Association at Fort Riley.[7]

The fort's next commanding officer asserted the government's jurisdiction over the townsite, ordering settlers off in August. His successor tore down the buildings late in November. Residents of Pawnee relocated. Within a few months they had founded Riley City, on the opposite bank of the river, and Ogden, downstream on the same side as the fort but off the reservation. These settlers clearly wished to stay close to the fort, with its post office, its surgeon, and its quartermaster's payroll. While destruction of the settlers' dwellings may seem draconian to modern readers, it was not unusual in territorial Kansas. In June 1855 Isaac T. Goodnow—a founder of Manhattan, a temperance advocate, and a devout Methodist who disliked traveling on the Sabbath—wrote in his diary, "Went to the city [Manhattan] to try Mr. Haskell condemned as a claim jumper. . . . Went with a body of men & drove off Haskell & tore down his house—Squatter Sovereignty. . . . Shouldered my gun and went to the city to drive Haskell from [the claim of Goodnow's brother William]. He fled as fast as his legs would carry him."[8]

Governor Reeder, the most prominent of the Pawnee Association's civilian members, convened a session of the territorial legislature at Pawnee in July 1855. It met in a stone building erected on the townsite by Robert Wilson, the post sutler at Fort Riley and himself a member of the Pawnee Association. After a couple of days the session adjourned to Shawnee Mission near the Missouri state line, where the proslavery legislators felt more secure. There they enacted a legal code based on Missouri's. This demonstration of Reeder's inability to control the legislature was one reason for his removal from office.

Twentieth-century historians have remarked that Reeder's land speculation, which included not only the Pawnee Association but other townsites and Indian land allotments as well, should have been sufficient cause for his removal. For the next fifty years, Free Staters and their associates and successors asserted that Reeder was removed for partisan reasons and that the town of Pawnee was destroyed because it was a free-state settlement composed mostly of Pennsylvanians like the governor. "It has been generally accepted that Jefferson Davis . . . extended the [boundary of the reservation] so as to destroy Pawnee, because it was a free-state settlement," George W. Martin, editor of the Junction City *Union* and a founder of the Kansas State Historical Society, wrote at the turn of the century, "but it is also claimed that the officers at the fort disregarded instructions concerning the limits of the reserve, and manipulated the lines in the interest of private speculation." The use of the conjunction *but* perhaps suggests that the two allegations are mutually exclusive. Of course, they are not.[9]

Town promoters in territorial Kansas acted in accordance with common contemporary practices. That rapacity was common did not make it less abhorrent in principle. Each side in the debate over slavery, for instance, stigmatized the other as grossly corrupt, and with a great deal of justice. Major Ogden, justifying his own and another officer's membership in the Leavenworth Association, wrote "that these persons in the Government employ are themselves of the people, and it is not in the commanding officer's power or mine to prevent them from exercising individual rights, which are common to all, by making claims upon lands subject to squatter occupancy." Six months later, a partisan of Governor Reeder wrote from Pawnee to the Leavenworth *Kansas Weekly Herald,* "The idea that a gentleman because he happens to be a Governor, has no right to avail himself of privileges guaranteed to every citizen, is so manifestly preposterous, and narrow minded as to excite no other feeling than that of contempt for the person who holds it." Army officer and civilian alike agreed that holding public office should not restrict a citizen's investment opportunities.[10]

The Pawnee Association was too flagrant an enterprise to be countenanced, though, even by Jefferson Davis. The Secretary of War had turned a blind eye to the speculative activities of two army officers in the Leavenworth Association. One of them, Ogden, was an old acquaintance of Davis, and Davis defended them and their associates against attacks by the Commissioner of Indian Affairs, George W. Manypenny, who had complained that the activities of the Leavenworth town company "have not only taken place under the eyes of the military officers stationed at the fort, but two of them . . . have been active agents in this discreditable business." Manypenny pointed out that if the Leavenworth Association's claim did not lie within the limits of the military reservation, which was closed to settlement, then it lay on the Delaware Indian lands immediately to the south of the fort, which were equally closed.[11]

For an official of one department of the executive branch to criticize the operations of another was a grave breach of etiquette, and Davis reacted angrily. "[I]t was to have been hoped that moral considerations would have prevented [Manypenny] from publishing his gratuitous accusations," he wrote to President Franklin Pierce, "even if he could not recognize the impropriety of invading the limits of a distinct Department of your Administration and of assuming to judge of matters which you had thought proper to consign to the care of another." Perhaps the effort of defending the Leavenworth Association had exhausted Davis's patience with land speculation by army officers. The members of the Leavenworth Association, proslavery Missourians for the most part, were certainly more sympathetic to his own point of view. The Pawnee Association, on the other hand, had failed to include the proslavery judge Samuel D. Lecompte or the Alabamian territorial secretary Daniel Woodson. Whatever Davis's reasons, Captain Montgomery, president of the Pawnee Association and Fort Riley's commanding officer from May 1854 to May 1855, faced a court martial that dismissed him from the service for conduct unbecoming an officer and a gentleman.[12]

The Pawnee Association's membership and its casual assemblage marked it from the start as a speculative venture and hastened its failure. Fourteen of the twenty-five members were army officers, ten of them stationed at Fort Riley. In contrast, the Leavenworth Association numbered only two army officers among its thirty-two members; the civilians could have settled in the new town they had staked out, had they so chosen. That only seven of them actually did so during the first six years of Leavenworth's existence was beside the point. Twelve of them, farmers and merchants, had substantial interests in Platte County, Missouri, which deterred them from moving; the men who relocated were doctors and lawyers, an editor, and a hotelier. The mobility of the army officers in the Pawnee Association, though, was so great that the idea of their settling anywhere permanently was laughable. Four of them had been ordered with their companies to Fort Laramie in September 1854, the month the association was organized; a fifth was ordered to duty in St. Louis in October; and three others, including Montgomery and Lyon, were en route to another post in May 1855 when they were intercepted by the board of officers sent to investigate Montgomery's reduction of the military reservation.[13]

The Pawnee Association admitted to membership all officers who served at Fort Riley in the late spring and early summer of 1854 and on into the following spring. Besides these officers there were Major Ogden and two others at Fort Leavenworth, as well as Major David H. Vinton, Chief Quartermaster of the Department of the West, in St. Louis. There seems to have been no sectional imbalance; five of the Fort Riley officers were from free states and five from slave states and the District of Columbia. Four of them were lieutenants who had graduated from West Point after 1850. The three captains and an assistant surgeon had much longer service, having received their first commissions between 1837 and 1841, while Montgomery was an 1825 graduate of West Point. Their combined military service totaled just over one hundred years. At least from the military, the Pawnee Association accepted for membership any and all.[14]

The Leavenworth Association, on the other hand, prided itself on the care with which it selected its members. One of them boasted in a letter to his father that the "association consists of 32 members they are persons of all descriptions. . . . They are the last crowd that would ever be selected to go into such an enterprise as this . . . & yet . . . it does seem as though any thing but this heterogeneous mass would have been completely defeated. . . . We have poverty enough among us to save us from the hatred of the lower classes & riches enough to command respect, dullness enough to excite pity & talent enough to make us formidable. Maj Ogden & Maj MacLain of the U.S.A. are two of our trustees, we have 4 lawyers 4 preachers & 3 doctors in the association."[15]

The civilian members of the Pawnee Association included five officials of the territorial government: Andrew H. Reeder, the governor; the U.S. attorney; the U.S. marshal; and two judges of the territorial court (although not the outspoken proslavery Justice Samuel D. Lecompte). That Reeder's name alone appears in the territorial census of 1855 demonstrates their tenuous connection with the territory, although all five appeared in Kansas at one time or another. Of the other six civilians, Robert Wilson, the post sutler at Fort Riley and one of the chief organizers of the Pawnee Association, remained in the neighborhood for years and was remembered with respect as an early settler. John N. Dyer, secretary of the association, was the quartermaster's clerk at Fort Riley. Lorenzo D. Bird and William S. Murphy were members of the Leavenworth Association, Bird a resident of Leavenworth and Murphy of Platte County, Missouri. Robert C. Miller, a merchant, lived somewhere north of the Kansas River and east of the Blue, in the Eleventh and Twelfth

Election Districts, although he had been in Leavenworth the previous year. Hiram Rich, a resident of the new town, had been the
post sutler at Fort Leavenworth for more than twelve years and was
"a high toned, honorable gentleman, well known in the West," according to one account. Dyer, Miller, and Wilson were among the
six signers of the September 1854 letter that led to the founding of
the Pawnee Association.[16]

The Pawnee Association's haphazard organization may have
added to its difficulties. Certainly Lyon's animosity towards Montgomery helped to precipitate the association's downfall. In contrast,
ten years later a handful of the fort's civilian neighbors began to or-
ganize carefully and by 1868 had succeeded in converting nearly
four thousand acres of Fort Riley's military reservation to their own
purposes. They operated quietly and effectively. Secrecy helped
them to succeed and made their operations more difficult to follow
than those of either the Pawnee Association or the scores of individuals who pillaged the reservation's resources for decades. There
is no trial record to consult. Their maneuvers can only be traced
through corporate charters, newspaper accounts, legislative records,
and a decision of the Kansas Supreme Court.

In November 1864 five residents of Junction City incorporated
the Republican River Bridge Company for the avowed purpose of
spanning the river with a toll bridge. Their real object, though, was
to obtain title to the part of the military reservation south of the
river and adjacent to town. Once in private hands, the land would
become valuable city lots. "For three years before the public knew
of any such scheme," they "were vigorously at work," the Junction
City *Union* claimed a year after the bridge had been built, the grant
secured, and the land parceled out and sold.[17]

The associates needed first to have Congress award the land to
the state of Kansas and then to have the state grant it to their company. In Washington, the House agreed to the measure without debate. During the brief Senate discussion of the bill, John Sherman
remarked, "That land must be of immense value. I will agree to
build all the bridges in Kansas for that." When word reached Junction City by telegraph that the congressional measure was in mo-

tion, a small party of the Bridge Company associates hastened to Topeka aboard a daily passenger train, scheduled to reach the capital from Junction City in four hours. There the state legislature was in the last week of its constitutionally mandated fifty-day session. State senator James M. Harvey, one of the company's stockholders, introduced the bill granting the land to the company. After intense lobbying (the *Union*'s account intimated that some legislators were "purchased"), the bill breezed through with a minimum of scrutiny. The governor signed it on the last day of the session.[18]

Thus using the latest technology, the telegraph and the railroad, the Republican River Bridge Company had attained its first goal. George W. Martin, the *Union*'s editor, exulted. "This measure is a source of gratification to every resident and property holder of Davis and adjoining counties," he wrote. "It throws open to settlement, cultivation, and taxation, over five thousand acres of rich, tillable land, and throws upon the market thousands of cords of wood, to which a conscientious title can now be had. It insures an expenditure in our midst of forty thousand dollars the coming season. It insures to our town and the surrounding country a permanent bridge across one of the meanest and most unreliable streams which exists, and all the incidental advantages of uninterrupted communication. Moreover, the land and the enterprise is in the hands of actual residents, men whose only interests are in Junction City." The editor of the Leavenworth *Times* saw a lesson for his own townsmen. "The fact is," he wrote, "Government should not hold a foot of land in settled States, not absolutely necessary for military purposes. Two sections would meet every necessity of Fort Leavenworth. The balance of the reservation should be sold in small lots" to pay for construction of a bridge across the Missouri River that the legislature, in its recent session, had refused to bankroll. Even residents of the largest city in Kansas (which Leavenworth was as late as 1885) had an eye for government money—if not state, then federal.[19]

Other editors were less sanguine about both the bridge company bill and the Kansas legislature in general. A Topeka newspaper summarized the last day of the legislative session:

The greater part of Tuesday was spent in earnest and well directed labor, the hours of the session drawing rapidly to a close, demonstrating to numerous members who had frittered away a good part of the session, eating apples, smoking, imbibing forty rod, and drinking in the essence of yellow backed novels, the startling fact that if they wished to make history for themselves and their posterity, it was necessary for them to act. . . . A number of our Junction City 'fellers' had a nice little repast which they now offered to the representatives . . . in which the State was asked to grant a donation of six thousand acres of the best land in Kansas, to the Republican bridge company for the purpose of enabling them to build a TOLL bridge over the Republican, which *modest* request was so amended . . . as to make it free to Kansas and the world, after which it passed.

The editor of the Manhattan *Kansas Radical* was predictably critical of any project originating in Junction City. Under the headline, "Another Fraud," he wrote:

Some wire pullers up at Junction have got a bill through Congress giving to the Republican bridge company six thousand and four hundred acres of land, comprising that portion of the Fort Riley reserve that lies between the Republican and Smoky Hill rivers. In return for this donation which is calculated to be worth a quarter of a million dollars, the company is to build a bridge across the Republican river, the cost of which will be about twenty thousand dollars. That is a soft take. The land was given to the State for the benefit of the company and the legislature was smart enough to require that the bridge should be free although our Senator Harvey voted to make it a toll bridge.

The grant had grown more munificent with each telling. When Samuel C. Pomeroy was trying to push the bill through the United

States Senate, he assured his colleagues that it amounted to a mere 2,000 acres. Township and section maps show that it included just over 3,922 acres. The United States deputy surveyor who signed the maps was one of the Bridge Company's original incorporators.[20]

Building the bridge was a straightforward task. That summer, a contractor from Leavenworth began construction; in December, Governor Samuel J. Crawford inspected the finished bridge and approved it. "Competent judges assert that this work will endure," a reporter from the Leavenworth *Conservative* concluded. It was natural that a Leavenworth newspaper should praise the work of a Leavenworth contractor and that a Junction City editor should quote favorable remarks about a Junction City bridge. Nineteenth-century newspapers were supposed to act as organs of community development. Within ten years, though, the bridge over the Republican River was gone and the issue of responsibility for its collapse was in the courts.[21]

The state of Kansas accepted the bridge, and the federal government transferred title to the land to the Bridge Company in 1868. The company sold the land in April 1869, mostly to its own stockholders, and "neglected"—one of several verbs later used by the state attorney general—the upkeep of the bridge. By the spring of 1873 the bridge was "impassable," the *Union's* editor wrote, "and the trade from that part of the county, including Fort Riley, is gradually dropping off. A few days ago a man in attempting to cross had a horse killed. A party of emigrants crossed over the other day by unloading their wagons and packing their goods over. The bridge has been in this condition for a month. We hear nothing about the purpose of the bridge company in this matter." Nor would there be any word from the company, despite official protests from Fort Riley. By 1877, when the bridge finally dropped into the river under the weight of a herd of ninety head of cattle, the *Union's* only comment was, "The much looked for event has come to pass."[22]

In the spring of 1877, before the collapse, Fort Riley's commanding officer had written repeated warnings to the War Department that "the bridge has been without repair until it is dangerous and al-

This photograph contains no hint of the ruinous state of Junction City's bridge over the Republican River. The partnership that built the bridge failed to honor the obligation to maintain it, and it collapsed in 1878. The driver of the wagon approaching the bridge may well have been taking his life—and his horse's—in his hands. (Kansas State Historical Society)

most impassable." According to "the positive statement of reliable citizens here," Colonel Richard I. Dodge complained, "the whole affair was a fraud from its inception. Certain parties leagued together to get possession of these valuable lands, held together as long as was necessary to effect sales and divide the plunder, and then dissolved. There is no such company now in existence. . . . In the mean time the bridge is rapidly going to pieces, and but for the repairs put on it from time to time by officers and men at this post it would now have been impassable. The county will not touch it. The farmers who use it daily will not even assist in its preservation so far as to haul a load or two of material to save the approaches." Dodge's letters initiated a correspondence between the War Department and the state of Kansas that went on until the bridge fell apart, "thus," an army quartermaster dutifully explained, "becoming worthless."[23]

The bridge's collapse attracted little attention in the Kansas press, but it did in Washington. The Secretary of War's annual report that year devoted two and a half pages to the bridge and its history. Under the terms of the federal land grant, the state had guaranteed "that said bridge shall be kept up and maintained in good condition . . . forever." Under pressure from the federal government, the state tried to force the company to rebuild the bridge in a case that reached the Kansas Supreme Court in January 1878. Unfortunately, "some of the members of the bridge company getting hard up and others recognizing what an elephant they had in 'keeping up and perpetually maintaining a free bridge,' [had] got tired and dropped quietly out," while, at some time during the previous ten years, the required security bond signed by the company's officers had disappeared.[24]

The state supreme court ruled that the Republican River Bridge Company had fulfilled all its obligations under the terms of the act of the legislature. The state had no remedy except a suit based on a nonexistent bond, some of whose signers had become insolvent or had left the state or had died. In his decision Chief Justice Albert H. Horton chided the legislature of 1867 for its "recklessness and improvidence," calling the act "unusually hasty and inconsiderate. . . . That such indecent haste should finally result in trouble, vexation, and perhaps disaster to the state, is neither unexpected nor startling." Not until 1885 did another bridge, paid for by state and county funds, span the Republican River. Nevertheless, the Republican River Bridge Company had achieved its goal of carving off a lucrative slice of Fort Riley's military reservation.[25]

Who were the organizers and stockholders of the Republican River Bridge Company? Of the five original incorporators in November 1864, four had settled in Davis County as early as 1860: two merchants, a lawyer, and one who listed his occupation as civil engineer (Daniel Mitchell, who would eventually, as United States deputy surveyor, sign the township and section maps of the Bridge Company's land grant). Indicating their prominence in the community, three of them served as president, secretary, and principal speaker at Junction City's memorial service for Abraham Lincoln the following spring.[26]

Of the Bridge Company's nineteen named associates (incorporators and stockholders), four had served as county commissioners; three as state representatives, city councilmen, or members of the Junction City board of education; and two as Davis County sheriff. The lawyer Anson W. Callen had served in all five capacities, and as probate judge as well. Daniel Mitchell, besides being United States deputy surveyor, served two terms as county clerk and as register of deeds simultaneously. Three of the company's stockholders—state senators Blakely and Harvey and Junction City's representative E. S. Stover—were in the legislature to vote in favor of the land grant. The Bridge Company associates took an active interest in public affairs.[27]

They also took part with a will in the feverish speculative promotions of the 1860s. Five of the early settlers among the associates had been delegates to the Topeka Railroad Convention of 1860. After the Civil War, five became incorporators of the Junction City and Smoky Hill Bridge Company; three, of the Junction City Stone Sawing Company, which set up a steam sawmill to turn local limestone into building material; two, of the Solomon River Bridge and Ferry Company; and one, of both the Fort Harker Bridge and Ferry Company and the nearby Ellsworth Townsite Company. That one of the state senators who held stock in the Republican River Bridge Company, William S. Blakely, had clerked for the Fort Riley quartermaster and was a former partner of the *Union*'s editor, George W. Martin, served only to widen the circle of the company's acquaintances. The members of the Republican River Bridge Company, in other words, were as well connected as those of the Leavenworth Association had been or as the backers of the Manhattan & Northwestern Railroad would be a few years later. This, and their ability to react quickly by rail and telegraph to changing circumstances, explains their success. That not all of them were uniformly successful in their subsequent business ventures explains their "getting hard up" and dropping "quietly out" of the Bridge Company, as the *Union*'s editor put it. Not even the federal presence could guarantee never-ending funds.[28]

While business leaders in Junction City schemed to gain title to parts of Fort Riley's military reservation with a few deft maneuvers, other civilians simply entered the reservation at will and took what they wanted of its resources: wood, hay, and sand. As soon as the Republican River Bridge Company had secured title to its slice of the reservation south of the river, it "commenced suit against several parties for stealing wood from [its] land," according to the Junction City *Union*. "For several years a number have made a good thing each winter by stripping the timbered portions of this tract," the writer added. Before the recent transfer, of course, "this tract" and its timber had been the army's. The fort's tiny, and frequently absent, garrison was powerless to stop these "depredations."[29]

Fort Riley's neighbors were heirs to the acquisitive, improvident attitude of the backwoods pioneers who had, in a couple of generations, advanced from the Appalachians to the tallgrass prairies. Backed by a legal system that preferred development to stasis, they stood poised on the edge of the grassland, looking for fresh opportunities. Historians who emphasize the federal role in the American West sometimes seem to suggest a government endowed with the awesome powers that it now possesses. But the federal government of the nineteenth century was tiny compared to today's. For instance, although the Department of the Interior was established in 1849 (the first addition to the president's cabinet in more than half a century), the next department, Agriculture, did not attain cabinet-level status until forty years later. Early westerners were not mere supplicants to the federal government. If the settlers had their hands outstretched, it was not so much to beg as to grab.[30]

The army could do little to prevent pillage of the reservation during the years of small garrisons, particularly when the troops were infantry and there were few horses at the post. Junction City newspapers downplayed the issue of trespassing, mentioning it only when the culprits were from Ogden, on the other side of the reservation in Riley County. In 1862, when the post quartermaster arrested "two or three men from Ogden, who were jayhawking timber from the reserve, after being repeatedly told to desist," a Junction City editor deplored "the wholesale pilfering which is carried on at times." Twenty-five years later, the *Union's* Fort Riley correspondent reported that Theodore Weichselbaum and Calvin M. Dyche, both of Ogden, were each grazing about one thousand head of cattle on the reservation. Weichselbaum and Dyche were well-known businessmen and had held many army contracts during the years since the Civil War. Large-scale operators like these led the assault on the reservation's assets. Most of the lesser trespassers remained anonymous, like the "jayhawkers" of earlier years.[31]

The need for a fence around the military reservation had become evident soon after Fort Riley became a cavalry station again in the early 1880s. Colonel Edward Hatch, commanding the fort in 1882, suggested that grazing on the reservation, "if properly enclosed . . . will more than pay all expenditures for [fencing] in one season." There was no money left in that year's budget, though, and not until the summer of 1884 did the reservation get about twenty-two miles of four-strand barbed-wire fence.[32]

By the time Colonel James W. Forsyth arrived with his regiment in the fall of 1887, the fence was "not in repair, and therefore," Forsyth wrote, was "of little or no service in keeping off the stock belonging to citizens living near the reservation lines." The *Union's* correspondent at the fort reported cattle "hovering about the fences all around the reservation," and adding that some farmers "drive their herds in the reserve at evenings and rush them out at daylight every morning." During the next three years, a combination of cavalry patrols and litigation—the United States prosecuted Weichselbaum for trespassing, Weichselbaum sued Forsyth, and Dyche sued a cavalry lieutenant for five hundred dollars' worth of damage to his herd—served to clear the reservation of unauthorized cattle. By the summer of 1890 Forsyth was able to report that Fort Riley was "freer of stock today than at any time since it has been surrounded by settlements." Its pastures were ready to accommodate the horses of the eight troops of cavalry and three batteries of artillery that would assemble there for training at the Mounted Branch School.[33]

Grazing was not the only use to which neighboring civilians put the reservation's grass. There was hay to be made and money to be got for it. When Robert Henderson received the 1882 hay contract and asked permission to cut on the reservation, the commanding officer pointed out that it had "been the custom of years" to allow the contractor to cut on the government's land. The Chief Quartermaster of the Department of the Missouri noted that the price of hay at Fort Leavenworth in the coming year would be $11 a long ton (2,240 pounds), while Henderson would deliver hay "stacked in the forage yard" at Fort Riley for $3.74. The Chief Quartermaster attributed the low cost of Fort Riley's hay to the contractors' traditional practice of cutting on the reservation, where there was plenty of good grass and contractors had not far to haul the hay to the post.[34]

But "the custom of years" could change gradually. Permitted to cut hay on the reservation, contractors had begun inviting outsiders to come in and take hay. Moreover, by 1887 the contractors felt free to take whatever hay was of such poor quality that the quartermaster would not accept it, and haul it to their own hay yards in Junction City. Shortly after his arrival that fall, Colonel Forsyth complained of the "custom of some people, not law-abiding, in this vicinity, to appropriate everything within their grasp." The contractors, as nearly as the post quartermaster could determine, had hauled off the reservation about two hundred tons of hay that they claimed was "of the same quality" as some that the quartermaster had already rejected, but which they had never bothered to submit for his inspection. "Why," Forsyth asked, "did they cut this hay, if they knew it would be rejected?" He supplied his own answer—"so that they could beat the Government out of this amount of hay"—and recommended that the cost of the two hundred tons be subtracted from the amount paid the contractors. The contractors, though, had already delivered enough acceptable hay to fulfill the terms of the contract, and had been paid.[35]

The department commander advised Forsyth that withholding pay for hay that had been delivered and accepted would be "clearly not legal." He urged "moderation," and suggested that the contractors "might plead, with a show of justice, their long immunity in the past" from prosecution. Employment of "a citizen range rider . . . , an old soldier of Junction City," to patrol the reservation may have been a deliberate part of the army's "moderate" approach to trespassers. Conrad Schmidt had served in Kansas with the Second Dragoons before the Civil War and was about fifty-five years old at the time of his appointment in the spring of 1889. A Junction City resident for more than fifteen years, he was well known in the neighborhood. His services "preventing depredations upon the hay & timber lands & encroachments upon the reservation" cost the government only forty dollars a month, a very moderate price. He continued on duty through the summer of 1894.[36]

Another form of encroachment that Colonel Forsyth moved to stop was civilians' taking sand from the reservation. The sand was used to mix concrete, and Forsyth wrote that Junction City businessmen shipped "from twenty to eighty car loads a month" of the sand during 1888. He added that "this was no doubt a profitable business, as they paid nothing for it." When he issued an order forbidding this "common pillage," a delegation of businessmen protested that sand was "one of the industries of their town." Forsyth pointed out that two landowners on the riverbank opposite the reservation offered sand for sale and that, as he told the U.S. attorney for Kansas, "instead of interfering with an industry of Junction City, I was in reality protecting their citizens (who had sand for sale) in a lawful business."[37]

But the colonel had an even more urgent reason for suppressing the traffic. Wagons that entered the reservation to haul off sand did not come empty. Residents of Junction City had long made Fort Riley's reservation the dumping ground for animal carcasses and other garbage. The wagoners, Forsyth pointed out, made money going and coming, for the sand cost them nothing, while they were paid to haul refuse. He complained that "last fall the stench from this deposit was so great that it was almost impossible to drive over the road" between the fort and the town. In December 1887 Forsyth warned the mayor of Junction City that if dumping "continued until warm weather it may result in disease and death." The mayor, himself a former regular army officer, cooperated by prosecuting one case in the local court and by sending the city marshal across the river to bury ten of the carcasses; "and he, and the Board of

Health," the mayor wrote, "will be vigilant in future in apprehending all violators." The cooperation seems to have been effective, for complaints about dumping on the reservation ceased. Municipal officials in Kansas and throughout the country were becoming increasingly aware of sanitation and other public health issues during the 1880s.[38]

Whether the attitude of most of Fort Riley's civilian neighbors changed, though, is doubtful. Some years later the post quartermaster requested barbed wire, staples, and oak fence posts with which to finish fencing the reservation, a project that had dragged on for more than a decade. The commanding officer's remarks endorsing the requisition perhaps best sum up civilian attitudes towards the reservation and its resources and towards the government itself, as well as the soldiers' opinion of the civilians. "The posts are on hand and are being put in place and it is desired to have the wire as soon as possible to complete the work and to prevent the posts being removed by citizens." Cutting the fence to let their cattle graze on the reservation was not enough; civilians would steal the fence itself. Several years earlier, some Junction City residents had removed the stone markers that the army had placed along the reservation boundary and used them as yard ornaments.[39]

What government would not bestow, westerners have always been content to take. Generations of historians, novelists, and politicians have idealized William H. Ashley's heading due west for the Rocky Mountains when the army could not guarantee safe passage up the Missouri River, and the consequent rediscovery of South Pass and a land route to the Pacific. The activities of the founders of the Pawnee Association, of the Republican River Bridge Company, and of the scores of neighboring civilians who "depredated" on Fort Riley's resources, represent the reverse side of the coin. Like Ashley's men, they were for the most part young, and they were demonstrably "enterprising." They belonged, though, more to the frontier of secondary settlement, in which farmers began to acquire legal title to their claims, lawyers thrived, and avarice and hope indeed joined partnership, than to our agreed-upon national epic. Still, they were no less characteristic of the spirit of expansionism than the more celebrated characters in western history. In fact, instances of nineteenth-century chicanery probably teach more about life in the present-day West than does the saga of the fur hunters and the overland emigrants. Cheating the government is still one of our national pastimes.

Chapter 7

"The Disbursement of Hundreds of Thousands of Dollars in our Midst"

FORT RILEY'S IMPORTANCE to its civilian neighbors varied directly with the Quartermaster Department's expenditures. The fort languished for more than fifteen years after the removal of its quartermaster depot in 1867. Garrisons were small; annual appropriations barely sufficed to keep roofs on existing buildings. Then, in the early 1880s General Sherman named Fort Riley as one of the large, central, permanent posts that the army would retain into the next century. The fort would be permanent, and a grain-purchasing cavalry station, at that: the site of a school where large bodies of horsemen could maneuver, and artillerymen could practice firing the new breech-loading field guns. That decided, federal officials began to work hand in hand with local businessmen to further their mutual interests. Between 1886 and 1891, the army would spend more than $750,000 to renovate and expand Fort Riley.

The reason for the fort's retention was its position in the middle of a rail network that had been promoted by many of these same businessmen during the years after 1867 when they had given up hope of deriving any immediate gain from the quartermaster's disbursements. It required large sums of money, though, to remedy the effects of nearly two decades' neglect and to turn Fort Riley into one of the army's largest, most modern posts. The money paid for construction of buildings, roads, and sewers. Work on the new Fort Riley turned at least one Junction City firm into a military contractor on a national scale and put wages in the pockets of an indeterminate number of artisans, laborers, and teamsters. The efforts of local railroad promoters had paid off unexpectedly years afterward.

By the time the Republican River Bridge collapsed in 1877, attempts to slice off pieces of Fort Riley's military reservation had ceased, and the fort's civilian neighbors had resigned themselves to pilfering the fort's hay, sand, and wood. John A. Anderson, the Kansas Fifth District's U.S. Representative from 1879 to 1891, introduced two bills that would have opened most of the reservation to settlement, but both died in the House Committee on Military Affairs. The bills specified that the land would be for "sale to actual settlers"—an indirect acknowledgment of the speculative nature of ventures like the Pawnee Association and the Republican River Bridge Company. Anderson conferred with General Sheridan and told him that a reduction of the reservation "would be to the advantage of our people in converting idle into profitable land." Sheridan was inclined to retain the reservation as a cavalry station because of its abundant hay lands and pasturage but promised to consider the matter carefully. "In any public notice," Anderson warned the editor of the Junction City *Union*, "don't put it so as to commit [Sheridan] or cause him to think that I am publishing his talk."[1]

Meanwhile, the army used Fort Riley as an enormous hay farm, shipping the crop far and wide via the nation's expanding rail network. Railroads also enabled the army to use the fort as a winter dormitory for troops who spent their summers guarding the Indian Territory against encroaching Boomers or supervising the removal of the Ute tribe from its extensive, mineral-rich lands in western Colorado. As railroads replaced wagon transportation in the West, military supply costs dwindled. The army sought to concentrate entire regiments at posts along major rail lines, where they could be supplied cheaply and large bodies of troops could receive military training instead of being "frittered away" in labor details, as they had been when they were stationed at scores of smaller posts.

The army located most of its large permanent posts close to major rail centers, where the troops would be handy in case of another railroad strike like the one in 1877. Business leaders in Chicago, the headquarters of the Military Division of the Missouri, had given the federal government some land, on which the army established Fort Sheridan in 1887—a year when anxiety about labor unrest and class conflict, exemplified by the hanging of the Haymarket anarchists, was high. Other regiment-strength posts were at Omaha and Cheyenne on the line of the Union Pacific; at San Antonio, Texas; and at Fort Leavenworth, about half an hour by rail from Kansas City. Fort Riley, too, was a logical site for a regimental station, on the main route between Kansas City and Denver, and with connections to the Union Pacific in Nebraska, as well as to roads leading south and southwest. As early as 1873, the editor of the Junction City *Union* had boasted that its rail connections made that town "the Indianapolis of Kansas"—a typical case of a local booster pointing at a map and mistaking his finger for the hand of destiny. In 1873 Junction City's rail connections lay mostly in the future; the town never managed to fulfill its vaunted promise.[2]

The army elected to retain Fort Riley for purely military reasons. Although the infantry and cavalry had begun soon after the Civil War to use breech-loading weapons that fired metallic cartridges, the horse-drawn cannons of the light artillery were still muzzle-loading smoothbores. Replacing old ordnance required instruction in new tactics. The army based its decisions on economy and the need for modernization, not the wishes of local businessmen and farmers. The officers making the decisions—Sherman, Sheridan, and Schofield—were well acquainted with western logistical requirements, particularly the demands of the mounted branches, both cavalry and field artillery. Their professional backgrounds and their thinking helped set the stage for events at Fort Riley during the 1880s.

William T. Sherman, the army's Commanding General since 1869, pondered its future needs as he neared the end of his career. In his annual report of 1882, he drew up a list of posts to be abandoned as soon as possible; posts to be active only a few years longer; and posts suitable for large bodies of troops, that could be regarded as permanent. He listed Fort Riley, with its stone buildings "meant to last forever," in the last category. Sherman retired a year later, turning the office of Commanding General over to Philip H. Sheridan.[3]

Sheridan had served in the Quartermaster Department of the Union Army early in the Civil War and then commanded cavalry—

first a regiment, then a brigade—in Mississippi. He went east in the spring of 1864 to lead the Cavalry Corps of the Army of the Potomac. His energetic leadership soon earned higher command, first in the Shenandoah Valley and, after the war, in Texas. Although Sheridan's cavalry experience during the war amounted to only about eight months, since 1869 he had commanded the Military Division of the Missouri, where eight of the army's ten cavalry regiments were usually stationed. He was well acquainted with the army's supply problems and with mounted troops' needs in particular.[4]

In his first annual report as Commanding General, Sheridan mentioned Fort Riley "on the line of the Kansas Pacific Railway," its "beautiful, large reservation," and the need for a cavalry school there. The headquarters of the army were in Washington, D.C., though, and not until May 1885 did Sheridan get a chance to visit the fort. Afterwards, he wrote to Secretary of War William C. Endicott, praising the fort's location in "the richest agricultural section of the state of Kansas." He went on to recommend the establishment of "a good cavalry school . . . and a place where we could take such horses as are worn out by hard service, if not disabled, and recuperate them. . . . [M]any of the horses now condemned and sold for little or nothing could, if gathered at a place like Fort Riley for recuperation, be made much more serviceable than green horses purchased at high prices every year in the market." Sheridan emphasized the fort's hay acreage, which "could not be exhausted." The report ended with an appraisal of existing structures and suggestions for future construction. Soon after writing to Endicott, Sheridan ordered Major General John M. Schofield, who had succeeded him as commander of the Military Division of the Missouri, to draw up plans for barracks to house four cavalry companies and quarters for their officers, to be built during the next fiscal year. "The money," Sheridan promised, "will be ready June thirtieth."[5]

While Sheridan was urging a school of instruction for cavalry, Schofield had revived his old idea of a school for field artillery. Calling it "the most difficult branch of modern military education," he told the Adjutant General that "the Light Artillery stands almost precisely where it did at the outbreak of the last war." Schofield hoped to establish the school close to his headquarters at Chicago, "upon a railway line having direct communication with all roads diverging from that city." Sheridan, though, insisted that since live artillery ammunition required a practice range of at least one mile wide and three and one-half miles long, Fort Riley was a better site. It was "central, easily accessible," he told the Secretary of War, "and probably the only one giving a sufficient [firing range] for the necessary target instruction." Sheridan recommended an appropriation of fifty thousand dollars for the construction of additional barracks to house the artillerymen.[6]

To secure support for the schools at Fort Riley, Sheridan began lobbying Edwin S. Bragg, a former brigadier general of U.S. Volunteers who, twenty years after the war, was chairman of the House Committee on Military Affairs. Because an appropriation bill for construction would have to begin in the House of Representatives, Bragg's support for the schools was essential. In January 1886 Sheridan sent Bragg a letter describing the costs of supply. "When the post is in the immediate vicinity of a line or lines of railway communication or in a country where beef, one of the principal articles of the ration, is cheap, the cost is reduced to a minimum." He included a statistical table comparing the costs of infantry and cavalry garrisons at "frontier" and "interior" posts. The "interior" posts Sheridan instanced were Fort Snelling at Minneapolis-St. Paul; the new infantry post at San Antonio, the Presidio of San Francisco; and Fort Riley. The "frontier" post he compared with Fort Riley was Fort Elliott, in the Texas Panhandle, where the estimated annual cost of maintaining a garrison of one thousand cavalry was $229,200 more than at Fort Riley. "In fact," Sheridan hammered the point home, "at this post of Fort Riley, besides the great advantage offered by its extensive reservation, cavalry or artillery can be maintained with much greater economy than at any other post in the United States."[7]

Later in the year, Sheridan told Bragg about the army's need for a recruit depot to provide basic training both for mounted troops and for their horses. "These two objects can well be combined at the same post, the horse broken and the recruit instructed in its proper management." He further told Bragg of the need for a place where worn-out horses could regain their health. "Fort Riley, in its fine climate, its ample reservation, and the moderate cost (less than at almost any other post in the army) with which both troops and animals can be maintained, enjoys an unequaled advantage," Sheridan wrote. Besides, he warned, foreign armies had all replaced their antiquated, muzzle-loading field artillery with breech-loading pieces; the United States would do so within a year or two. Where better than Fort Riley's twenty thousand acres to instruct four or five batteries at a time in the new weaponry? Before the year was out, Bragg was able to notify Sheridan of the appropriation's passage. Sheridan expressed himself "greatly gratified" and "much obliged."[8]

A glance at the size of Fort Riley's garrison during the fifteen years after 1871, when General Schofield's first attempt at a field artillery school was discontinued, shows the amount of work needed to prepare the fort for a large body of troops. The overall average troop strength, counting the months of March, June, September, and December, was 149. The smallest garrisons were 98 in 1874 and 61 in 1876, years when hostilities demanded the troops' presence elsewhere; the largest were 220 and above in 1883 and 1884, by which time rail links to Colorado and Indian Territory had long since made possible the concentration of a larger force. Fort Riley's post returns show that from 1871 to 1886 its average troop strength during the month of March was 196; June, 81; September, 102; and December, 218. The seasonal averages clearly show Fort Riley's dormitory function as a winter station for troops who conducted warm-weather operations elsewhere. Large sums of money would be necessary to turn the post into a year-round home for the equivalent of an entire regiment.

The fort would need improved maintenance, too. Deterioration of existing structures had plagued the post's commanding officers and quartermasters since the Civil War. An inspection just after the Civil War revealed "neither Storehouses, Granaries nor workshops. In fact there is not a storehouse at the post, and the Corn Cribs look as if they might tumble any day. . . . One of the Cavalry Stables is used as a Storehouse for Subsistence and Qr.Master's Stores. There are Quarters and Stabling here for six Cavalry Companies—the former need extensive repairs, and the Company Quarters owing to a faulty construction of the Chimneys are in great danger of fire, and . . . if not repaired during the coming season the expence will be almost doubled in another year, the Stables also require repairing." The post quartermaster spent the year 1866 repairing roofs and floors, gutters and spouts, which were "Indispensible in procuring drinking water." He admitted that there was "not a stable at the Post . . . but what leaks badly," and the commanding officer soon addressed him on the topic. "*Something must be done* to make the roof of the Commissary building water proof: during the recent rain it leaked so badly that many of the stores were wet and some were spoiled; in this way the U.S. will lose more than it would cost to put an entire new shingle roof on the building, in the place of the miserable apology for a roof which now disgraces it. In this connection I would call your early attention to the condition of all the roofs on the stables; they are all flooded with water and not fit for man or beast to stop in. Something must be done, and that as soon as possible." After a year of repairs to the buildings, the quartermaster was still keeping his supplies in a vacant barracks and a stable.[9]

Tight budgets kept the quartermaster from employing local civilian workers to make needed repairs. Four years of intermittent labor by soldier-artisans made most of the barracks, storehouses, workshops, and stables reasonably safe, but some other buildings suffered neglect. "The horse appears to have had a monopoly of the good things," the post surgeon fumed in 1871, while "the most trifling repairs or improvements in the hospital have been looked upon as a matter of little moment—perhaps unworthy of attention." As a result, he "found its condition anything but satisfactory. A more dreary, forlorn, dilapidated-looking hospital I have rarely if ever seen. Decay, ruin and general neglect are the marked features. . . . On entering it now the foul and fetid effluvia . . . reminds one most forcibly of those so often found in the crowded, ill-ventilated prison-rooms of not a few of our military guardhouses." The officers' quarters were in little better shape, with plaster cracked and

Two views of Fort Riley during the mid-1870's, a time of small garrisons, when the military reservation lay open to the "depredations" of settlers who grazed cattle, cut hay and timber, helped themselves to sand, and dumped animal carcasses and other refuse there. The hospital building (shown below) appears at the left of the panoramic view, taken from a hill west of the post. Six two-story company barracks—most of them empty when the picture was taken—flank the parade ground. Three sets of officers' quarters face the parade ground and its flagstaff, with their kitchens and privies towards the camera. (Kansas State Historical Society)

George E. Pond served in the Civil War as an enlisted man before entering West Point. After eleven years as a cavalry officer, he transferred to the Quartermaster Corps and was in charge of construction at Fort Riley between 1885 and 1891. (U.S. Cavalry Museum, Fort Riley)

falling, and walls and ceilings discolored by smoke from faulty chimneys. An inspector complained of "debris of all kinds, cow's manure being prominent in the case of the Commanding Officer's Quarters." While some of the quarters had brick or board floors, others had only bare earth. Annual appropriations provided for scarcely enough material and labor to keep buildings from collapsing entirely.[10]

During the next fifteen years, officers noted Fort Riley's deficiencies in every department from cisterns ("almost useless") to the post cemetery ("extreme dilapidation and neglect"). In 1885 the new quartermaster, Captain George E. Pond, "found the buildings, with but very few exceptions, greatly out of repair, porches rotten and leaky, plastering cracked or entirely off. Two or three Stone walls of Barracks bulged and falling down, wood work generally in bad order, fences and outbuildings . . . dilapidated where not entirely gone, all of which necessitates early repairs to put them in proper condition for habitation." Pond was the first officer of the Quartermaster Department to be assigned to Fort Riley since the quartermaster depot had moved to Fort Harker in the summer of 1867. He would stay at Fort Riley, superintending construction and renovation, for the next six years.[11]

Pond's predecessors had survived from year to year on entirely inadequate budgets. Besides normal wear and tear, the fort's buildings suffered from occasional natural disasters. In 1880, when the commanding officer learned that the Department of the Missouri had budgeted no money for maintenance at Fort Riley, he wrote to headquarters, pointing out "decay and consequent injury to the public buildings. The floors now as well as the roofs are giving away and are in a very dangerous condition." Two months afterward, a windstorm tore the roof off one building and damaged the guttering and spouts that furnished much of the garrison's drinking water. The commanding officer's telegram describing the damage to department headquarters ended with the words, "Please answer." The tone may have been either plaintive or exasperated; in any case, the department authorized Fort Riley's quartermaster "to expend not to exceed $100.00" on repairs.[12]

Two years later, in April 1882, a tornado tore roofs off barracks, stables, the quartermaster and commissary storehouses, and several of the officers' quarters. The commanding officer estimated the cost of repairs at thirty thousand dollars; the assistant quartermaster general in Washington, D.C., was able to allocate four thousand dollars for the task. Damage was so extensive that a correspondent of the *Army and Navy Journal* surmised that the post might be abandoned rather than rebuilt. By 1882, though, Fort Riley had become a cavalry station again; the railroads facilitated its use as a hay farm and dormitory; and General Sherman had probably already decided on its retention, which he was to announce in his report at the end of the year. A crew of sixteen civilian carpenters and "several other mechanics" went quickly to work repairing the roofs. "It will take only a couple of weeks . . . to expend all the money to be had," the Junction City *Union* commented.[13]

Without question, Fort Riley needed more money if the War Department intended to keep it open. Natural disasters and normal maintenance aside, the fort's retention as a cavalry post housing a regimental headquarters and a four-company squadron demanded new buildings. Construction of barracks, officers' quarters, and stables got under way while Sheridan's and Schofield's projected school for cavalry and field artillery was still in the planning stage. Most of the government's expenditures on these projects during the next five years wound up in the pockets of Davis County's contractors, workers, and merchants.[14]

Representatives of Junction City's commercial interests at once began to cultivate federal officials. When Sheridan visited Fort Riley in the spring of 1885, the Junction City *Union* reported that the mayor and a delegation "expressed to him the interest our people feel in the improvement of Riley, to which the General responded that he had desired for some time to improve Riley, and hoped yet to do it. He would say nothing definite, however, as to what would happen." A month later, though, Sheridan wrote to tell Schofield that thirty thousand dollars had been appropriated for new barracks and officers' quarters at Fort Riley. It was the first step in the fort's renovation and expansion.[15]

Construction did not get well under way until 1887, when Congress appropriated two hundred thousand dollars, "or so much thereof as may be necessary," for "a permanent school of instruction for drill and practice for the cavalry and light artillery service." Plans called for quarters and stables for a twelve-company regiment of cavalry (or three four-company squadrons from different regiments, in rotation) and five horse-drawn batteries, one from each artillery regiment. The Department of War in Washington, D.C., rather than the Chief Quartermaster of the Department of the Missouri at Fort Leavenworth, advertised these contracts, which drew bidders from as far away as Chicago, Cincinnati, and Pittsburgh. Nevertheless, Kansas contractors, particularly those from Junction City, got most of the work and most of the money.[16]

The first year's appropriation, though, went largely to G. D. and L. E. Hullinger of Springfield, Illinois. Their low bid of $124,998 on the entire contract for the new artillery buildings was $20,500—14 percent—less than the next lowest, offered by a Junction City firm. The Hullingers underbid five contractors from Junction City, one each from Chicago and Kansas City, and a partnership of men from Clay Center and Manhattan, Kansas. What was left of the appropriation went to the partnership of Ziegler and Dalton (four brothers who lived in Junction City) and another partnership that consisted of Gottlieb G. Griese, a Junction City resident, and a brother of his from Cleveland, Ohio. Hullinger and Son got nearly 64 percent of the appropriated funds, Junction City residents just over 28 percent, and the Griese brother from Cleveland about 7.25 percent. A plumber from Topeka did $438 worth of work on the officers' quarters.[17]

Hullinger and Son had difficulty completing their contract and had to ask for two extensions, totaling three months. Their huge bid, meant to monopolize construction of the artillery post, was uncharacteristic. Smaller, more manageable bids were the rule. By way of comparison, during the previous year Griese Brothers had received $24,135 for building a pair of barracks and a wall around the post cemetery, Ziegler and Dalton $15,320 for officers' quarters, and a Leavenworth contractor $2,909 for work on latrines and sewers. The Fort Riley quartermaster's money usually stayed close to home. In 1888 things were back to normal, with Junction City residents winning $83,989 in contracts (46.4 percent); other Kansans $52,472 (29 percent); and a firm from Kansas City, Missouri, building the fort's new waterworks for $44,509.[18]

Junction City residents old and new gained from the boom. James Tully had lived in the neighborhood since he came to work as a stonemason with Major Ogden's crew in the summer of 1855. In the years since, he had married and raised eight children, acquired a farm worth $1,500, and served as township treasurer and county commissioner. In the summer of 1888 he received $3,815 for building culverts and sewers at Fort Riley.[19]

John K. Wright, the Civil War veteran, state legislator, and army contractor, had for years graded railroad rights-of-way and laid track. Whether or not he employed more men and "built more miles of railroad than any other man in the state," as his obituaries later declared, brief newspaper accounts of his activities through the years show that his field of operations did extend from Nebraska to Louisiana. He put his graders to work at Fort Riley and moved forty-six thousand cubic yards of earth.[20]

The construction at Fort Riley was just what the new firm of

Contractors from Davis and Riley Counties begin grading Fort Riley's parade ground in the fall of 1887. (U.S. Cavalry Museum, Fort Riley)

Ziegler and Dalton needed. The Ziegler brothers had come to Junction City from Pennsylvania in 1883 and became partners with John and William Dalton, two Yorkshiremen who had arrived five years earlier. They put up several buildings for John K. Wright and Dustin Sands, another prominent army contractor, as well as a city schoolhouse, and began bidding on jobs at the fort in 1886. Within two years, they had engaged to build more than $130,000 worth of barracks and officers' quarters.[21]

Ziegler and Dalton had done more than $185,000 worth of work at Fort Riley before the Mounted Branch School opened officially in 1892. By that time, the firm was prosperous enough to bid on contracts at Fort Ethan Allen, a new cavalry post in Vermont, where they built sixteen structures. During the next two decades, the partners put up at least forty-five buildings for the army at Forts Leavenworth, Sam Houston (San Antonio), and D. A. Russell (Cheyenne). Like Fort Riley, all were large posts on major rail lines. Although a number of Ziegler and Dalton's nonmilitary buildings still stand in Junction City, the partnership's huge success within ten years of the Zieglers' arrival was due almost entirely to army contracts and shows clearly the effect of quartermaster's disbursements on the local economy.[22]

The growth of that economy, though, since the days when the Quartermaster Department had to bring contract laborers from Cincinnati and St. Louis to put up Fort Riley's first buildings, makes it hard to estimate how many wage earners took part in the boom of the 1880s. The army awarded contracts building by building, and the contractors, whose records have long since disappeared, hired men by the job. According to the Junction City *Union*, the Griese Brothers had sixty men at work in March 1887, and Ziegler and Dalton had twenty. In December of that year, Fort Riley's commanding officer gave a round figure of "500 citizens at work in the Quartermaster's department, and this number . . . will have to be employed for more than a year, to complete the post in accordance with its present plans." The quartermasters' reports for that month list only sixteen employees on monthly salaries: clerk, superintendent, steam engineer, forage master, blacksmith, and teamsters. The balance of the 500 must have been working for the contractors.[23]

The commanding officer's figure of 500 may have included both workers and their families, who lived in shacks on the reservation. The Fort Riley correspondent of the Junction City *Republican*, who provided that paper with a weekly column of gossipy news, estimated the number of workers in November 1887 at "about 200" and in December at "upwards of three hundred and," he predicted, "in the spring the number will be greatly increased." Meanwhile, the post trader added to his stock of groceries so that workers' families could "buy everything they need right here at home without having to pay fifty cents [to ride a horse-drawn omnibus into town] to buy what little necessaries they may need." The fort's post trader, too, was doing well out of the boom.[24]

When spring rolled around, Fort Riley's construction projects competed for labor with Junction City's own building boom: a municipal waterworks, projected to cost fifty thousand dollars; a steam-driven flour mill, to cost thirty thousand dollars; two railroad depots, with a combined cost of twenty thousand dollars; a hotel and nine other commercial buildings downtown; and a possible forty thousand dollars' worth of private houses. It is hard to say how much of this nonmilitary construction was inspired by the prospect of long-term economic growth due to Fort Riley's expansion. If the newspapers' editorial comments accurately reflected businessmen's opinions, hopes were high.[25]

The Junction City newspapers commented briefly from time to time on the progress of construction downtown. The builders' names show that private and municipal projects sustained local contractors in 1888 while the outsiders Hullinger and Son enjoyed a practical monopoly at Fort Riley. Jobs were plentiful, with wages at least comparable to those offered by the Quartermaster Department. "Men with teams are getting three dollars a day," the *Republican*'s correspondent wrote; artisans received $2 or $3 a day, and laborers between $1.25 and $1.50. By way of comparison, the quartermaster's blacksmith at the fort earned $60 a month; the teamsters, $30. When budget restrictions in the Department of the Missouri forced the quartermaster to lay off some of his teamsters, they at once found work, digging a trench for the sewer contractor. Junction City was a seller's market for labor in the late 1880s, and when the next year's federal appropriation looked sure to pass, the *Republican*'s editor wrote that it was "glorious news to the people of Junction City and Davis county and especially to our mechanics and laborers, insuring as it does employment for them during the coming year. The improvements going on at the post have been a God-send to our laboring population during the past two years, affording them, as it has, work at fair wages. Had it not been for this, many families would have suffered for the necessities of life." However overstated the *Republican*'s praise for the accomplishment of a Republican senator may seem, Fort Riley's construction boom certainly spread a good deal of money among Davis County's wage earners.[26]

Not all of the money went directly from the Quartermaster Department to contractors to employees; some of the work was subcontracted, and sometimes the contractors bought supplies from local manufacturers. There seems to be no record of how much of Hullinger and Son's massive contract was subcontracted, or to whom, but Ziegler and Dalton used the same painter on all their jobs at Fort Riley. The painter himself "employs about fifteen hands," according to the *Republican*, "and keeps them busily at work." William W. Cook and John O. Heaton, who built the fort's steam-heating plant, bought 1,025,000 bricks from the Junction City Pressed Brick Company, which employed fourteen workers but never signed a contract with the army. Thus the quartermaster's disbursements percolated through Davis County's economy.[27]

The army's budget, of course, ran only from year to year, and required annual replenishment. In March 1888 Sheridan wrote to Preston B. Plumb, the junior U.S. senator from Kansas, recommending an appropriation of three hundred thousand dollars to go on with construction at Fort Riley. Plumb gave a copy of the letter to the Junction City *Union*, and it appeared in the issue of March 10, two columns to the left of a set of resolutions that the Junction City Board of Trade had passed a few days earlier. The aggrieved, self-righteous tone of the resolutions makes them worth quoting, because it places them in a direct line of descent from the *Kansas Weekly Herald*'s remarks in 1854 about "the fostering aid of our government."

The board of trade began by complaining that the army "during years of neglect and the practical abandonment of Fort Riley, persistently refused to reduce the military reservation, or open any part of it to settlement, thus retarding the growth of this section." The board then noted that the previous year's appropriation was nearly exhausted and "that the desires of the military department with respect to Fort Riley are of great consequence to Central Kansas, providing for the disbursement of hundreds of thousands of dollars in our midst, now expended for the same purpose elsewhere, which will make a horse, stock and grain market equal to the best in the country; and for the absolute necessities of the Government more can be obtained for the money expended in this way at Fort Riley than for any other disbursement of public funds." The board of trade then urged the Kansas congressional delegation "to assist the military authorities in securing liberal appropriations for the continuance of the work they have in hand at Fort Riley, as a matter of interest to this portion of their constituents, and as an important factor in the general development of the State." The resolutions ended with a defensive slap at military construction "in cities where the Government could rent for less expense, and overlooking a military establishment [Fort Riley] where a whole brigade can be housed for the cost of one of these buildings, thus adding for all time to the various productive industries of several counties, and bringing into our midst, according to the designs of the military, the most important post of the Government." This last rush of prose, by turns assertive and fawning, was inspired by the army's plans for new construction in Atlanta, Chicago, Omaha, St. Louis, and San Antonio, all of them rail centers that were to be protected against labor disturbances by garrisons of regimental strength. The board of trade sent copies of its resolutions to all members of the Kansas congressional delegation.[28]

Congress came through with $150,000 for Fort Riley in 1888. By November disbursements were under way, and Captain Pond, the quartermaster in charge of construction, wanted to assure more. With the help of Bertrand Rockwell, one of Junction City's leading merchants, Pond initiated a newspaper campaign to flatter Senator Plumb and to press for further appropriations. Only three letters from this correspondence survive, but they show clearly how federal officials could work with local businessmen and editors to promote a project.[29]

On November 24, Rockwell wrote to the newspaper editor and former Junction City resident George W. Martin. Martin had been one of the founders of the Junction City *Union*, but by 1888, after a few years in Topeka as state printer, he was editing the Kansas City, Kansas, *Gazette*. He was a staunch Republican who still took an interest in Junction City and, just as important, had always regarded Fort Riley and its reservation as a vital part of the Kansas economy. Rockwell told him:

> The other day Capt Pond rec[eive]d a letter from
> Plumb. . . , saying that the people outside of Davis Co. in

The interior of Bertrand Rockwell's general merchandise store in Junction
City during the 1880s. Rockwell helped to launch the newspaper campaign
to flatter Senator Preston B. Plumb and secure appropriations for construction at Fort Riley. (Kansas State Historical Society)

the state did not care a d—n about appropriations for Fort
Riley, that the J. C. Union was the only paper that had
given him any credit for doing what he had &c. &c. . . .
Now I wish you would take this matter in hand in your
paper—tell of the great improvements. You can get a detailed statement of them by writing to Capt Pond—of
Sheridan's ideas—which we have no doubt will be approved
by Genl Schofield of making all purchases of Horses for
Cavalry & Artillery in Kansas, . . . of the great interest
Senator Plumb has from the start taken in the matter, and
of it being one of the most important things for the benefit of the State, he has assisted in. . . . Now George block
this out in nice shape—so that it will be copied in most of
the State papers—and do all you can to make the path
easy for another appropriation this winter.[30]

Martin did not have to write to Pond because a letter from the quartermaster was already on its way to him. Pond wrote that Rockwell had already asked him

> to give you some points for an article commending Senator Plumb, for his successful efforts in behalf of the Riley appropriations. . . . Gen. Sheridan recommended $300,000 for this great work, which is about as large a sum as can well be handled in one year. The committee in the House cut this down to $100,000 and when it reached the Senate, Mr. Plumb raised it to $200,000, and the conference left the amount as it now stands $150,000. . . . Without men like Plumb . . . , the Generals may recommend all they please, & have but their paper for their pains. . . . The immense benefits to accrue to the service, and incidentally to this section of Kansas, you, and all far seeing men, can realize. . . . I am glad to give you . . . all the information possible, only dont let it appear as coming direct from me, for reasons you can understand.[31]

Martin went to work at once, and on the last day of November the *Gazette* printed "The Rebuilding of Fort Riley," which ran more than an entire column on the editorial page. The fort's expansion, Martin wrote, "will send a throb through Kansas agriculture . . . almost as important as that which will follow a full development of the sorghum industry" that was then being introduced into the state. Passages from Pond's letter describing the budget seesaw, current construction at Fort Riley, and future plans all found their way into the editorial without attribution. "We predict that in ten years Central Kansas will be one of the most valuable horse regions in the world," Martin soared to his peroration, "and that Riley will be the heart that will furnish the pulse-beats to a great interest. . . . When fully equipped this means the disbursement of two or three millions a year. Senators Ingalls and Plumb and Representatives Ryan and Anderson, have each visited Riley, and made a careful inspection of the work, and in view of its apparent value to a large portion of the state it is not to be wondered at that they have pushed it so vigor-

Longtime Junction City resident George Martin edited the *Weekly Union* for years. He had moved to the Kansas City *Gazette* by 1888, when Bertrand Rockwell recruited him to write an editorial extolling Fort Riley and Senator Preston B. Plumb that would "make the path easy for another appropriation this winter." (Kansas State Historical Society)

ously, and that they are enthusiastic in backing the military to the end of the handsome job they have in hand." Words like "industry," "valuable," "disbursement," and "job" made the message plain: Fort Riley was going to be an economic asset to Kansas, and the state's senators, as well as the representatives from the Kansas River valley, were to be congratulated for their activities in the fort's behalf.

It was not a propitious time to launch an editorial campaign. Martin's Fort Riley piece had to compete for space with the president's annual message—"Grover's Growl," the Leavenworth *Times* called it—and the proceedings of the 50th Congress, to which some papers devoted several columns of small type in each issue. Nevertheless, the Emporia *Republican* copied Martin's article in its entirety, and editors in Atchison, Fort Scott, Hutchinson, Newton, and Wichita contributed their own praise of Plumb's work. Rockwell was pleased with the results, and both the Junction City *Republican* and Martin's old paper, the *Union*, wound up the campaign with an entire page devoted to Fort Riley, including Martin's edito-

Table 6. Fort Riley Construction, by Residence of Contractor

	Davis County	Other Kansas	Out of State
1886–87	$29,388	$2,909	$12,607
1887–88	$61,679	$438	$138,809
1888–89	$78,376	$66,732	$153,624
1889–90	$86,296	$19,246	$30,951
1890–91	$53,493	$6,745	$1,111
Totals	$309,243	$96,070	$336,562

Source: Quartermaster Department, Register of Contracts 2 (1886–1887); 3 (1888–1889); and 4 (1890–1891), RG92.

rial and comments from other papers around the state. Senator Plumb's reaction has not survived, but appropriations for Fort Riley continued. Junction City's contractors garnered about one hundred thousand dollars in 1889, more than 60 percent of the total appropriations.[32]

Expenditures for the five-year period of construction—including 1886–87, a year when Fort Riley was merely being renovated as a one-squadron cavalry post, before passage of the bill creating the Mounted Branch School—show the Davis County contractors' predominance (Table 6). Of the out-of-state contracts, $124,998 went to Hullinger and Son for building the artillery school; $81,363 to a Pittsburgh, Pennsylvania, firm for the steam-heating plant; and $44,509 to Kansas City, Missouri, contractors for the waterworks. When these three contracts, amounting to $250,870, are subtracted from the total, the gross income of Davis County's contractors looks even more impressive: they handled nearly 63 percent of the grading, sewer work, and above-ground construction at Fort Riley during the five years.[33]

Construction of the school for cavalry and artillery at Fort Riley brought contracts and jobs to the fort's neighbors. The businessmen, editors, and politicians of Davis County and Kansas had cooperated to an unprecedented degree with each other and with the army officers who needed their help and had earned enormous profits. The fort's renovation and expansion evinced a maturing economy in Kansas and in the West as a region: an economy that could produce its own brick but needed outside expertise to install steam-heating and federal money to pay for both bricks and boilers. Skillful lobbying was partly responsible for the appropriations, but the original impetus, modernizing the army, was beyond local control. This tension between local and national interests, as well as the unprecedented scale of the operation—the size of the garrison, of the physical plant, and of the disbursements—presaged Fort Riley's history, and that of the American West, for a hundred years to come.

Epilogue

"The Fostering Aid of Our Government"

FROM THE MOMENT it acquired the territory, the federal government, and the army in particular, profoundly influenced the economy of the American West. At the outset, this involvement took the form of exploring and appraising the new lands and attempting to manage Indian relations by controlling trade through the factory system. The Department of War was responsible for the factory system through one of its branches, the Office of Indian Affairs, while the army's Ordnance Department controlled mineral leases on the public lands. Even after the factories shut down in 1822 and the Office of Indian Affairs moved to the Department of the Interior in 1849, the army remained to manifest the federal presence in the West. The Corps of Topographical Engineers was still largely responsible for exploration until it merged with the Corps of Engineers in 1863.

The army's economic influence worked in two conflicting directions. Sequestering tracts of land for military reservations, keeping them closed to settlement, shrinking the tax base of local governments, and reserving the land's resources for the army's use tended to dampen local economic growth. On the other hand, pumping money into local economies through cash payments to contractors and wage earners promoted western development. In the neighborhood of army posts, these payments fostered a class of frontier capitalists whose wealth derived partly from supplying the troops with food, forage, and firewood, although they always kept an eye turned towards land speculation and the civilian economy that developed as settlers moved into the region. Some of these settlers came with the army, either as contract laborers or as soldiers who stayed after their enlistments expired.

Other settlers seem to have been attracted by the economic possibilities that the army offered. Their numbers may have been small compared with those of the farmers who merely sought good, cheap land, but they included some of the future leaders of the new civilian communities that sprang up near army posts. These men favored the army's presence when they thought that its contracts could work to their benefit, but sought to get rid of it when contracts were few and small. At those times the military reservation merely posed a vast obstacle, as they saw it, to the economic expansion of their communities.

Settlers sought connection, whether by river, wagon road, or railroad, to markets and to assistance from government, whether federal, state, or local. In the earliest days, at the local level, this meant licensing ferries, for bridge building required a sum of money beyond the reach of county governments in territorial Kansas. During this early stage of development, towns like Manhattan donated ox teams to a wagon-road survey expedition, and the post trader at Fort Riley, a federally licensed merchant, donated provisions from his stock. After the Civil War, county bond issues supported construction of short-line railroads that linked Manhattan and Junction City on the line of the Kansas Pacific with the main line of the Union Pacific to the north and with the Katy and Santa Fe lines to the south. The coming of the Kansas Pacific in 1866 caused the army to move Fort Riley's quartermaster depot, and with it a large government payroll, farther west. The bond issues represented local civilians' efforts to strengthen their economic position by connections with railroads that would offer competitive freight rates. An incidental consequence of the connecting short lines was to put Fort Riley squarely in the middle of the growing national rail network.

In the long run, Fort Riley's central position proved far more important to the local economy than the hoped-for lower shipping costs. The rail connections led the army to keep Fort Riley open during the 1880s, a decade during which it abandoned all its other posts in Kansas except Fort Leavenworth. The Quartermaster Department used Fort Riley's military reservation as a huge hay farm, shipping the product by rail to posts in more arid regions. By the 1880s the fort's rail links in all directions made it the cheapest post in the United States to supply. For this reason, and because the army's field artillery needed a large reservation to practice with its new breech-loading rifled cannon, Fort Riley became the site of the Mounted Branch School. The army would continue to pour money into the local economy throughout the next century.[1]

National rather than local considerations determined federal policy, although businessmen, newspaper editors, and their elected representatives strove to influence it for their own ends. Fort Riley's selection as a permanent station with a large garrison was part of the army's changing strategic deployment during the 1880s and '90s. This plan relied on the railroads to supply large bodies of troops—regiments numbering between five hundred and eight hundred men—at central points on major rail lines and to transport them quickly to wherever they might be needed. Labor disturbances during the strikes of 1877 lent urgency to the rail-based policy of troop concentration. The railroads (whose operations were characterized by holding companies and stock rigging) on the one hand, and militant labor unions on the other, stood for all that was changing in American society during the last third of the nineteenth century: concentration of economic power and growing class conflict that caused grave apprehension in middle-class property owners.[2]

In the industrializing, urbanizing United States, the middle class—and this included most merchants and property owners, newspaper editors and publishers, and public officials, both civil and military—felt ground between the stones of great corporate wealth and cheap, foreign-born wage labor. After the Paris Commune in 1871, and particularly after newspaper exploitation of the Haymarket explosion in 1886 raised the specter of Anarchism in the United States, alien political ideologies as well as labor unrest nettled the minds of the middle class. When the army went to Chicago during the strikes of 1877, a correspondent of the *Army and Navy Journal* remarked, it had been "to help out the people during the Railroad

Riots." This view was common among army officers. One of its foremost exponents was Nelson A. Miles, who attained general rank in 1880 and by the early 1890s commanded the Military Division of the Missouri, with headquarters at Chicago. His opinions were translated into action during the strikes of 1894.[3]

The first major test of the army's new strategic system of large garrisons at central points on major railroad lines came during the Pullman Strike in the summer of 1894. The Pullman Company, a manufacturer, owner, and operator of railroad sleeping cars, had cut its workers' wages by more than half during the previous year. The American Railway Union, fresh from a strike victory over the Great Northern, refused to run trains that included Pullman cars. The U.S. Attorney General used the interruption of the mails as an excuse to summon the regular army to clear the Chicago railroad yards and run the trains. Four troops of cavalry and three batteries of artillery came from Fort Riley.[4]

The Pullman Strike collapsed, largely because of the economic power of the company and because of dissension between the American Railway Union (an industry-wide organization) on the one hand and the brotherhoods (engineers, firemen, and others) and the American Federation of Labor on the other. The army had little direct influence on the course of the strike. Nevertheless, the speed with which it was able to concentrate its force at Chicago proved the efficacy of having fewer, larger garrisons along transportation arteries. Besides Fort Riley's contingent of 370, troops had assembled from posts on the Great Lakes and from Forts Leavenworth and Niobrara. The soldiers from Fort Riley had covered the 650 miles to Chicago in two days. Sixty-five years earlier, it had taken Bennet Riley and his men thirty-five days to cover the 485 miles from Fort Leavenworth to Chouteau's Island in the Arkansas River. The army's new mobility was proven, and future administrations could bear in mind the possible use of military force to suppress civil unrest.[5]

Army officers, whose overwhelmingly middle-class origins or aspirations made them apt agents of the simultaneous advance of capitalism and federal authority into the West, staunchly favored law and order and thoroughly sympathized with the aims of management. The strike was barely over and the troops withdrawn from Chicago to the recently established Fort Sheridan just north of the city, when Nelson Miles, the commanding general, wrote a short essay on "The Lesson of the Recent Strikes." The *North American Review* published it, along with three others on the topic, in August. Miles saw the strike as a struggle between "red-hot anarchy, insurrectionary and revolutionary, . . . mob violence, and universal chaos under . . . socialism" and "the supremacy of law, the maintenance of good order, . . . absolute security of life and property, [and] the rights of personal liberty." Miles favored the latter. He urged urban workers to "get out into the country, into the pure air and among the birds, flowers, and green fields, where they may cultivate the ground; for really all wealth comes from the ground, directly or indirectly." Miles was fond of pointing out that he himself was a Massachusetts farm boy; his fustian rhetoric expressed the alarm at industrialization and class stratification that characterized the American middle class during the last quarter of the nineteenth century.[6]

Miles's own property interests were intimately tied to cities, though, and to Washington, D.C., real estate in particular. "Like most of his army colleagues," his most recent biographer writes, "Miles found it unnecessary to separate personal profit from professional development." Several officers who had served at Fort Riley continued to own lots in Junction City, although their duties took them elsewhere. Fort Riley's commanding officer between 1885 and 1887, Lieutenant Colonel Charles E. Compton of the Fifth Cavalry, owned a ranch in Wyoming, where his regiment had served before moving to Kansas. Most officers had similar interests; as an anonymous "old Army officer" told one reporter, "From time immemorial Army officers have always done a little money-making as they went along out on the plains." In that respect, little had changed since the days of the Pawnee Association. During the post–Civil War era, though, many officers invested in enterprises like agriculture or mining that depended on the railroads to move goods to market. Army officers' business contacts, as well as their social origins, attuned them to the railroads' needs.[7]

The Civil War had brought millions of Americans face to face with the federal government and its army for the first time, whether as soldiers, military dependents, contractors, or civilian employees. The chief engineers of the transcontinental railroads were former generals: the Union volunteer Grenville M. Dodge on the Union Pacific, the Confederate West Pointer Thomas L. Rosser on the Northern Pacific. The idea of the railroad united the nation's mind as the rails themselves connected its regions. Long after the war, a Confederate veteran (himself a president of the Maryland Bar Association) recalled the abilities of Stonewall Jackson. "What a splendid railroad manager he would have made." Professional conflict between "progressive" junior officers and fossilized Civil War veterans, or the degree of isolation from the larger society that soldiers endured in the late nineteenth century, are tangential issues because most army officers and many enlisted men, as the careers of several Junction City residents show, rejoiced in the expansion of capitalism.[8]

So did most of their civilian neighbors, to one degree or another. Although editors wrote in the language of entitlement, demanding "the fostering aid of our government," local residents were not passive recipients of government largesse. Eager to exploit the land and its resources, whether or not these were reserved for use by the federal government or by Indian tribes, they reached avidly to connect their communities to larger markets. On the local level, the connection could be as cheap as a county ferry license or as costly and potentially ruinous as an issue of ten-year bonds to promote railroad construction. Although farmers balked at bonded indebtedness, they lined up to sell their corn and oats to army contractors, and when the federal government ignored local wishes, an editorial campaign could cajole a United States senator into renewed efforts on behalf of his constituents.

By the time the Mounted Branch School opened at Fort Riley in 1892, the state and the market were more firmly wedded than they had been sixty-five years earlier when George Sibley's government survey crew marked the Santa Fe Trail. During the twentieth century the federal government's economic role in the West, although evident from the outset, would become manifest on a far grander scale. So, too, would Westerners' ambivalence towards both the market and the federal government. The first forty years of Fort Riley's history and the century that has followed exemplify the interplay among federal activity, local interests, and market forces that has characterized the entire history of the American West.

Abbreviations

AAG	Assistant Adjutant General (of a Department or Military Division)
AAQM	Acting Assistant Quartermaster (post quartermaster)
ACS	Acting Commissary of Subsistence (post commissary)
AG	Adjutant General (Department of War, Washington, D.C.)
AGO	Adjutant General's Office
CCF	Consolidated Correspondence File
CG	Commanding General (of a Department or Military Division)
CIA	Commissioner of Indian Affairs, Annual Report
CO	Commanding Officer (of a military post or unit)
KSHS	Kansas State Historical Society
LC	Library of Congress
LR	Letters Received
LS	Letters Sent
NA	National Archives, Washington, D.C.
QM	Quartermaster
QMD	Quartermaster's Department
QMG	Quartermaster General (Department of War, Washington, D.C.)
RG	Record Group
RPA	Report of Persons and Articles Hired
SWAR	Secretary of War, Annual Report

Notes

Preface

1. Nancy O. Lurie, "Ethnohistory," 78–92.

2. Wilbur S. Nye, *Carbine and Lance*; Robert C. Carriker, *Fort Supply*; Robert Lee, *Fort Meade*; Ty Cashion, *A Texas Frontier*.

3. Paul L. Hedren, *Fort Laramie in 1876*; John C. Hudson, *Plains Country Towns*; Frank N. Schubert, *Outpost of the Sioux Wars*. Schubert's study was first a Ph.D. dissertation, "Fort Robinson, Nebraska: The History of a Military Community, 1874–1916," at the University of Toledo in 1977 and later appeared in hard cover as *Buffalo Soldiers, Braves, and the Brass: The Story of Fort Robinson, Nebraska* (Shippensburg, Pa.: White Mane, 1993).

4. Statistics from annual Economic Impact Statements, prepared by Fort Riley's Directorate of Resource Management, available from the fort's Public Affairs Office.

Introduction

1. During the depression of the 1890s, one-quarter of the nation's railroads, representing one-third of its rail mileage, came under the care of receivers at one time or another, and the Union Pacific was prominent among them. Its affairs were particularly complicated because of a massive debt to the federal government, dating from the time of the road's construction three decades earlier (Maury Klein, *Union Pacific*, especially 14–15, 31–32, 375–84, 450, 532–33, 626, and 654–57). Quotation from Junction City *Republican*, March 29, 1895.

2. Joyce Appleby has pointed out that even before the nineteenth-century transportation revolution rising European grain prices were sufficient incentive for American farmers to plant wheat and so take part in the international economy ("Commercial Farming and the 'Agrarian Myth,'" especially 840–42). James Henretta, while acknowledging the influence of grain prices, maintains that cultural factors, principally kinship, impeded a headlong rush towards the market ("Families and Farms"). Allan Kulikoff concludes that, although some farmers "welcomed the higher standard of living and bourgeois culture" that accompanied commercial farming, others "rejected capitalism because it threatened the economic independence they valued" (*Agrarian Roots of American Capitalism*, 264). The same stresses operate today when people like what money buys but don't like what they have to do to get it. Someone has remarked that "so-called 'country music' is the music of people who have moved to the city and don't like it."

3. The railroads "closed time and distance across the western interior of North America. . . . [T]echnical application of steam power to land travel therefore vastly advanced the geographic reach of capital; as a consequence the rail links everywhere boosted speculation in western land and resources" (William G. Robbins, *Colony and Empire*, 67). Sherman's remarks are in the Secretary of War's Annual Report (hereafter SWAR [date]) for 1883, 45–46.

4. *Far West*, August 11, 1836; *Kansas Weekly Herald*, September 22, 1854; *Army and Navy Journal*, December 4, 1880; *Junction City Union*, October 20, 1888; *Junction City Republican*, November 4, 1887.

5. [Thomas Hart Benton], *Thirty Years' View*, 2:469.

6. Quotation in 39th Cong., 2nd sess., H. Ex. Doc. 23, "Protection Across the Continent," 19.

7. Percentages based on tables in Erik F. Haites et al., *Western River Transportation*, 157, 162, which shows four-decade averages for freight and passengers, both upstream and down, between Louisville and New Orleans.

8. Patricia N. Limerick lists federal money as one of "five principal resources . . . ready for exploitation" by early settlers (*Legacy of Conquest*, 82).

9. Troops came to Kansas from posts along the line of the

Union Pacific between Omaha, Nebraska, and Rawlins, Wyoming (*Army and Navy Journal*, July 18, 1885).

10. Sherman in SWAR 1882, 10–17; Sheridan to Bragg, January 13, 1886, Sheridan Papers, LC.

11. White, "*It's Your Misfortune and None of My Own*," 58.

Prologue

1. Donald Jackson, ed., *Journals of Zebulon Montgomery Pike*, 2:19; Edwin James, *Account of an Expedition from Pittsburgh to the Rocky Mountains*, 2:361.

2. 22nd Cong., 1st sess., S. Doc. 90, "Fur Trade, and the Inland Trade to Mexico," 33; [Thomas Hart Benton], *Thirty Years' View*, 2:469.

3. According to Donald Worster, the maxim of twentieth-century wheat farmers is, "Do not interfere with us when we are making money, but rescue us when we are going bankrupt" (*Dust Bowl*, 154).

4. Storrs's estimate is in 18th Cong., 2nd sess., S. Doc. 7, "Trade and Intercourse, Between Missouri and . . . New Mexico," 6; Benton is quoted in Kate L. Gregg, ed., *Road to Santa Fe*, 5.

5. "Trade and Intercourse," 4.

6. James, *Account of an Expedition*, 2:353, 355, 361.

7. Louise Barry, *Beginning of the West*, 65–67, 107; Gregg, *Road to Santa Fe*, 10, 24. Senator Benton introduced the bill to abolish the factories. "Some light is thrown upon lobbying practices of a century ago by the fact that Benton was retained as an attorney for the American Fur Company in the same year in which he pushed through a bill so favorable to its interests" (Kenneth W. Porter, *John Jacob Astor, Business Man*, 2:714).

8. John R. Stilgoe outlines the folklore of pedology in *Common Landscape of America*, 140–48; John M. Faragher describes Illinois farmers' experiences in *Sugar Creek*, 62–67; on Anglo settlers' experience in Texas during the 1820s, see Terry G. Jordan, "Vegetational Perception and Choice of Settlement Site."

9. Willard H. Rollings, *Osage*, 69–75, and Richard White, *Roots of Dependency*, 158–67, describe the annual cycle of village life.

10. Rollings, *Osage*, 78.

11. George R. Brooks, ed., "Sibley's Journal," 170, 176.

12. Sibley quoted in William E. Unrau, *Kansas Indians*, 105–106.

13. Gregg, *Road to Santa Fe*, 58, 63, 65; Barry, *Beginning of the West*, 100–101, 107. Merchants' advertisements in Kansas newspapers during the 1850s and '60s show the same concern with freight costs and credit, thirty and forty years after Sibley.

14. Gregg, *Road to Santa Fe*, 181, 183.

15. Joseph T. Manzo, "Emigrant Indian Objections to Kansas Residence," "Indian Pre-Removal Network," and "Native Americans, Euro-Americans."

16. "Trade and Intercourse," 6; Josiah Gregg, *Commerce of the Prairies*, 332; Barry, *Beginning of the West*, 145–46.

17. Josiah Gregg, ibid.; Barry, *Beginning of the West*, 110, 121, 145–46, 150–51.

18. Barry, *Beginning of the West*, 158–65; Leo E. Oliva, *Soldiers on the Santa Fe Trail*, 26–33. Riley's journal is reprinted in Fred S. Perrine, ed., "Military Escorts on the Santa Fe Trail." Although popular imagination, then and since, has attributed most raiding on the Santa Fe Trail to Comanches, the Indians who killed the trader in 1829 remain unidentified. Thomas W. Kavanagh, *Comanche Political History*, 215–19.

19. Statistics from Josiah Gregg, *Commerce of the Prairies*, 332. Leavenworth's failure, though, had as important a result as Riley's success. Unable to get past the Arikara village, Ashley's men turned due west and headed straight for the Rocky Mountains. They soon found South Pass, which became the most important route across the Continental Divide for the next forty years.

Chapter 1

1. John D. Unruh, Jr., *Plains Across*, 185; Francis B. Heitman, *Historical Register*, 2:400–401.

2. SWAR 1844, 132a; SWAR 1849, 188a, d, e.

3. SWAR 1851, 109–10, 219. The usual rate of travel was one hundred miles in twelve days (Henry P. Walker, *Wagonmasters*, 148).

4. Fauntleroy to QMG, July 31, 1852, in SWAR 1852, 137. Post surgeons thought the deforestation might lead to an increase in disease, particularly malaria. 34th Cong., 1st sess., S. Ex. Doc. 96, "Statistical Report," 167; Simons to Winship, July 2 1854, quoted in Winship to AG, September 27, 1854, AGO LR, 1822–1860, RG94 (NA Microfilm Publication M567, roll 508).

5. 33rd Cong., 2nd sess., S. Ex. Doc. 68, "Appropriation of Lands for Military Purposes," 3.

6. Commissioner of Indian Affairs (hereafter CIA [date]), Annual Report for 1851, 333, 335.

7. Louise Barry, *Beginning of the West*, 1103, 1121, 1131; Woodbury F. Pride, *History of Fort Riley*, 61.

8. Details of officers' careers are in Heitman, *Historical Register*, vol. 1; monthly post returns list the strength of Fort Riley's garrison and the assignment of officers. Returns From U.S. Military Posts, 1800–1916, RG94 (M617, rolls 1011–15).

9. E. A. Ogden, RPA May 1853, RG92, NA; Ogden, "Estimate of Cost of Barracks," Box 912, CCF, RG92; SWAR 1853, 131; Ogden to QMG, November 7, 1853, and March 11, 1854, Box 912, CCF; Winship to AG, September 27, 1854, AGO LR; SWAR 1854, 73; Post Return, Fort Riley, September 1854.

10. Hancock to Ogden, June 25, 1855, vol. 1, Department of the West LS, RG393, NA; Ogden to QMG, July 4 and July 14, 1855, Box 911, CCF.

11. John B. Garver, Jr., "Role of the United States Army in the Colonization of the Trans-Missouri West," 445–48; Ogden to QMG, October 26, 1853, Box 912, CCF; Albert R. Greene, "Kansas River—Its Navigation," 322; 33rd Cong., 2nd sess., S. Ex. Doc. 46, "Contracts Made Under Authority of the War Department," 7; Ogden to QMG, June 13, 1854, Box 912, CCF; *Independence (Missouri) Messenger*, June 24, 1854, quoted in Greene, 323.

12. Winship to AG, September 27, 1854, AGO LR; *Leavenworth, Kansas Weekly Herald*, October 6, 1854.

13. Greene, "Kansas River," 318–19; James C. Malin,

Grassland of North America, 133; Edgar Langsdorf, "First Survey of the Kansas River," 155–56. The Quartermaster General was aware of the seasonal flow of rivers in the plains but seemed to think that it occurred only in Texas and in the tributaries of Red River (SWAR 1852, 72).

14. CIA 1851, 314; CIA 1852, 380; CIA 1853, 342, 344; CIA 1854, 310, 314, 318. What I call a "subjective" judgment is the remark of the Sac and Fox farmer in 1854 that "the potatoes will not return the amount of seed planted." The missionary at St. Mary's was an ardent fan of navigation. "Steamboats will certainly ascend the Kanzas next spring," he wrote in 1853, "come up to our landing, discharge freight, and make us forget that we live in the Indian country."

15. CIA 1851, 326; CIA 1854, 310–11.

16. Barry, *Beginning of the West,* 1203; Greene, "Kansas River," 323; QMD Register of Contracts, 1819–1870, 12:87, 120, RG92; George R. Taylor, *Transportation Revolution,* 52, 64.

17. CIA 1856, 671, 675, 682; CIA 1857, 454, 458, 465; Corley to QMG, September 14, 1855; Buford to QMG, June 14, 1857; and Ogden, "Estimate," all in Box 912, CCF; SWAR 1853, 131.

18. 33rd Cong., 2nd sess., H. Rept. 36, "Military Roads—Kansas," 2–3; 34th Cong., 3rd sess., H. Rept. 172, "Military Road from Fort Leavenworth to Fort Riley," 1–3.

19. QMD Register of Contracts, 1819–1870, 12:167; 36th Cong., 1st sess., H. Ex. Doc. 22, "Contracts with the War Department," 6; *Leavenworth, Kansas Weekly Herald,* March 9, 1855; Lewis Atherton, *Main Street on the Middle Border,* 23.

20. Corley, RPA August 1855; Post Returns, Fort Riley, July-December 1855; Ogden to QMG, July 4, 1855, Box 911, CCF. Local residents made up a small percentage of the fort's civilian work force during the early years; on the other hand, the Quartermaster Department employed, at one time or another, three-fourths of the men listed in the 1855 territorial census who did not give their occupation as farmer or one of the professions (clergyman, doctor, lawyer).

21. Ogden to QMG, July 4 and 31, 1855, Box 911; Corley to Hancock, August 15, 1855, Box 912; Brent to QMG, December 15, 1855, Box 911, CCF. Corley was Ogden's successor as quartermaster, and his letter to Hancock (AAG Department of the West) says that fifty-six persons

died of cholera, of which he itemized seventeen soldiers and military dependents. Corley's RPA for August 1855, though, gives no hint of anything
like thirty-nine deaths among the civilian employees.

22. The number of troops present at Fort Riley is taken
from the March, June, September, and December Post Returns, June
1853–March 1860. Post returns also list the number of cavalry and artillery horses present but not the quartermaster's "public mules." Troop
strength was usually much lower in the summer, when the mounted troops
were in the field. The number of officers is disproportionately low because
many of them took leave during the winter, when the full enlisted strength
was present. Fort Riley hay contracts are in QMD Register of Contracts,
1819–1870, 12:79, 157, 400, 467.

23. Winship to AG, September 27, 1854, AGO LR; Donald J. Berthrong, *Southern Cheyennes*, 125.

24. Berthrong, *Southern Cheyennes*, 114, 134–35; George
B. Grinnell, *Fighting Cheyennes*, 112–13; John Stands in Timber and Margot Liberty, *Cheyenne Memories*, 163–65; Heitman, *Historical Register* 2:401–
4; Richard White, *Roots of Dependency*, 168–70.

25. Unruh, *Plains Across*, 120.

26. John H. Moore, *Cheyenne Nation*, 185–202, quotation
on 192.

27. CIA 1865, 571.

28. On the comparative effectiveness of military action
and the market as means of subjugation, see White, *Roots of Dependency*,
xiv–xv. New tanning processes developed about 1870 made possible the industrial use of buffalo hides, but the slaughter on the southern plains did
not get well under way until the Santa Fe railroad reached Dodge City in
1872, and in the north not until the Northern Pacific reached Miles City,
Montana, in 1881.

29. There were 35,085 miles of track in 1865 and 52,922
in 1870 (*Historical Statistics of the United States*, 2:731). "Perhaps with
sounder analysis the railroad's achievement should be stated in terms of
density rather than frontiers" (Edward C. Kirkland, *Industry Comes of Age*,
47). Sherman to Hancock, January 9, 1867, Box 28, Department of the
Missouri LR, 1861–67, RG393; *Junction City Union*, May 6 and September
16, 1865.

30. *Junction City Union*, September 23, November 18, and December 16, 1865, and February 10, 1866; 39th Cong., 1st sess., H. Ex. Doc. 76, "Report of General John Pope," 3.

31. SWAR 1865, 848; 40th Cong., 1st sess., S. Ex. Doc. 2, "Protection of Trains," 2; *Junction City Union*, September 23 and November 17, 1866; Post Returns, Fort Riley, June–December 1866.

32. SWAR 1868, 829; SWAR 1869, 391; Easton to AAG Department of the Missouri, May 17, 1867, Box 29, Department of the Missouri LR, 1861–67; *Junction City Union*, July 6 and 13, 1867. Langdon C. Easton, a lieutenant colonel by 1867, had helped select the site of Fort Riley fifteen years earlier.

33. Davidson to Jones, May 16, 1866, vol. 1, Fort Riley LS, RG393; Bradley to Easton, May 29, 1867, Box 29, Department of the Missouri LR, 1861–67.

Chapter 2

1. Charles B. Boynton and T. B. Mason, *Journey Through Kansas*, 107, 112.

2. 33rd Cong., 2nd sess., S. Ex. Doc. 78, "Reports of Explorations," 20. Later in his career, Pope would command the Department of the Missouri, with headquarters at Fort Leavenworth.

3. The discussion that follows is based on the Kansas census of 1855, KSHS; Fort Riley Post Returns, RG94 (NA Microfilm Publication M617, roll 1011); and RPAs of T. L. Brent, J. L. Corley, L. C. Easton, H. Heth, E. A. Ogden, M. T. Polk and A. Sargent for the years 1853–55, RG92, NA.

4. Five years later, after the counties of Davis and Riley had been organized, Davis still lagged behind Riley with 201 farmers (46.3 percent of residents reporting an occupation) to Riley's 261 (52.8 percent). Quotation from Isaac T. Goodnow Diary, December 11, 1856, KSHS.

5. Wages seem to have declined later as the construction boom subsided and the supply of labor increased. In 1857 Riley County farmer Thomas Wells wrote to his relatives in the East, "Labor is in good demand; common laborers getting from $1.75 to $2. per day while masons,

carpenters &c get $2.50 and $3. a day" (Wells, "Letters of a Kansas Pioneer," 316).

6. Government employees worked a ten-hour day. Lieutenant Henry Heth's RPA for November 1853 credits one teamster with "38 hours extra time=3 days 8 hours" that month, and his notes in the "Remarks" column also indicate the observance of the ten-hour day.

7. W. R. Montgomery, RPA December 1854; Montgomery to QMG, November 10, 1854, and January 5, 1855, Box 912, CCF, RG92; Ogden to QMG, July 4 and 31, 1855, Box 911, CCF.

8. *Report of the Adjutant General of the State of Kansas, 1861–65*, 2:334.

9. "Personal Records, Officers Q. M. Corps, Civil war," 1:24–25, a two-volume bound manuscript on the reference shelf in the Military Records consultation room, NA.

10. Anonymous letter dated May 21, 1863, Box 910, CCF.

11. Ibid. Langdon C. Easton was one of the officers who selected the site of Fort Riley in 1852.

12. QMD Registers of Contracts, 1819–1870, 14:186 and 15:28, 30 and 34, RG92; Subsistence Department, Registers of Contracts, 1819–1907, 7:49, 57–58, RG192, NA. The only instance I have found of a contractor's publishing a price for farmers' produce was in the *Junction City Smoky Hill and Republican Union* of August 23, 1862, when Streeter and Strickler, a Junction City firm, needed six thousand bushels of corn for Fort Larned and offered thirty cents a bushel for it. There is no record of Streeter and Strickler's corn contract, but to buy from farmers at thirty cents and to sell to the government at fifty-five cents, if Fort Riley prices were like those at Fort Scott and Fort Leavenworth, represents an 83 percent markup. There is a record, though, of an April 1862 corn contract at Fort Riley in which the government paid only thirty-six cents a bushel (QMD Registers of Contracts, 1819–1870, 13:389).

13. "Personal Records, Officers Q. M. Corps"; Elliott to Bell, September 30, 1865, Box 18, Department of the Missouri LR, 1861–67, RG393.

14. "Personal Records, Officers Q.M. Corps"; Elliott to Bell, September 30, 1865, Department of the Missouri LR, 1861–67; *Junction City Smoky Hill and Republican Union*, February 20, 1862.

15. D. W. Scott, RPA January 1865; manuscript census returns, Ninth District (1855) and Davis County (1865, 1870); *United States Biographical Dictionary. Kansas Volume*, 223–24.

16. D. W. Scott, RPA January 1865; manuscript census returns, Davis County (1860, 1865, 1870); *Junction City Union*, April 15, 1865.

17. D. W. Scott, RPA January 1865. "Boss" is the word used in the report.

18. The inflation figure is from James M. McPherson, *Battle Cry of Freedom*, 447. This sample of teamsters and freighters is too small to permit comparison with Don H. Doyle's finding that the rate of upward mobility in Jacksonville, Illinois, was twice the rate that Stephan Thernstrom found in Boston, but it does tend to support Doyle's observation that the "relationship between property and persistence was reciprocal—those with a 'stake in the community' were inclined to stay, and those who stayed improved their chances of acquiring property" (Doyle, *Social Order of a Frontier Community*, 107).

19. *Junction City Union*, February 3 and 17, 1866.

20. Jones to Sawyer, January 23, 1866, Box 913, CCF. According to the *Junction City Union* of June 17 and July 15, 1865, several volunteer regiments had not been paid for a year; one of them, not for eighteen months.

21. Unless otherwise noted, this paragraph and those that follow are based on the monthly Regimental Returns, RG94, which list all soldiers discharged from companies stationed at Fort Riley; the post quartermasters' monthly RPAs; and manuscript census returns of 1860, 1865, 1870, and 1875 for Davis County. Newspaper lists of Grand Army of the Republic members and manuscript census returns for Riley County show that although many Union army veterans settled there, many more regular soldiers settled in Davis County. The regulars were either discharged at Fort Riley or had served in companies that had been stationed there; the soldiers' stay at the fort had provided their first exposure to the region and, presumably, influenced their decision to settle there.

22. Clarke received his ferry license within six months of his discharge. Davis County Commissioners' Proceedings, October 1,

1860. The *Junction City Union*, August 3, 1867, listed Henderson as senior vice commander of the Grand Army of the Republic.

23. McFarland Family file, Geary County Historical Society.

24. Davis County Commissioners' Proceedings, November 10, 1865; November 8, 1867; November 5, 1869; February 10, 1880; February 10, 1885.

25. Cosgrove's moving his saloon is in the *Junction City Union*, August 28, 1880.

26. Kansas census forms in 1865, 1885, and 1895 listed veteran status, including a former soldier's company and regiment. The *Junction City Union*, September 9, 1882 and June 2, 1883, printed lists of veterans living in Davis County.

27. Quotation from *Junction City Union*, October 7, 1865. Lockstone's cash must have become part of the egg money of many Davis County women. The careers of Lockstone, Rizer, and Wright are encapsulated from the records of the Junction City council and Davis County commissioners and the files of the *Junction City Union* for this period.

28. *Junction City Union*, June 4, 1865.

29. *Junction City Union*, August 19 and September 9, 1865.

30. Post Returns, Fort Riley, 1866–1870; manuscript census of Davis County, 1870 and 1875.

31. *Junction City Union*, July 13, 1867.

Chapter 3

1. Thomas C. Wells, "Letters of a Kansas Pioneer," 317.

2. Quotation from Richard R. Rees, justice of the peace in Jackson County, Missouri, certifying Samuel C. Owens as surety for Aaron Overton and Lewis Jones, January 25, 1838. Office of Indian Affairs LR, 1824–1881, RG75 (NA Microfilm Publication M234, roll 307).

3. Francis P. Prucha, *Sword of the Republic*, 233–48. The average strength of the infantry garrison during the year before the dragoons' arrival had been 93 officers and men; the dragoons' strength dur-

ing their first year at Fort Leavenworth averaged 177; from 1835 to 1839 the garrison numbered about 300 officers and men. Post Returns, Fort Leavenworth, October 1833-July 1839, RG94 (M617, roll 610).

4. QMD Registers of Contracts, 1819–1870, vols. 3–6 (1829–1839), RG92.

5. Prucha, *Broadax and Bayonet*, 156. Abstracts of Bids were compiled by post quartermasters and listed bidders on a contract, the price asked, and sometimes the names of each bidder's sureties. Abstracts of Bids for Fort Leavenworth are in Box 539, CCF, RG92.

6. Manuscript census of 1840 for Clay and Platte Counties, Missouri. A long ton weighs 2,240 pounds.

7. The county histories I consulted are *History of Clay and Platte Counties, Missouri* and *Illustrated Historical Atlas of Clay County, Missouri*. They contain lists of early inhabitants in each township, local officeholders, and members of religious congregations, besides the subsidized autobiographical puffery common to "mug books."

8. QMD Registers of Contracts, 1819–1870, 5:52, 6:82, and 8:264.

9. Prucha, *Sword of the Republic*, 339–48; Grant Foreman, *Indians and Pioneers*, describes intertribal conflict, particularly between the Cherokees and the Osages, from about 1815 on; *Far West*, August 11, 1836; QMD Registers of Contracts, 1819–1870, 7:106–12.

10. QMD Registers of Contracts, 1819–1870, 12:79, 120; *History of Buchanan County*, 853–54; Louise M. Barry, *Beginning of the West*, 961, 985, 1070, 1109. One Kansas settler in 1855 estimated an allowance of one ton of hay per head to "winter" cattle (Wells, "Letters of a Kansas Pioneer," 159).

11. *Junction City Union*, April 1, 1871; Barry, *Beginning of the West*, 719, 791, 894, 1108, 1171; QMD Registers of Contracts, 1819–1870, 12:157.

12. Barry, *Beginning of the West*, 313, 433, 621, 717, 1130; QMD Registers of Contracts, 1819–1870, 12:400.

13. Barry, *Beginning of the West*, 769, 879, 949, 1016, 1059, 1108; *Leavenworth, Kansas Weekly Herald*, March 9, 1855; QMD Registers of Contracts, 1819–1870, 12:204.

14. Horace Greeley's stagecoach was delayed twenty-four

hours by high water in Wildcat Creek, near Manhattan, in May 1859. Greeley, *Overland Journey*, 71.

15. Abstract of Bids, May 16, 1857, and Buford to QMG, June 14, 1857, Box 912, CCF, RG92.

16. J. R. McClure, "Taking the Census," 229–30; G. W. Martin, "Territorial and Military Combine," 377. That Pawnee, the projected capital, lay in the Ninth Census District of 1855 may explain why the concentration of lawyers there was three times as high as in the Tenth District. The Virginia-born P. Z. Taylor was apparently no relation to "Taylor Brothers" of Manhattan, who came from New York.

17. Griffin to QMG, August 25, 1858, Box 912, CCF; QMD Registers of Contracts, 1819–1870, 12:467. In his letter accompanying the abstract of bids, Lieutenant Charles Griffin offered the opinion "that there is no doubt but what treble the amount of corn might be purchased, and that there is no post in the army that possesses such advantages, for Cavalry or Light Artillery, in the way of grazing and drill grounds as this."

18. Albert Griffin, ed., *Illustrated Sketch Book of Riley County*, 53; *Historical Plat Book of Riley County*, 23, 25; *Portrait and Biographical Album of Washington, Clay, and Riley Counties*, 268, 852; *United States Biographical Dictionary*, Kansas Volume, 549.

19. Abstract of Bids for Corn, 1858, Box 912, CCF.

20. Elliott to Bell, September 30, 1865, Box 18, Department of the Missouri LR, 1861–67, RG393; QMD Registers of Contracts, 1819–1870, 16:142.

21. Abstract of Bids for Corn, 1858, Box 912, CCF; Prucha, *Broadax and Bayonet*, 156.

22. Goodnow Diary, November 27 and 30, 1855, KSHS. Perry's 1854 contract is recorded in QMD Registers of Contracts, 1819–1870, 12:120.

23. There was 50 percent deflation during the decade after the Civil War, a further 20 percent in 1875–85, and another 6 percent decline in the ten years after that. Edward M. Coffman, *Old Army*, 265. Statistics for 1864 and 1868 are in QMD Registers of Contracts, 1819–1870, 16:65, 79 and 17:43–44, 47. Thomas Dixon's contracts are in QMD Registers of Contracts, 1871–1880, 2:59.

24. Figures for 1866 are in QMD Registers of Contracts, 1819–1870, 16:154–55, 164, 166, and 168; the 1890 corn contract is in QMD Registers of Contracts, 1881–1912, 4:126.

25. QMD Registers of Contracts, 1819–1870, 15:34, 50; 16:142.

26. QMD Registers of Contracts, 1819–1870, 16:150, 154, 213, 215, 223, 241; 17:43, 64, 74, 78, 79, 89, 93, 115, 123, 214.

27. Mattie M. Coons, *Pioneer Days in Kansas*, 35–36. In light of Coons's anecdote, a few sentences from G. W. Higinbotham's "mug book" entry are worth quoting. "By the application of rare good judgment and faithful attention to the details of business, Mr. Higinbotham has enjoyed almost uninterrupted prosperity. . . . With a strong native sense of justice, and large social qualities, he takes a deep interest in all movements for the public good, and actively furthers them. He is exceptionally liberal toward rivals in business; never seeks to monopolize the avenues to wealth, but seems to rejoice in the prosperity of others" (*United States Biographical Dictionary*, Kansas Volume, 39). This style of writing belongs to the same realm as horoscopes and fortune cookies.

28. *Manhattan Independent*, August 17, 1863; *United States Biographical Dictionary, Kansas Volume*, 143; *Report of the Adjutant General of the State of Kansas, 1861–65*, 1:1058; censuses of Riley County for 1860 and 1865.

29. *Manhattan Standard*, May 22, 1869; *Manhattan Independent*, August 11, 1866, September 22, 1866, and August 10, 1867. Henry Booth had been a sergeant in Company G of the Eleventh Kansas when Adams commanded it. When the regiment expanded and Company L was formed, Booth became its captain. Membership in a local unit of the Union army could confer some of the same advantages that, say, a Rhodes Scholarship can today.

30. *Manhattan Standard*, November 28, 1868; QMD Registers of Contracts , 1819–1870, 16:229, 241. Beginning in 1868, Elliott served as agent for the lands that had been granted to the Kansas Pacific Railroad, and from 1873 to 1883 he was agent for the state agricultural college lands (*Portrait and Biographical Album of Washington, Clay, and Riley Counties*, 490).

31. QMD Registers of Contracts, 1819–1870, 17:8, 10, 13–14, 27, 33, 43–45, 47–48, 53–54.

32. The tenth contractor, A. H. Whitcomb, moved from Grasshopper Falls, in Jefferson County, to Lawrence, on the line of the Kansas Pacific, sometime between 1865 and 1870.

Chapter 4

1. According to Robert R. Dykstra, rural taxpayers were irritated at having to pay for criminal prosecutions in the county seats (*Cattle Towns*, 184–85). The discontent ran far deeper than that. In 1873 a Farmer's Convention declared, "[T]he practice of voting municipal bonds is pernicious in its effects, and will inevitably bring bankruptcy and ruin upon the people, and we are therefore opposed to all laws allowing the issuance of such bonds" (James E. Boyle, *Financial History of Kansas*, 60). My assertion about "every county commission" is based on an examination of the original county records of Clay (1866–79), Davis (1856–94), Dickinson (1861–79), and Riley (1857–87) Counties at the courthouses or county office buildings in Clay Center, Junction City, Abilene, and Manhattan, and on transcriptions of the records of Cloud (1868–75), Ottawa (1867–80), and Saline (1868–87) Counties by the WPA Federal Writers' Project at KSHS.

2. George R. Taylor, *Transportation Revolution*, 79.

3. *Junction City Smoky Hill and Republican Union*, May 15, 1862. The name of the railroad was actually the Leavenworth, Pawnee & Western, but the town of Pawnee had been defunct for more than six years by the spring of 1862.

4. *Kansas City Western Journal of Commerce*, January 2, 1858. The Irish bishop George Berkeley wrote the poem, "On the Prospect of Planting Arts and Learning in America," which contains the line, "Westward the course of empire takes its way."

5. Timothy R. Mahoney, "Urban History in a Regional Context," 329, 333; Charles N. Glaab, *Kansas City and the Railroads*, 43–44.

6. Alfred D. Chandler, *Visible Hand*, 81; William Cronon discusses river and lake navigation in *Nature's Metropolis*, 86.

7. *Manhattan Express*, September 24 and October 1, 1859.

8. *Leavenworth Times*, March 30 and May 18 and 21,

1860; *Manhattan Express*, April 7, 1860. Russell agreed to a one-third discount if his trip took less than forty days; he may have received as little as $2,300.

9. *Leavenworth Times*, May 23 and June 2, 1860; *Manhattan Express*, May 25, 1860; Manhattan City Council Minutes, May 28, 1860. The editor, Charles F. deVivaldi, did indeed "have City property"—according to the 1860 census, twenty-four thousand dollars worth. Since no records of the Junction City Council before 1871 have survived, it has been impossible to check the accuracy of deVivaldi's statement about their pledge of municipal bonds.

10. *Leavenworth Times*, May 21, 1860; *Manhattan Express*, May 26, 1860. Patricia N. Limerick writes, "Nothing so undermines the Western claim to a tradition of independence as this matter of federal support to Western development" (*Legacy of Conquest*, 82).

11. *Leavenworth, Kansas Weekly Herald*, September 22, 1854. On the memory of old-timers and the role of early settlers' associations in shaping the group recollection that colors so much local history, see Clyde A. Milner II, "The Shared Memory of Montana's Pioneers."

12. *Leavenworth Times*, June 2, 6, and 16, July 23 and August 28, 1860; *Junction City Statesman*, June 30, 1860.

13. *Manhattan Express*, April 20, 1861; *Junction City Smoky Hill and Republican Union*, June 5 and 12, 1862; *Atchison Freedom's Champion*, March 23 and 30, 1865. Historians do not devote much space to the Smoky Hill route, and their opinions conflict. According to Henry P. Walker, the Smoky Hill route offered poor water, wood, and grass, but his source is a Council Grove newspaper of 1863, and Council Grove was, of course, interested in the Arkansas River route (*Wagonmasters*, 42). William E. Lass writes that the Smoky Hill "was used briefly by emigrants but was not at all attractive for conventional freighting" (*From the Missouri to the Great Salt Lake*, 83). Oscar O. Winther, on the other hand, says the route "gained great popularity with staging firms and wagon freighters." (*Transportation Frontier*, 4).

14. On the Santa Fe trade, see Josiah Gregg, *Commerce of the Prairies*, 25; for the fixed costs of railroads, Cronon, *Nature's Metropolis*, 84–87. New Mexican wool delivered to Kansas City amounted to 865,000 pounds in 1857 and more than 950,000 in 1862 (Walker, *Wagonmasters*,

149). During the 1850s, the number of sheep in New Mexico (almost all in settlements along the line of the Rio Grande) increased from 377,271 to 830,116. Robert W. Frazer suggests that the army's presence may have provided greater security for the flocks (*Forts and Supplies*, 187). Readers of Robert M. Utley's *Frontiersmen in Blue*, particularly 165–74, might conclude that New Mexico's security depended more on the peaceable disposition of the Navajos than on the army's efforts.

15. Quotation in Glaab, *Kansas City and the Railroads*, 57. On page 39, Glaab mentions the difficulty experienced by the Pacific Railroad of Missouri in collecting money from the subscribers to its issue of stock. The charter of the Kansas River Navigation Company is in *Laws of the Territory of Kansas*, 167. The same volume contains the charters of the Central Gulf Railroad, the Atchison & Fort Riley, the Missouri River & Rocky Mountain, the Atchison & Palmetto City, the Prairie City & Missouri State Line, the Atchison & Lecompton, and the St. Joseph & Topeka, all of which specify that 10 percent of the subscribed stock must have been "actually paid" before the company's organization could proceed further. Among the organizers of the Kansas River Navigation Company were Charles A. Perry, the army contractor who owned the steamer *Excel*; and William F. Dyer, the builder of a bridge on the road between Fort Leavenworth and Fort Riley and president of the Osawkee town company.

16. Organizers of railroad companies are named in the corporate charters published in *Statutes of the Territory of Kansas*, 904–27. I checked the names against the index in Louise M. Barry, *Beginning of the West*. Names of organizers will be followed by page references to Barry's work, as: Duff, 1119; Passmore, 1152.

17. Findlay, 343, 1131, 1173; Grover, 1204; Rively, 1108, 1171, 1226–27. H. Craig Miner and William E. Unrau have pointed out that concentration on the affairs of a single railroad or of a single tribe will reveal only a fragment of the railroad organizers' activities. "To say there were conflicts of interest is merely to scratch the surface. They used the multiplicity of their interlocking interest to conceal their precise gain or loss and to befuddle Indians and government clerks" (*End of Indian Kansas*, 35).

18. Boone, 130, 350; Chouteau, 102; Stinson, 502, 798, 975.

19. Johnson, 179; Lykins, 204. Glaab calls Lykins one of "the most prominent of the early Kansas City railroad advocates. First president of the Chamber of Commerce, president of the Mechanics' Bank, commission agent, real-estate developer, Dr. Lykins by the mid-fifties was eminently a man of affairs" (*Kansas City and the Railroads*, 30). Glaab also mentions the effect of "Bleeding Kansas" on the economic growth of Kansas City (46). For the effect of the Panic of 1857 on railroad building, see Taylor, *Transportation Revolution*, 350.

20. Robert G. Athearn, *William Tecumseh Sherman and the Settlement of the West*, 18, 20; *Junction City Union*, September 16, 1865 and October 13, 1866; Sherman to Hancock, January 9, 1867, Box 23, Department of the Missouri LR, 1861–67, RG393. Until 1869 the railroad through the Kansas River valley was called the Union Pacific Eastern Division, but I have called it Kansas Pacific throughout.

21. SWAR 1865, 848; Richard N. Ellis, "General Pope's Report on the West, 1866," 354. Pope's report first appeared as 39th Cong., 1st sess., H. Ex. Doc. 76.

22. Quotations from *Junction City Union*, June 22, 1867 and May 1, 1869. For mention of Chicago, see the *Union*, April 20, 1867; *Manhattan Standard*, April 17, 1869; and an article from the *Chicago Republican* that was reprinted in the *Pottawatomie Gazette*, January 1, 1868: "It is now a matter of certainty that in the further development and prosperity of Kansas, Chicago is more interested than any other city."

23. Manhattan City Council Minutes, November 15, 1865 and July 27, 1867. The names of Manhattan's city parks show that residents have always taken the town's name seriously and that automobile bumper stickers advertising it as "The Little Apple" are no aberration. Junction City's surviving municipal records go back only to 1871, so there is no record of the inducements the city offered the Kansas Pacific to place its machine shops there. Employment statistics are from the federal manuscript census of Davis County for 1870.

24. Boyle, *Financial History of Kansas*, 57; Kansas Board of Railroad Commissioners, *First Annual Report*, 43, 45.

25. Kansas Corporation Charters, 1:595, KSHS.

26. Riley County Commissioners' Proceedings, May 1, 1869; *Manhattan Standard*, May 8, 1869.

27. *Manhattan Standard*, June 5 and 12, 1869. Shortly afterward, Henry Booth became post trader (sutler) at Fort Larned and ceased to take an active part in Manhattan's railroad projects for a while.

28. *Pottawatomie Gazette*, June 11, 18, and 25, 1869. The Pottawatomie County census of 1865 lists Sprague's age as twenty-three. He was not married, lived with his parents, and owned land valued at $150.

29. *Manhattan, Kansas Radical*, July 20 and December 21, 1867.

30. *Manhattan Standard*, August 7 and December 18, 1869; *Manhattan Nationalist*, December 23, 1870. The Manhattan & Nebraska was to run up the Big Blue River to the state line; the Manhattan & Southern was to connect with the Missouri, Kansas & Texas.

31. *Manhattan Independent*, October 5, 1867, and May 23, 1868; *Manhattan, Kansas Radical*, May 25, 1867; *Manhattan Standard*, June 5, 1869, February 5, 1870. *Proceedings of the M. W. Grand Lodge of the Ancient, Free & Accepted Masons, of Kansas, 1871*, 157. Higinbotham's running as first pro-, then antilicense does not necessarily indicate duplicity or opportunism. In 1869 the name of Samuel G. Hoyt, who was then (and continued to serve as) county clerk, appeared on both tickets for city council. Hoyt was elected with 203 votes, nearly double the tally of any of the candidates who enjoyed the backing of only one faction. Political opinions diverged again during the presidential election of 1872, when Griffin, Higinbotham, and Purcell campaigned for Grant's reelection while Adams, Elliott, and Gove helped form a Greeley Club—along with Higinbotham's brother William and W. H. Fagley, an outspoken opponent of railroad bond issues.

32. Quoted in Glaab, *Kansas City and the Railroads*, 54.

33. *Manhattan Standard*, May 22, 1869; *Manhattan Nationalist*, July 14 and November 3, 1871; Riley County Commissioners' Proceedings, July 12, 1871.

34. Riley County Commissioners' Proceedings, November 10, 1871, September 1, 1873, and September 7, 1874. On refunding the bonds, ibid., from January 6, 1880, to November 8, 1884.

35. SWAR 1882, 10; 1883, 45–46, 105. On the army's role in the strikes of 1877, and the effect on military thought and troop dispositions, see Jerry M. Cooper, *Army and Civil Disorder*.

Chapter 5

1. Jones to AAG Department of the Missouri, January 23, 1866, Box 913, CCF, RG92, NA.

2. Robert G. Athearn, *William Tecumseh Sherman and the Settlement of the West*, 186, 194; Paul A. Hutton, *Phil Sheridan and His Army*, 120–21 and 174–75; and Robert M. Utley, *Frontier Regulars*, 93–94, all emphasize the importance of supply routes, and of railroads in particular.

3. Post Returns, Fort Riley, June 1867, October and November 1876, RG94 (NA Microfilm Publication M617, roll 1012). Other troop movements by rail were recorded in June, July, and September 1877; April and September 1878; and May and October 1879 (roll 1013).

4. *Junction City Union*, May 18, 1872.

5. Charles J. Kappler, *Indian Affairs. Laws and Treaties*, 2:988, 1002. The Fort Laramie treaty ended the war with the Sioux along the Bozeman Trail to Montana. Sherman favored abandonment of the forts along the Bozeman Trail as soon as the Union Pacific reached Utah, opening a shorter, safer route to the goldfields. SWAR 1868, 3.

6. Pope's reports in SWAR 1870, 11 (quotation); SWAR 1872, 46; SWAR 1873, 43. The Cheyenne and Arapaho hunts are mentioned in their agents' reports in CIA 1871, 885, 887; CIA 1872, 633–34; CIA 1873, 589.

7. SWAR 1865, 113; SWAR 1869, 391; SWAR 1870, 248; SWAR 1872, 47.

8. Fort Hays lay 166 miles, and Fort Dodge 86 miles, north of Camp Supply. John S. Billings, *Report on Barracks and Hospitals*, 261. Sheridan's late-autumn campaign was in retaliation for Cheyenne raids in the valleys of the Saline and Solomon Rivers in August 1868. Although Kit Carson had commanded New Mexico volunteers in a winter campaign against the Navajos in 1863–64, Sheridan's campaign required logistical support on a scale made possible only by the railroad in order to keep eight hundred regular soldiers, mounted on grain-fed horses, in the field.

9. Post Returns, Fort Hays, February 1868–December 1869 (M617, roll 469). Post returns during the late 1860s were more complete than those kept during the Civil War but less so than those from the

1870s and later. The newly expanded army of 1866–69 contained many officers whose only military experience was in the volunteers during the war; volunteers tended to keep records haphazardly or not at all.

10. Post Returns, Fort Dodge and Fort Hays, January 1872–December 1873 (M617, rolls 319 and 469).

11. The texts of these orders, or summaries of them, were published in the *Junction City Union*, March 10, 1866, and March 16 and May 4, 1867. The number of teamsters employed at Fort Riley is listed in the Post Returns, April–December 1865 and May–September 1866. Quotation from Sherman to Rawlins, August 17 and 24, 1866, is in 39th Cong., 2nd sess., H. Ex. Doc. 23, "Protection Across the Continent," 3, 7.

12. Advertisements for passenger service on the Kansas Pacific in the fall of 1867 show that it took five hours and thirty minutes to travel between Junction City and Ellsworth; three years later, with the line open all the way to Denver, the trip took only four and a half hours (Junction City Union, November 23, 1867, and September 10, 1870).

13. *Junction City Union*, July 13, 1867; Ingalls to Meigs, July 2, 1866, and Meigs to Sherman, July 11, 1866, Box 910, CCF.

14. Endorsement by L. C. Easton, August 1866, 21, Box 910, CCF.

15. Post Returns, Fort Riley, September 1865–March 1869 (M617, roll 1012).

16. Based on biographical sketches of Schofield in Heitman, *Historical Register*, and Mark M. Boatner, *Civil War Dictionary*.

17. John M. Schofield, *Forty-six Years in the Army*, 426. When Schofield commanded the Military Division of the Missouri, he set forth his views in a letter to the adjutant general, August 29, 1884, supporting another attempt to set up a school for light artillery (Schofield Papers, LC).

18. Schofield to Hamilton, June 1, 1869, Fort Riley Telegrams Received, RG393, NA. Hamilton, a major in the First Artillery, was Fort Riley's commanding officer during the artillery school's brief existence.

19. Data from fifteen muster rolls for Batteries K, First Artillery; A, Second Artillery; and C, Third Artillery, dated between April 30, 1869, and February 28, 1871. Muster Rolls of Regular Army Organiza-

tions, RG94. Three of the muster rolls showed more than 25 percent of the men assigned to these tasks; three, as few as 10 percent.

20. Hamilton to AAG Department of the Missouri, June 4, 1869, and Hamilton to AG, August 7, 1869, both in vol. 2, Fort Riley LS, RG393; Easton to AAG Department of the Missouri, May 4, 1869, Department of the Missouri, Registers of LR, 1868–98, 3:44, RG393.

21. David A. Dary, *Buffalo Book*, 94–95, lists several attempts to make leather of buffalo hides. Before the 1870s the only commercial demand was for tanned buffalo skins with the hair on, as robes.

22. Fort Sill figures in William T. Hagan, *United States–Comanche Relations*, and Fort Reno in Donald J. Berthrong, *Cheyenne and Arapaho Ordeal*. On the cost of these operations, see the remarks of W. T. Sherman in SWAR 1879, 6; John Pope in SWAR 1882, 99, and SWAR 1883, 130; and C. C. Augur in SWAR 1884, 118–19.

23. Carl C. Rister, *Land Hunger*. Rister's account is adulatory; for instance, "Payne's indomitable will and amazing resourcefulness enabled him to weather every storm" (143).

24. Schurz to McCrary, May 1, 1879, in 46th Cong., 1st sess., S. Ex. Doc. 20, "Occupation of Indian Territory by White Settlers," 16–18.

25. Four companies of the Twenty-second Infantry took a lake steamer from Fort Mackinac to Chicago and continued from there to Kansas by rail. Sheridan to Sherman, May 7, 1879, in "Occupation of Indian Territory by White Settlers," 30. *Coffeyville Journal*, May 17 and 31 and June 7, 1879. Report of F. H. Weaver, Southern Ute Agency, August 18, 1878, in CIA 1878, 513.

26. CIA 1880, 93; CIA 1881, 55; CIA 1883, 147; CIA 1884, 33–34; SWAR 1883, 70, and SWAR 1884, 118–19. These last two were the annual reports of John Pope and C. C. Augur, Pope's successor as commander of the Department of the Missouri, whose troops were directly involved in restraining and removing the Boomers. See also 47th Cong., 1st sess., H. Ex. Doc. 145, "Prevention of Trespass on Indian Lands," 2; and 48th Cong., 1st sess., H. Ex. Doc. 17, "Trespass on Indian Lands," 2.

27. *Arkansas City Republican*, February 28 and March 7, 1885.

28. *Kiowa Herald*, August 20 and 27 and September 3 and 10, 1885.

29. Post Returns, Fort Riley, July–August 1877 and November 1880–October 1881; *Army and Navy Journal*, December 4, 1880. Jerry M. Cooper, *Army and Civil Disorder*, 59–60, mentions the movement of troops to St. Louis from as far away as Colorado during the railroad strikes of 1877.

30. About the Utes, Sherman remarked, "Their management is complicated by the fact that their country is known to possess mineral deposits, which attract a bold and adventurous class of white men" (SWAR 1879, 7). When the Utes finally left Colorado, John Pope wrote, "The whites who had collected in view of their removal were so eager and so unrestrained by common decency that it was absolutely necessary to use military force to keep them off the reservation until the Indians were fairly gone" (SWAR 1881, 116). Estimates of Navajo population and sheep are in the agents' reports in CIA 1881, 195, and CIA 1883, 180. In Edward H. Spicer's opinion, "The original land arrangement simply was not sufficient to support the increasing numbers of Navajos and livestock" (*Cycles of Conquest*, 222). Richard White comments, "Reservation boundaries had little immediate impact on Navajo life" (*Roots of Dependency*, 216). The results of the cavalry patrols are in SWAR 1883, 139.

31. Quotation from the military novelist Charles King's aptly entitled volume of essays, *Trials of a Staff Officer*, 12. Alfred D. Chandler dismisses the idea of the army as a model for business organization, although he acknowledges the Ordnance Department and the Corps of Engineers as "two of the very few professionally manned, hierarchical organizations in antebellum America" (*Visible Hand*, 95). At least one late nineteenth-century army officer, though, saw railroad managers as models for military professionals; he is quoted in Peter Karsten, "Armed Progressives," 221–22.

32. SWAR 1879, 12; Department of the Missouri, QM Registers of LR, 29:116–18, RG393; quotations from Pope's annual report in SWAR 1880, 83.

33. Department of the Missouri, QM Registers of LR, 30:113–14 and 31:105–8; quotation from 31:106.

34. Department of the Missouri, QM Registers of LR,

40:233, 236; Department of the Missouri, Register of LR, 1868–98, 46:178, 184, 265, and 52:55, 132; QM Department of the Missouri to AAG Department of the Missouri, May 18, 1883, Box 115, Department of the Missouri LR, 1868–98, RG393. Darlis A. Miller discusses the effect of drought on the New Mexico hay crop in *Soldiers and Settlers*, 102–103.

35. Quotations from Department of the Missouri, QM Register of LR, 31:108 and 32:182, 184.

36. SWAR 1882, 12; SWAR 1883, 45–46. Sherman must have been thinking of the railroad strikes that had occurred six years earlier when he wrote that railroads "require a station, with siding, every ten miles, water stations at convenient and short intervals, and costly repair-shops every hundred miles. These constantly call for protection of the military usually posted on or near the lines" (SWAR 1883, 46).

Chapter 6

1. Joseph G. Baldwin, *Flush Times of Alabama and Mississippi*, 87.

2. A copy of the settlers' letter, dated September 4, 1854, is in William R. Montgomery's General Court Martial Case File, HH566, RG153, NA. Unless otherwise attributed, the following account is based on the more than four hundred manuscript pages of testimony and exhibits that make up HH566.

3. Page to CO Fort Riley, March 21, 1854; Post Orders No. 84, Fort Riley, June 14, 1854; Montgomery to Winship, February 20, 1855; all in HH566. Davis to Hitchcock, April 13, 1853, in Lynda L. Crist, ed., *Papers of Jefferson Davis*, 5:7. "Even now," Montgomery complained to Winship about the liquor traders, "individuals engaged in that baneful traffic are obtruders upon the reserve, and will compel me to eject them by force."

4. Wilson et al. to Montgomery, September 4, 1854; Montgomery to Wilson et al., September 20, 1854; both in HH566. Wilson was the post sutler at Fort Riley; another of the signers was his clerk; a third was the civilian clerk employed by the post quartermaster; and a fourth was in the neighborhood because of a contract to furnish hay for the fort.

5. "Constitution of the Pawnee Association," November 25, 1854; Post Orders No. 217, Fort Riley, December 25, 1854; both in HH566.

6. Christopher Phillips, *Damned Yankee*, 81–103, covers Lyon's service at Fort Riley and his conflict with Montgomery.

7. Post Return, Fort Riley, May 1855, RG94 (NA Microfilm Publication M617, roll 1011).

8. George W. Martin, "Territorial and Military Combine," 370–73; Isaac T. Goodnow Diary, June 11, 12, and 23, 1855, KSHS. Post surgeons could treat private patients in their spare time and sometimes treated indigent civilians at government expense.

9. Paul W. Gates, *Fifty Million Acres*, 39–40; James A. Rawley, *Race and Politics*, 91–92; Miner and Unrau, *End of Indian Kansas*, 20–24. Martin, "Territorial and Military Combine," 371. Martin quotes the *New York Times*, January 9, 1856, to the effect that Pawnee was a settlement of Pennsylvanians and that Montgomery's court martial came about because he, too, was a Pennsylvanian.

10. 33rd Cong., 2nd sess., H. Ex. Doc. 50, "Delaware Indians," 19; *Kansas Weekly Herald*, February 16, 1855. A text with which that generation of West Point graduates should have been familiar was William Paley's *Principles of Moral and Political Philosophy*, which was used at the U.S. Military Academy from 1820 to 1843. Paley wrote, "As the right of property depends upon the law of the land, it seems to follow, that a man has a right to keep and take every thing which the law will allow him to keep and take; which in many cases will authorize the most manifest and flagitious chicanery" (91).

11. Ogden entered West Point in 1827, a year before Davis graduated, so they may have become acquainted there. They served together at Fort Crawford, Wisconsin, in the early 1830s, when both were lieutenants in the First Infantry Regiment (*Davis Papers*, 5:95n; CIA 1854, 217).

12. Davis to Pierce, December 16, 1854, *Papers of Jefferson Davis*, 5:94; the charge against Montgomery is in HH566.

13. Rita G. Napier, "Squatter City," 107–8; Post Returns, Fort Riley, September and October 1854, May 1855 (M617, roll 1011).

14. The tenth Fort Riley officer was an assistant surgeon

commissioned in 1849. The Fort Leavenworth officers had opportunities to talk to Ogden, whose duties took him to Fort Riley from time to time, and Lieutenant Marshall T. Polk, AAQM and ACS at Fort Riley, who visited Fort Leavenworth several times on official business in 1854 (Fort Riley Post Returns, July, October, and November 1854). Jefferson Davis entered West Point in 1824, a year before Montgomery graduated. Personal antipathy cannot be discounted as a possible motive for Davis's actions in 1855.

15. Starr to his father, August 1, 1854. Frederick Starr, Jr. Papers, Western Historical Manuscript Collection, University of Missouri at Columbia.

16. The fulsome description of Rich occurs on page 7 of *Papers Relative to the Proceedings of a Court Martial*, an attempt to exculpate Montgomery and reinstate him in the army. Although Lecompte was not a member of the Pawnee Association, Robert C. Miller may have represented a proslavery viewpoint. He and three other men with interests in Leavenworth signed a letter that appeared in the *Missouri Republican*, July 31, 1854: "To Missourians especially we would say, do not leave the best portion of the Territory to be taken up by thieves and paupers to be exported from the sinks of abolitionism" ("Delaware Indians," 13). "Sinks" was a nineteenth-century term for "latrines." The signers of the letter to Montgomery who did not join the association were E. Francis Mezick, Wilson's clerk in the sutler's store; John Heth, brother of Lieutenant Henry Heth, the AAQM and ACS at Fort Riley from November 1853 to April 1854, who had come west for his health; and Anthony Grable, whom I have been unable to identify.

17. Kansas Corporation Charters, 1:14, 283–84, KSHS. The original incorporators capitalized the firm at $30,000; in February 1867, when they began intense activity, they added five more associates, capitalizing the new corporation at $160,000. Quotations from *Junction City Union*, November 21, 1868.

18. *Congressional Globe*, 39th Cong., 2nd sess., 1867, 37, 1868; *Junction City Union*, November 21, 1868. Another state senator, William S. Blakely, a former Junction City resident, also owned stock in the Bridge Company (*Kansas Supreme Court Reports*, 20:406). In the Kansas Senate, the bill was read twice, referred to the judiciary commit-

tee, received a third reading and passed, all during the morning session on February 25, the day before the legislature's fifty-day limit expired (*Senate Journal of the Legislative Assembly of the State of Kansas*, 771–72, 778).

19. *Junction City Union*, March 23, 1867; *Leavenworth Times*, March 6, 1867. The *Leavenworth Daily Conservative*, December 22, 1867, was also envious of Junction City: "The United States having established a precedent in Kansas, by devoting a portion of the Fort Riley reservation to construct this bridge, why cannot Leavenworth insist on a reduction of the Fort Leavenworth reservation, and obtain aid in bridging the Missouri?" Lewis Atherton's dictum is clearly applicable to the *Union's* observation about the interests of Junction City's residents: "Every country town had an inner circle whose own personal interests were so tightly interwoven with those of the community at large that one cannot determine where self-interest ended and public spirit began" *Main Street on the Middle Border*, 23.

20. *Topeka Weekly Leader*, February 28, 1867; *Manhattan Kansas Radical*, March 2, 1867; *Congressional Globe*, ibid. "Bills pass with very little consideration, or are rejected, with or without cause, according to the humor members happen to be in at the time. . . . The late Legislature was far behind any of its predecessors of which we have any knowledge, in capacity, and there have been none that could not show as fair a record for integrity" (*Leavenworth Daily Conservative*, February 26 and 28, 1867).

21. *Leavenworth Daily Conservative*, December 22, 1867, quoted in *Junction City Union*, December 28, 1867.

22. *Junction City Union*, April 24, 1869, March 22, 1873, and August 25, 1877; *Junction City Tribune*, August 25, 1877. The state attorney general alleged that the Bridge Company "has neglected, failed, and omitted to keep up and maintain said bridge in good condition and repair" (State v. Republican River Bridge Company, *Kansas Supreme Court Reports*, 20:408).

23. SWAR 1877, 218–20.

24. SWAR 1877, 218–20; *Junction City Union*, August 25, 1877, and August 15, 1885.

25. *Kansas Supreme Court Reports*, 20:413.

26. The occupations of William K. Bartlett, Robert

McBratney, Daniel Mitchell, and Philemon Z. Taylor are in the 1860 federal census of Davis County; the township and section maps signed by Mitchell are at KSHS. Bartlett, McBratney, and Taylor officiated at the Lincoln memorial service; *Junction City Union*, April 22, 1865.

27. Since the extant municipal records of Junction City go back only to 1871, this paragraph is based on the Proceedings of the Davis County Commissioners, 1860–71, and election returns published in the *Junction City Union*, 1866–71, every April (municipal elections) and November (county and state elections). By 1871 the Republican River Bridge Company had accomplished its purpose and was about to vanish quietly.

28. *Manhattan Express*, October 6 and 20, 1860; *Junction City Union*, April 15 and November 4, 1865, May 26, 1866, January 26 and February 9, 1867; Kansas Corporation Charters, 1:303, KSHS.

29. *Junction City Union*, November 28, 1868. "These depredations are causing great injury to the reservation," Fort Riley's commanding officer wrote to department headquarters in 1874. "It is impossible for me to prevent it" with a garrison numbering nine enlisted men. Whistler to AAG Department of the Missouri, December 22, 1874, Fort Riley LR by Endorsement, RG 393, NA. "Depredations" was the same word used to describe the raids of hostile Indians. One commanding officer, indeed, requested "a new fence, to protect us from raids from the south bank of the river . . . a constant source of annoying duty, since within an hour after being driven across the river, the stock returns, and are probably driven back by the owners" (Forsyth to AAG Department of the Missouri, February 16, 1889, vol. 7, Fort Riley LS, RG393).

30. Terry G. Jordan admits that backwoods culture was "flawed in diverse ways and perhaps partly responsible for certain ecological problems that plague us yet today," but remains awed by the speed with which backwoodsmen swept out of Pennsylvania to cover the eastern half of the United States (Jordan and Matti Kaups, *American Backwoods Frontier*, 62). Confusion, or willful refusal to distinguish, between "public lands" and "reservations" has persisted into and throughout the twentieth century; see Peter Iverson, *When Indians Became Cowboys*, especially 109–15.

31. *Junction City Smoky Hill and Republican Union*, February 20, 1862; *Union*, June 4, 1887.

32. Hatch to AAG Department of the Missouri, November 18, 1882, and AG to CG Department of the Missouri, December 16, 1882, Box 93, AGO Reservation File, RG94. Endorsement by E. Swift, October 11, 1887, on Forsyth to AAG Department of the Missouri, October 9, 1887, Box 143, Department of the Missouri LR, 1868–98, RG393.

33. Forsyth to AAG Department of the Missouri, October 9, 1887, Box 143, Department of the Missouri LR, 1868–98; *Junction City Union*, June 25, 1887; Forsyth to AAG Department of the Missouri, July 15, 1890, vol. 8, Fort Riley LS. The average number of cavalry and artillery horses at Fort Riley rose from 432 in 1889 to 585 in 1894; these numbers do not include animals belonging to the Quartermaster Department (Post Returns, Fort Riley, January, April, July and October 1889–1894 [M617, roll 1014]).

34. Endorsements of E. Hatch and J. D. Bingham on Henderson to Bingham, May 30, 1882, Box 109, Department of the Missouri LR, 1868–98. Henderson was one of the discharged cavalry troopers mentioned in chapter 2 who settled near Fort Riley in the 1850s. He had become a substantial farmer by 1882. On the troublesome growth of "custom," in 1881 Fort Riley's commanding officer pointed out that "the people have taken wood from the reservation without hinderance for so long a time that it may be considered by them to be a sanctioned privilege" (Hughes to AAG Department of the Missouri, December 14, 1881, vol. 3, Fort Riley LS).

35. Forsyth to AAG Department of the Missouri, September 29 and October 11, 1887, and endorsement of W. W. Robinson, October 6, 1887, on James Brumbough's "Statement relative to cutting Hay on reservation," Box 143, Department of the Missouri LR, 1868–98. As for the quality of hay, in 1885 the post quartermaster "insisted on all hay being thoroughly dried for at least one half day upon the ground and then stacked in stacks of not less than 8 tons to undergo a sweat and be cured before being put in large ricks in the hay yard" (Department of the Missouri, QM Registers of LR, 40:245, RG393).

36. AAG Department of the Missouri to CO Fort Riley, October 11, 1887, vol. 48, and June 17, 1889, vol. 51, Department of the Missouri LS, 1869–98, RG393. Schmidt returned to Kansas after the Civil War and was farming in Davis County by 1875, according to that year's

census. His salary was the same as that of the firemen (stokers) at the pump house and the mess hall. The post blacksmith received sixty dollars a month; teamsters, thirty. E. B. Fuller, RPA June 1889, and S. R. Jones, RPA August 1894, RG92.

37. Forsyth to AAG Department of the Missouri, March 2, 1888, vol. 5, and Forsyth to Perry, November 25, 1888, vol. 6, Fort Riley LS.

38. Forsyth to Mullins, December 8, 1887, vol. 5, Fort Riley LS; Mullins to Forsyth, December 12, 1887, Box 143, and Forsyth to AAG Department of the Missouri, March 2, 1888, Box 145, Department of the Missouri LR, 1868–98. On public health issues, see William A. Dobak, " 'One of the Nastiest Rivers That I Know Of.' "

39. Department of the Missouri, QM Register of LR (unnumbered vol. for 1895), 152. Forsyth to AG, January 2, 1889, vol. 7, Fort Riley LS.

Chapter 7

1. *Congressional Record*, 46th Cong., 2nd sess., 1880, 10, 654, and 47th Cong., 1st sess., 1881, 13, 100. Anderson, a Presbyterian minister, had served as president of the state agricultural college from 1873 to 1879. His letters, and many of his sermons, are part of the Anderson Family Papers, KSHS. Unfortunately, they include only one letter that dates from his years in Congress, written shortly after his arrival in Washington in 1879. Quotation from Anderson to Martin, January 9, 1884, George W. Martin Collection, KSHS. This letter, and one quoted later in this chapter, contain the only admissions of impropriety or furtive conduct among all those that I have read.

2. *Junction City Union*, January 18, 1873. The *Army and Navy Journal*, November 5, 1887, commented that the establishment of Fort Sheridan "will be worth columns to the scribblers flooding the country with stories about general alarm here over the impending execution of the Anarchists. It is needless to say that there is no connection between the Government taking formal possession of a piece of its property and the hanging of seven criminals 20 miles distant."

3. SWAR 1882, 10–14. As for accommodating local interests, Sherman had grumbled years earlier that "people west of the Missouri river look to the army as their legitimate field of profit and support and the quicker they are undeceived the better for all" (Sherman to Rawlins, September 30, 1866, in 39th Cong., 2nd sess., H. Ex. Doc. 23, "Protection Across the Continent," 18–19).

4. Sheridan's career is sketched in Mark M. Boatner, *The Civil War Dictionary*, 747–48, as well as Paul A. Hutton, *Phil Sheridan and His Army*.

5. SWAR 1884, 50; Sheridan to Endicott, June 5, 1885, and Sheridan to Schofield, June 11, 1885, in Sheridan Papers, LC. Sheridan had passed through Fort Riley occasionally during his years in command of the Military Division of the Missouri; the visit in 1885 was not his first.

6. SWAR 1884, 105; Schofield to AG, August 29 and November 18, 1884, in Schofield Papers, LC; Sheridan to Endicott, November 10, 1885, Sheridan Papers.

7. Sheridan to Bragg, January 13, 1886, ibid.

8. Sheridan to Bragg, March 31 and December 7, 1886, ibid.

9. Jones to Sawyer, January 23, 1866, and Owen to Easton, June 4, 1866, Box 913, CCF, RG92, NA; Noyes to Owen, July 19, 1866, vol. 1, Fort Riley LS, RG393; Davidson to McKeever, January 16, 1867, Box 28, Department of the Missouri LR, 1861–67, RG393. L. C. Easton, who by 1866 had become the Chief Quartermaster of the Division of the Mississippi, was the same Easton who helped select the site for Fort Riley in 1852.

10. Irwin to Williams, May 20, 1871, and Gibson to Williams, May 15, 1871, Box 25, Department of the Missouri LR, 1868–98, RG393. Irwin had been an army surgeon for fifteen years by 1871; Gibson's evaluation of the hospital is similar, though less vivid. Irwin's attention to "effluvia" was consonant with accepted medical theory before the development of bacteriology.

11. On the cisterns, see Department of the Missouri, Register of LR, 1:436, October 31, 1868, RG393; on the cemetery, ibid., 54:142, April 9, 1886. Quotation from Pond to AAG, Department of the Missouri, June 6, 1885, Box 913, CCF. A soldier whose company trans-

ferred to a small post on Wyoming's Wind River Indian Reservation wrote that the "quarters are such a decided improvement on those at Riley that it gives one the 'shivers' to think of Riley in winter" (*Junction City Union*, October 13, 1885).

12. Pennypacker to AAG Department of the Missouri, February 20 and April 19, 1880; post adjutant to post quartermaster, April 22, 1880, vol. 3, Fort Riley LS.

13. Proceedings of a Board of Officers, April 8, 1882; Dudley to AAG, Department of the Missouri, April 10, 1882; and endorsement of S. B. Holabird, April 13, 1882; all in AGO LR, 1881–89, RG94 (NA Microfilm Publication M689, roll 94). *Army and Navy Journal*, April 15, 1882; *Junction City Union*, May 6, 1882.

14. A two-year gap in the Quartermaster Department's Register of Contracts covers 1884 and 1885, the years when construction at Fort Riley first began to gather momentum.

15. *Junction City Union*, May 9, 1885; Sheridan to Schofield, June 11, 1885, Sheridan Papers.)

16. *U.S. Statutes at Large*, 24(1887):372; Endorsement by S. B. Holabird on Chandler to Pond, July 28, 1887, Box 142, Department of the Missouri LR, 1868–98.

17. QMD Register of Contracts, 1881–1890, 2:269, 334, 343, RG92; Pond to post adjutant, September 10, 1887, Box 142, Department of the Missouri LR, 1868–98. The Quartermaster Department does not seem to have kept Abstracts of Bids for construction projects during the 1880s, as it did for bids on forage in the pre–Civil War period, but the *Junction City Union*, September 17, 1887, printed that year's bids.

18. QMD Register of Contracts, 1881–1890, 2:181, 211, 214, 263; 3:19–20, 25, 77, 137–38. I use "winning" advisedly; when Hullinger and Son got their enormous contract, the Junction City *Republican* of September 16 commented, "Our home contractors were scooped," as if it had been reporting a baseball game.

19. Tully's name appears in the Fort Riley quartermaster's RPAs, RG92, from August to November 1855; in censuses of Davis County from 1860 on; and in the Davis County Commissioners' Proceedings, February 10, 1880, and November 7, 1884. His construction contracts are listed in the QMD Register of Contracts, 1881–1890, 3:20, 25.

20. Wright's career has been sketched earlier, in chapter 2. Quotation from *Kansas City Star*, January 15, 1904. For a brief sample of Wright's railroad-building, see *Junction City Union*, November 6 and 13, 1886, and January 29, February 26, and June 11, 1887. His construction contract is in QMD Register of Contracts, 1881–1890, 3:287.

21. *Junction City Union*, September 8, 1930; QMD Register of Contracts, 1881–1890, 2:211, 214, 334; 3:20, 138.

22. Frank W. Blackmar, ed., *Kansas*, 3:815. If Vermont seems an odd place for a cavalry station, it must be remembered that Vermont was sheep country then, as it is dairy country now, and that the Secretary of War, Redfield Proctor, was a Vermonter. One of the Zieglers may have heralded a new era in public rectitude in 1899, when he resigned from the county commission before submitting a bid to construct the courthouse in Junction City (*Union*, February 4, 1944). No such scruples had troubled Manhattan's city treasurer when he got the contract to grade Poyntz Avenue in 1859 (Manhattan City Council Minutes, September 5, 1859).

23. *Junction City Union*, March 19, 1887. The brief notices of numbers of men at work are entirely different in tone from the *Union*'s usual boasting about the Fort Riley boom, and since, when the paper quoted the dollar-amounts of individual contracts, its figures always agreed with those of the Quartermaster Department, their employment figures may be close to the mark. Quotation from Forsyth to AAG Department of the Missouri, December 9, 1887, vol. 5, Fort Riley LS. G. E. Pond and E. B. Fuller, RPAs December 1887.

24. *Junction City Republican*, February 18, November 11 and 18, and December 9, 1887. The post trader was a general merchandiser licensed by the War Department to operate at an army post and within the bounds of its military reservation.

25. Figures from *Junction City Republican*, April 27, 1888, and *Union*, April 9, 1888.

26. *Junction City Republican*, April 15, 1887 (discharged teamsters), April 27, 1888 (wages), and August 3, 1888 (quotation). Quartermasters' RPAs from Forts Harker, Larned, and Riley show that by 1868 the earnings of teamsters and laborers had declined to thirty dollars a month from a Civil War high of forty-five dollars and stayed at thirty dollars through the 1880s. Examples of comment on the progress of construc-

tion are in the *Republican*, May 25, July 6, August 3, and September 28, 1888, and the *Union*, May 5, June 2 and 30, July 14 and 28, and September 8, 1888.

27. *Junction City Republican*, August 24 and December 21, 1888, and May 24, 1889.

28. *Junction City Union*, March 10, 1885. The army received a copy of the resolutions, too; it is in Box 913, CCF. Sheridan to Bragg, January 13, March 31, and December 7, 1886, Sheridan Papers.

29. A five-year gap, from 1887 to 1891, in the Department of the Missouri Quartermaster's Register of LR blots out the period of most extensive construction at Fort Riley, but the volumes for the years just before and after show substantial outlays immediately after the beginning of the fiscal year. Most of the appropriation for 1888–89 was probably spent, or at least allocated, by November 1888.

30. Rockwell to Martin, November 24, 1888, George W. Martin Collection, KSHS. To say that Martin saw Fort Riley as an important part of the Kansas economy is not to imply that he was a constant partisan of the army. In the absence of large disbursements by the Quartermaster Department, he had urged opening the reservation to settlement or turning it over to the state as the site of some public institution.

31. Pond to Martin, November 25, 1888, G. W. Martin Collection, KSHS.

32. *Atchison Champion*, December 6, 1888; *Fort Scott Daily Monitor*, December 5, 1888; *Hutchinson Daily News*, December 4, 1888; *Junction City Union*, December 15, 1888; Wichita *Eagle*, December 5, 1888. Rockwell to Martin, December 9, 1888, G. W. Martin Collection, KSHS. QMD Register of Contracts, 1881–90, 3:286–87, 310, 312, 319, 321. Some of the contracts were for grading and paving and did not list the number of cubic yards of earth moved or the total area paved.

33. Totals from QMD Register of Contracts, 1881–1890, vols. 2 (1886–87), 3 (1888–89), and 4 (1890–91).

Epilogue

1. By 1995 the Fort Riley military reservation had grown to 100,671 acres, of which 56,046 were "leased to the public for hay pro-

duction." The garrison consisted of more than 12,500 soldiers, 15,300 dependents, and 3,300 civilian employees. The annual payroll amounted to more than $572,000,000, with purchases (concessions, construction, supplies) of more than $78,700,000. The fort's "direct economic impact on Kansas" was $665,985,532, according to the Economic Impact Summary for fiscal 1995, prepared by the Fort Riley Directorate of Resource Management.

2. Jerry M. Cooper, *The Army and Civil Disorder*, 85–86.

3. *Army and Navy Journal*, September 14, 1878.

4. See Stanley Buder, *Pullman*, 178–201; and Nick Salvatore, *Eugene V. Debs*, 126–138.

5. SWAR 1894, 109; Cooper, *Army and Civil Disorder*, 149 ff. The strength of Fort Riley's contingent is in Post Returns, July–September 1894, RG94 (NA Microfilm Publication M617, roll 1014); time and distance traveled in Regimental Return, 3rd U.S. Cavalry, July 1894, RG94 (M744, roll 33). Bennet Riley's 1829 journal is in Fred S. Perrine, "Military Escorts on the Santa Fe Trail." In April 1916 Woodrow Wilson's aide Edward M. House conferred with the secretary of war about the availability of troops to suppress German and Irish rioting if the United States entered the First World War on Britain's side (Charles Seymour, ed., *The Intimate Papers of Colonel House*, 2:232).

6. Nelson A. Miles et al., "The Lesson of the Recent Strikes"; quotations from 186–88. "Equally removed from poverty and wealth . . . the early years of my life were passed. I attended the district school, participating in the sports and pastimes customary in those days among boys of the rural districts. I also took my full share in the occupations incident to life on a New England farm" (Miles, *Personal Recollections and Observations*, 1:23).

7. Robert Wooster, *Nelson A. Miles and the Twilight of the Frontier Army*, 137–38; "old Army officer" quoted in the *Army and Navy Journal*, May 24, 1884. The *Army and Navy Journal* mentions other military investors, August 6, 1881 (mining in Arizona), January 13, 1883 (stock-growing in Idaho, Montana, and Wyoming), July 3, 1886 (Chicago grain futures), and October 8, 1892 (orange groves in Florida)—all businesses intimately linked with rail transportation. Edward M. Coffman, *The Old Army*, 222–223, contrasts the middle-class backgrounds of army officers

during the post–Civil war era with those of officers in the U.S. Navy and British Army. See also Cooper, *Army and Civil Disorder*, 155–57, 258–59.

8. Quotation in Charles Royster, *The Destructive War*, 162. See also John M. Gates, "The Alleged Isolation of U.S. Army Officers in the 19th Century"; and Peter Karsten, "Armed Progressives."

Sources Cited

Manuscript Sources

LIBRARY OF CONGRESS
John M. Schofield Papers.
Philip H. Sheridan Papers.

NATIONAL ARCHIVES
Record Group 75, Records of the Office of Indian Affairs.
        Letters Received, 1824–1881 (Microfilm Publication M234).
Record Group 92, Records of the Office of the Quartermaster
    General.
        Consolidated Correspondence File, 1794–1890.
        Personal Records, Officers, Q.M. Corps, Civil War.
        Registers of Contracts, 1819–1870.
        Registers of Contracts, 1871–1880.
        Registers of Contracts, 1881–1912.
        Reports of Persons and Articles Hired, 1818–1905.
Record Group 94, Records of the Office of the Adjutant General.
        Letters Received, 1822–1860 (Microfilm Publication M567).
        Letters Received, 1861–1870 (Microfilm Publication M619).
        Muster Rolls of Regular Army Organizations, 1784–1912.
        Reservation File.
        Returns from Regular Army Artillery Regiments, 1821–1901
          (Microfilm Publication M727).
        Returns from Regular Army Cavalry Regiments, 1833–1916
          (Microfilm Publication M744).

Returns from Regular Army Infantry Regiments, 1821–1916 (Microfilm Publication M655).

Returns from United States Military Posts, 1800–1916 (Microfilm Publication M617).

Record Group 153, Records of the Office of the Judge Advocate General.

Court-Martial Records, 1808–1939.

Record Group 192, Records of the Office of the Commissary General of Subsistence.

Registers of Contracts, 1819–1907.

Record Group 393, Records of U.S. Army Continental Commands.

Department of the Missouri.

Letters Received, 1861–1867.

Letters Received, 1868–1898.

Registers of Letters Received, 1868–1896.

Letters Sent, 1868–1898.

Quartermaster, Registers of Letters Received, 1880–86 and 1892–98.

Department of the West.

Letters Sent, 1853–1861.

Fort Riley.

Letters Received by Endorsement, 1864–1891.

Letters, Endorsements, and Telegrams Sent, 1866–1906.

Telegrams Received, 1869–1891.

Kansas State Historical Society.

Federal censuses of 1840, 1850, 1860, 1870, and 1880.

State censuses of 1865, 1875, and 1885.

Territorial census of 1855.

Isaac T. Goodnow Diary.

Kansas Corporation Charters.

George W. Martin Collection.

Western Historical Manuscript Collection, University of Missouri.

Frederick Starr, Jr., Papers.

GEARY COUNTY HISTORICAL SOCIETY.
Newspaper clippings files.

COUNTY AND MUNICIPAL RECORDS.
Davis County Commissioners, Proceedings, 1856–1882 (Geary
    County Office Building, Junction City).
Junction City Commission, Minutes, 1871–1887 (Junction City
    Municipal Building).
Manhattan City Council, Minutes, 1857–1886 (Riley County His-
    torical Society, Manhattan).
Riley County Commissioners, Proceedings, 1857–1887 (Riley
    County Office Building, Manhattan).

Published Sources

CONGRESSIONAL DOCUMENTS
Annual Reports of the Commissioner of Indian Affairs.
Annual Reports of the Secretary of War.
Congressional Globe, 1867–1868.
Congressional Record, 1880–1881.
18th Cong., 2nd sess., S. Doc. 7, "Trade and Intercourse, Between
    Missouri and . . . New Mexico." (serial 108)
22nd Cong., 1st sess., S. Doc. 90, "The Fur Trade and the Inland
    Trade to Mexico." (serial 213)
33rd Cong., 2nd sess., S. Ex. Doc. 46, "Contracts Made Under Au-
    thority of the War Department." (serial 752)
———. S. Ex. Doc. 68, "Appropriation of Lands for Military Pur-
    poses." (serial 756)
———. S. Ex. Doc. 78, "Reports of Explorations and Surveys," v. 2.
    (serial 759)
———. H. Ex. Doc. 50, "Delaware Indians." (serial 783)
———. H. Rept. 36, "Military Roads—Kansas." (serial 808)
34th Cong., 1st sess., S. Ex. Doc. 96, "Statistical Report on Sickness
    and Mortality." (serial 827)

————. 3rd sess., H. Rept. 172, "Military Road from Fort Leavenworth to Fort Riley." (serial 912)

36th Cong., 1st sess., H. Ex. Doc. 22, "Contracts with the War Department." (serial 1047)

39th Cong., 1st sess., H. Ex. Doc. 76, "Report of General John Pope." (serial 1263)

————. 2nd sess., H. Ex. Doc. 23, "Protection Across the Continent." (serial 1288)

40th Cong., 1st sess., S. Ex. Doc. 2, "Protection of Trains." (serial 1308)

46th Cong., 1st sess., S. Ex. Doc. 20, "Occupation of Indian Territory by White Settlers." (serial 1869)

47th Cong., 1st sess., H. Ex. Doc. 145, "Prevention of Trespass on Indian Lands." (serial 2030)

48th Cong., 1st sess., H. Ex. Doc. 17, "Trespass on Indian Lands." (serial 2193)

NEWSPAPERS

Arkansas City (Kansas) Republican, 1885.

Army and Navy Journal. New York, 1878–82.

Atchison (Kansas) Freedom's Champion, 1865.

Coffeyville (Kansas) Journal, 1879.

Fort Scott (Kansas) Daily Monitor, 1888.

Hutchinson (Kansas) Daily News, 1888.

Junction City (Kansas) Republican, 1887–89.

Junction City (Kansas) Smoky Hill and Republican Union, 1861–63.

Junction City (Kansas) Statesman, 1860.

Junction City (Kansas) Weekly Union, 1865–94.

Kansas City (Missouri) Star, 1904.

Kansas City (Missouri) Western Journal of Commerce, 1858.

Kiowa (Kansas) Herald, 1885.

Leavenworth (Kansas) Daily Conservative, 1867.

Leavenworth Kansas Weekly Herald, 1854–55.

Leavenworth (Kansas) Times, 1860.

Liberty (Missouri) The Far West, 1836.

Louisville (Kansas) Pottawatomie Gazette, 1868–69.

Manhattan (Kansas) Express, 1859–61.

Manhattan (Kansas) Independent, 1863–68.
Manhattan Kansas Radical, 1867.
Manhattan (Kansas) Nationalist, 1870–71.
Manhattan (Kansas) Standard, 1868–70.
New York Army and Navy Journal, 1878–82.
Topeka (Kansas) Weekly Leader, 1867.
Wichita (Kansas) Eagle, 1888.

ARTICLES AND BOOKS

Appleby, Joyce. "Commercial Farming and the 'Agrarian Myth' in the Early Republic." *Journal of American History* 68, no. 4 (March 1982):833–49.

Athearn, Robert G. *William Tecumseh Sherman and the Settlement of the West.* Norman: University of Oklahoma Press, 1956.

Atherton, Lewis. *Main Street on the Middle Border.* Bloomington: Indiana University Press, 1954.

Baldwin, Joseph G. *The Flush Times of Alabama and Mississippi: A Series of Sketches.* Edited by James H. Justus. Baton Rouge: Louisiana State University Press, 1987.

Barry, Louise. *The Beginning of the West: Annals of the Kansas Gateway to the American West, 1540–1854.* Topeka: Kansas State Historical Society, 1972.

[Benton, Thomas Hart]. *Thirty Years' View: Or, a History of the Working of the American Government. . . .* 2 vols. New York: D. Appleton, 1854.

Berthrong, Donald J. *The Cheyenne and Arapaho Ordeal: Reservation and Agency Life in the Indian Territory, 1875–1907.* Norman: University of Oklahoma Press, 1976.

———. *The Southern Cheyennes.* Norman: University of Oklahoma Press, 1963.

Billings, John S. *Report on Barracks and Hospitals.* Washington, D.C.: Government Printing Office, 1870.

Blackmar, Frank W., ed. *Kansas: A Cyclopedia of State History.* Chicago: Standard Publishing, 1912.

Boatner, Mark M. *The Civil War Dictionary.* New York: David McKay, 1959.

Boyle, James E. *The Financial History of the State of Kansas*. Madison: University of Wisconsin Press, 1908.

Boynton, Charles B., and T. B. Mason. *A Journey Through Kansas*. Cincinnati: Moore, Wilstach, Keys, 1855.

Brooks, George R., ed. "George C. Sibley's Journal of a Trip to the Salines in 1811." *Bulletin of the Missouri Historical Society* 21, no. 3 (April 1965): 167–207.

Buder, Stanley. *Pullman: An Experiment in Industrial Order and Community Planning, 1880–1930*. New York: Oxford University Press, 1967.

Carriker, Robert C. *Fort Supply, Indian Territory*. Norman: University of Oklahoma Press, 1970.

Cashion, Ty. *A Texas Frontier: The Clear Fork Country and Fort Griffin, 1849–1887*. Norman: University of Oklahoma Press, 1996.

Chandler, Alfred D. *The Visible Hand: The Managerial Revolution in American Business*. Cambridge: Harvard University Press, 1977.

Coffman, Edward M. *The Old Army: A Portrait of the American Army in Peacetime, 1784–1898*. New York: Oxford University Press, 1986.

Coons, Mattie M. *Pioneer Days in Kansas*. Manhattan: privately printed, 1939.

Cooper, Jerry M. *The Army and Civil Disorder: Federal Military Intervention in Labor Disputes, 1877–1900*. Westport, Conn.: Greenwood Press, 1980.

Crist, Linda L., ed. *The Papers of Jefferson Davis*, vol. 5. Baton Rouge: Louisiana State University Press, 1985.

Cronon, William. *Nature's Metropolis: Chicago and the Great West*. New York: W.W. Norton, 1991.

Dary, David A. *The Buffalo Book*. Chicago: Swallow Press, 1974.

Dobak. William A. " 'One of the Nastiest Rivers That I Know Of': Municipal and Rural Sanitation in Nineteenth-Century Kansas." *Kansas History* 19, no. 1 (Spring 1996): 52–63.

Doyle, Don H. *The Social Order of a Frontier Community: Jacksonville, Illinois, 1825–70*. Urbana: University of Illinois Press, 1978.

Dykstra, Robert R. *The Cattle Towns*. New York: Knopf, 1968.

Ellis, Richard N. "General Pope's Report on the West, 1866." *Kansas Historical Quarterly* 35, no. 4 (Winter 1969): 345–72.

Faragher, John M. *Sugar Creek: Life on the Illinois Prairie.* New Haven: Yale University Press, 1986.

Foreman, Grant. *Indians and Pioneers: The Story of the American Southwest Before 1830.* New Haven: Yale University Press, 1930.

Frazer, Robert W. *Forts and Supplies: The Role of the Army in the Economy of the Southwest, 1846–1861.* Albuquerque: University of New Mexico Press, 1983.

Gates, John M. "The Alleged Isolation of U.S. Army Officers in the Nineteenth Century." *Parameters* 10, no. 3 (September 1980): 32–45.

Gates, Paul W. *Fifty Million Acres: Conflicts Over Kansas Land Policy, 1854–1890.* Ithaca: Cornell University Press, 1954.

Glaab, Charles N. *Kansas City and the Railroads: Community Policy in the Growth of a Regional Metropolis.* Lawrence: University Press of Kansas, 1993.

Greeley, Horace. *An Overland Journey.* New York: C. M. Saxton, Barker, 1860.

Greene, Albert R. "The Kansas River—Its Navigation." *Transactions of the Kansas State Historical Society* 9 (1905–1906): 317–58.

Gregg, Josiah. *Commerce of the Prairies.* Norman: University of Oklahoma Press, 1954.

Gregg, Kate L., ed. *The Road to Santa Fe: The Journal and Diaries of George Champlin Sibley. . . .* Albuquerque: University of New Mexico Press, 1952.

Griffin, Albert. *An Illustrated Sketch Book of Riley County, Kansas.* Manhattan: The Nationalist, 1881.

Grinnell, George B. *The Fighting Cheyennes.* Norman: University of Oklahoma Press, 1956.

Hagan, William T. *United States–Comanche Relations: The Reservation Years.* New Haven: Yale University Press, 1976.

Haites, Erik F., et al. *Western River Transportation: The Era of Internal Development, 1810–1860.* Baltimore: Johns Hopkins University Press, 1975.

Hedren, Paul L. *Fort Laramie in 1876: Chronicle of a Frontier Post at War.* Lincoln: University of Nebraska Press, 1988.

Heitman, Francis B. *Historical Register and Dictionary of the United States Army.* 2 vols. Washington, D.C.: Government Printing Office, 1903.

Henretta, James. "Families and Farms: *Mentalité* in Pre-Industrial America." *William and Mary Quarterly* 3rd ser., 35, no. 1 (January 1978): 3–32.

Historical Plat Book of Riley County, Kansas. Chicago: Bird & Mickle, 1881.

Historical Statistics of the United States. 2 vols. Washington, D.C.: Bureau of the Census, 1975.

History of Buchanan County, Missouri. St. Joseph: Birdsall, Williams, 1881.

History of Clay and Platte Counties, Missouri. St. Louis: National Historical Company, 1885.

Hudson, John C. *Plains Country Towns.* Minneapolis: University of Minnesota Press, 1985.

Hutton, Paul A. *Phil Sheridan and His Army.* Lincoln: University of Nebraska Press, 1985.

An Illustrated Historical Atlas of Clay County, Missouri. Philadelphia: Edwards Brothers, 1877.

Iverson, Peter. *When Indians Became Cowboys: Native Peoples and Cattle Ranching in the American West.* Norman: University of Oklahoma Press, 1994.

Jackson, Donald, ed. *The Journals of Zebulon Montgomery Pike.* 2 vols. Norman: University of Oklahoma Press, 1966.

James, Edwin. *An Account of an Expedition from Pittsburgh to the Rocky Mountains.* Philadelphia: Carey and Lea, 1823.

Jordan, Terry G. "Vegetational Perception and Choice of Settlement Site in Frontier Texas." In *Pattern and Process: Research in Historical Geography*, edited by Ralph E. Ehrenberg. Washington, D.C.: National Archives, 1979.

Jordan, Terry G., and Matti Kaups. *The American Backwoods Frontier: An Ethnic and Ecological Interpretation.* Baltimore: Johns Hopkins University Press, 1989.

Kansas Board of Railroad Commissioners. *First Annual Report.* Topeka: State Printer, 1884.

Kappler, Charles J. *Indian Affairs. Laws and Treaties.* 2 vols. Washington, D.C.: Government Printing Office, 1904.

Karsten, Peter. "Armed Progressives: The Military Reorganizes for the American Century." In *Building the Organizational Society: Essays on Associational Activities in Modern America,* edited by Jerry Israel. New York: Free Press, 1972.

Kavanagh, Thomas W. *Comanche Political History: An Ethnohistorical Perspective, 1706–1875.* Lincoln: University of Nebraska Press, 1996.

King, Charles. *Trials of a Staff Officer.* Philadelphia: L. R. Hamersly, 1891.

Kirkland, Edward C. *Industry Comes of Age: Business, Labor, and Public Policy, 1860–1897.* New York: Holt, Rinehart and Winston, 1961.

Klein, Maury. *Union Pacific: Birth of a Railroad, 1862–1893.* Garden City: Doubleday, 1987.

Kulikoff, Allan. *The Agrarian Roots of American Capitalism.* Charlottesville: University Press of Virginia, 1992.

Langsdorf, Edgar. "The First Survey of the Kansas River." *Kansas Historical Quarterly* 18, no. 2 (May 1950): 146–58.

Lass, William E. *From the Missouri to the Great Salt Lake: An Account of Overland Freighting.* Lincoln: Nebraska State Historical Society, 1972.

Laws of the Territory of Kansas. Lecompton: R. H. Bennett, 1857.

Lee, Robert. *Fort Meade and the Black Hills.* Lincoln: University of Nebraska Press, 1991.

Limerick, Patricia N. *The Legacy of Conquest: The Unbroken Past of the American West.* New York: Norton, 1987.

Lurie, Nancy O. "Ethnohistory: An Ethnological Point of View." *Ethnohistory* 8, no. 1 (Winter 1961): 78–92.

McClure, J. R. "Taking the Census and Other Incidents in 1855." *Transactions of the Kansas State Historical Society* 8 (1903–1904): 227–50.

McPherson, James M. *Battle Cry of Freedom: The Civil War Era.* New York: Oxford University Press, 1988.

Mahoney, Timothy R. "Urban History in a Regional Context: River Towns on the Upper Mississippi, 1840–1860." *Journal of American History* 72, no. 2 (September 1985): 318–39.

Malin, James C. *The Grassland of North America: Prolegomena to Its History*. Lawrence: privately printed, 1961.

Manzo, Joseph T. "Emigrant Indian Objections to Kansas Residence." *Kansas History* 4, no. 4 (Winter 1981): 246–55.

———. "The Indian Pre-Removal Network." *Journal of Cultural Geography* 2, no. 2 (Spring–Summer 1982): 72–83.

———. "Native Americans, Euro-Americans: Some Shared Attitudes Toward Life on the Prairies." *American Studies* 23, no. 2 (Fall 1982): 39–48.

Martin, George W. "The Territorial and Military Combine at Fort Riley." *Transactions of the Kansas State Historical Society* 7 (1902): 361–90.

Miles, Nelson A. *Personal Recollections and Observations of General Nelson A. Miles*. 2 vols. Chicago: Werner, 1896.

Miles, Nelson A., et al. "The Lesson of the Recent Strikes." *North American Review* 159, no. 453 (August 1894): 180–206.

Miller, Darlis A. *Soldiers and Settlers: Military Supply in the Southwest, 1861–1885*. Albuquerque: University of New Mexico Press, 1989.

Milner, Clyde A., II. "The Shared Memory of Montana's Pioneers." *Montana* 37, no. 1 (Winter 1987): 2–13.

Miner, H. Craig, and William E. Unrau. *The End of Indian Kansas: A Study of Cultural Revolution, 1854–1871*. Lawrence: University Press of Kansas, 1978.

Moore, John H. *The Cheyenne Nation: A Social and Demographic History*. Lincoln: University of Nebraska Press, 1987.

Nye, Wilbur S. *Carbine and Lance: The Story of Old Fort Sill*. Norman: University of Oklahoma Press, 1969.

Oliva, Leo E. *Soldiers on the Santa Fe Trail*. Norman: University of Oklahoma Press, 1967.

Paley, William. *Principles of Moral and Political Philosophy*. Boston: Richardson and Lord, 1825.

Papers Relative to the Proceedings of Court Martial in the Case of Brevet

Lieut. Col. Wm. R. Montgomery. Philadelphia: C. Sherman & Son, 1858.

Perrine, Fred S. "Military Escorts on the Santa Fe Trail." *New Mexico Historical Review* 3, no. 3 (July 1928): 265–300.

Phillips, Christopher. *Damned Yankee: The Life of General Nathaniel Lyon.* Columbia: University of Missouri Press, 1990.

Porter, Kenneth W. *John Jacob Astor, Business Man.* 2 vols. Cambridge: Harvard University Press, 1931.

Portrait and Biographical Album of Washington, Clay, and Riley Counties, Kansas. Chicago: Chapman Brothers, 1890.

Pride, Woodbury F. *The History of Fort Riley.* Fort Riley: privately printed, 1926.

Proceedings of the M. W. Grand Lodge of the Ancient, Free & Accepted Masons of Kansas, 1871. Leavenworth: J. C. Ketcheson, 1871.

Prucha, Francis P. *Broadax and Bayonet: The Role of the United States Army in the Development of the Northwest, 1815–1860.* Madison: University of Wisconsin Press, 1953.

———. *The Sword of the Republic: The United States Army on the Frontier, 1783–1846.* New York: Macmillan, 1969.

Rawley, James A. *Race and Politics: "Bleeding Kansas" and the Coming of the Civil War.* Philadelphia: Lippincott, 1969.

Report of the Adjutant General of the State of Kansas, 1861–65. 2 vols. Leavenworth: Bulletin Cooperative Printing, 1867.

Reports of Cases Argued and Determined in the Supreme Court of the State of Kansas, vol. 20. Leavenworth: State Printer, 1887.

Rister, Carl C. *Land Hunger: David L. Payne and the Oklahoma Boomers.* Norman: University of Oklahoma Press, 1942.

Robbins, William G. *Colony and Empire: The Capitalist Transformation of the American West.* Lawrence: University Press of Kansas, 1994.

Rollings, Willard H. *The Osage: An Ethnohistorical Study of Hegemony in the Prairie-Plains.* Columbia: University of Missouri Press, 1992.

Royster, Charles. *The Destructive War: William Tecumseh Sherman, Stonewall Jackson, and the Americans.* New York: Knopf, 1991.

Salvatore, Nick. *Eugene V. Debs: Citizen and Socialist.* Urbana: University of Illinois Press, 1982.

Schofield, John M. *Forty-six Years in the Army.* New York: Century, 1897.

Schubert, Frank N. *Outpost of the Sioux Wars: A History of Fort Robinson.* Lincoln: University of Nebraska Press, 1995.

Senate Journal of the Legislative Assembly of the State of Kansas. Leavenworth: State Printer, 1867.

Seymour, Charles, ed. *The Intimate Papers of Colonel House.* 4 vols. Cambridge: Harvard University Press, 1926–28.

Spicer, Edward H. *Cycles of Conquest: The Impact of Spain, Mexico, and the United States on the Indians of the Southwest, 1533–1960.* Tucson: University of Arizona Press, 1962.

Stands In Timber, John, and Margot Liberty. *Cheyenne Memories.* New Haven: Yale University Press, 1982.

Statutes of the Territory of Kansas. Shawnee, Kans.: Shawnee Manual Labor School, 1855.

Stilgoe, John R. *Common Landscape of America, 1580 to 1845.* New Haven: Yale University Press, 1982.

Taylor, George R. *The Transportation Revolution, 1815–1860.* New York: Holt, Rinehart and Winston, 1961.

United States Biographical Dictionary. Kansas Volume. Chicago: S. Lewis, 1879.

U.S. Statutes at Large 24 (1887): 372.

Unrau, William E. *The Kansas Indians: A History of the Wind People.* Norman: University of Oklahoma Press, 1971.

Unruh, John D., Jr. *The Plains Across: The Overland Emigrants and the Trans-Mississippi West.* Urbana: University of Illinois Press, 1979.

Utley, Robert M. *Frontier Regulars: The United States Army and the Indian, 1866–1891.* New York: Macmillan, 1973.

———. *Frontiersmen in Blue: The United States Army and the Indian, 1848–1865.* New York: Macmillan, 1967.

Walker, Henry P. *The Wagonmasters: High Plains Freighting from the Earliest Days of the Santa Fe Trail to 1880.* Norman: University of Oklahoma Press, 1966.

Wells, Thomas C. "Letters of a Kansas Pioneer, 1855–1860." *Kansas Historical Quarterly* 5, no. 2 (May 1936): 143–79; no. 3 (August 1936): 282–318; no. 4 (November 1936): 381–418.

White, Richard. *"It's Your Misfortune and None of My Own": A History of the American West*. Norman: University of Oklahoma Press, 1991.

———. *The Roots of Dependency: Subsistence, Environment, and Social Change Among the Choctaws, Pawnees, and Navajos*. Lincoln: University of Nebraska Press, 1983.

Winther, Oscar O. *The Transportation Frontier: Trans-Mississippi West, 1865–1890*. New York: Holt, Rinehart and Winston, 1964.

Wooster, Robert. *Nelson A. Miles and the Twilight of the Frontier Army*. Lincoln: University of Nebraska Press, 1993.

Worster, Donald E. *Dust Bowl: The Southern Plains in the 1930s*. New York: Oxford University Press, 1979.

DISSERTATIONS

Garver, John B., Jr. "The Role of the United States Government in the Colonization of the Trans-Missouri West: Kansas, 1804–1861." Syracuse University, 1981.

Napier, Rita G. "Squatter City: The Construction of a New Community in the American West, 1854–1861." American University, 1976.

Index

Adams, Nathaniel A., 85–88, 101–107, 205
Agriculture, 4, 12, 21, 24–25, 32, 46–47, 52, 64, 71, 79–81, 188; and soil, 14, 16–18
Anderson, John A., 156, 173, 216
Arkansas River, 12, 14, 17, 19–20, 22, 33–34, 38, 41, 45, 60, 66, 74, 81, 113, 123
Ashley, William H., 13, 20, 153, 190

Benton, Thomas H., 6, 12–14, 18–20, 189
Blakely, William S., 59, 148, 212
Booth, Henry, 86, 103, 200, 205

Cheyenne, Wyoming, 113, 157, 167
Cheyenne and Arapaho Agency, 9, 123, 126
Cheyenne Indians. See Indian Tribes: Cheyennes
Chicago, 40, 100, 102, 111, 131, 156, 159, 165, 171, 179–81, 204
Cincinnati, 29, 35, 45, 47, 131, 165, 168
Construction. See Fort Riley: construction

Contracts. See U.S. Army: contracts
County bond issues, 5, 8, 69, 89, 101–109, 178, 201; rural opposition to, 102–103, 108–109, 178, 201

Davis, Jefferson, 133–34, 138–40
Davis (Geary) County, Kansas, 45, 55, 59–61, 63–65, 68, 79, 81, 88, 100–101, 169, 176, 194, 196
Denver, Colorado, 40–41, 45, 92–93, 111, 113, 157, 207
Dixon, Thomas, 57, 80, 82–85, 87–88
Dyche, Calvin M., 61, 78–80, 150
Dyer, John N., 53, 141–42
Dyer, William F., 35, 76, 96, 203

Easton, Langdon C., 26, 57, 119, 122, 194, 217
Elliott, L. Richard, 86, 102–104, 106–107, 200, 205
Ellsworth, Kansas, 41, 44, 68, 81, 86, 100, 113, 119, 148, 207
Emporia, Kansas, 41, 68, 100, 109